Against the Grain

Against the Grain

Couples, Gender, and the Reframing of Parenting

GILLIAN RANSON

University of Toronto Press

LIBRARY AND ARCHIVES CANADA CATALOGUING IN PUBLICATION

Ranson, Gillian
Against the grain : couples, gender, and the reframing of parenting / Gillian Ranson.

Includes bibliographical references and index.

ISBN 978-1-4426-0358-5 (pbk.).—ISBN 978-1-4426-0357-8 (bound)

1. Parenting—Canada. 2. Sex role—Canada. 3. Work and family—Canada. 4. Sexual division of labor—Canada. 5. Social change—Canada. I. Title.

HQ755.8.R355 2010   306.8740971   C2009-906446-4

We welcome comments and suggestions regarding any aspect of our publications — please feel free to contact us at news@utphighereducation.com or visit our internet site at www.utphighereducation.com.

North America
5201 Dufferin Street
Toronto, Ontario, Canada, M3H 5T8

2250 Military Road
Tonawanda, New York, USA, 14150
ORDERS PHONE: 1-800-565-9523
ORDERS FAX: 1-800-221-9985
ORDERS EMAIL: utpbooks@utpress.utoronto.ca

UK, Ireland, and continental Europe
NBN International
Estover Road, Plymouth, PL6 7PY, UK
TEL: 44 (0) 1752 202301
FAX ORDER LINE: 44 (0) 1752 202333
enquiries@nbninternational.com

This book is printed on paper containing 100% post-consumer fibre.

The University of Toronto Press acknowledges the financial support for its publishing activities of the Government of Canada through the Book Publishing Industry Development Program (BPIDP).

Designed by Daiva Villa, Chris Rowat Design.

Printed in Canada

For Matthew and Caroline, with love

Contents

Acknowledgements

This book was a labour of love. I was writing about something that mattered deeply to me, and I really did love the writing itself. But the labour was not mine alone, and I am indebted to many people who helped along the way. Chief among them are the 32 couples who participated in the study on which the book is based. I am immensely grateful for the gift of time they gave me, and for their willingness to share their thoughts and experiences as parents. They stayed in my mind long after our interviews were done, and I hope I have done them justice in the pages that follow.

Colleagues and friends have also been invaluable. Among them, Liza McCoy deserves special mention. In many meetings, both work-oriented and social, she listened patiently to my ideas, made excellent suggestions, and helped me work through blocks and problems. She also read successive drafts of the manuscript and offered constructive advice. I deeply appreciate her friendship and collegiality. I would also like to thank Glenda Wall for helpful comments on conference presentations about this research and for other occasionally very well-timed expressions of interest and encouragement.

Outside the university setting, other friends have also offered great support. Yvonne Stanford took a lively interest in the project from the start. Her perspective on many of the issues I was grappling with often helped me to see things in a broader context. I have warm memories of our walks, and the conversations that accompanied them, over the time the book was taking shape. Trish McBride is another friend whose support was practical, as well as moral, and also much appreciated.

I am also grateful for the ongoing encouragement provided by Anne Brackenbury, Executive Editor, Higher Education, University of Toronto Press. In spite of various ups and downs I encountered along the way, she always gave me the sense that she thought the book was worth writing, and that meant a lot. Once the book went into production, I had the pleasure of working with Karen Taylor, and thank her for her thoughtful and sensitive copy-editing.

Research often grows out of the researcher's own life experiences, and my research is no exception. As the mother of two children, I was drawn to the study of family life and work-family balance out of personal interest and commitment. But my kids did more than suggest the course of my research. For more than 20 years — ever since they were in elementary school and I was just embarking on graduate studies — they have cheered me on and sustained me with humour, practical help, and lots of love. It's hard to imagine how my personal experience of parenting could have been much better, and I dedicate this book to them as a way to tell them so.

Part I

Setting the Scene

Introduction

The arrival of a child turns a couple into a new kind of family. Indeed, for many couples in permanent, long-term relationships, it is the signal that family life has officially begun. When it is taken seriously, as an event with consequences beyond the purely biological facts of reproduction, the transition to parenthood is one of the most significant milestones of adult life. It ushers in a whole new set of responsibilities, interests, joys, worries, and time demands in a complex web of relationships that will last for each parent's lifetime.

All the daily details of life — the paid and unpaid work that both partners may have been doing, without much negotiation, to earn the rent or mortgage money, put food on the table, keep on top of the laundry and housework, and remain emotionally connected to one another — assume new significance when a dependent and vulnerable child also needs their care. The dual responsibilities of earning enough to support the family and providing appropriate care to the new arrival are fundamental. So how partners divide up these responsibilities when they become parents is critical to their experience of family life.

In Canada, there have been changes over the years in the ways families have organized this division — changes linked to economic, social and political events, and upheavals that have often been global in scale. Perhaps the best-known slice of this history is the half-century since World War II, which has seen women (and more particularly married women with children) enter the paid labour force in unprecedented numbers. This trend has been even sharper in the past three decades. Between 1976 and 2005, the proportion of dual-earner families increased from 36 per cent to 69 per cent. Women's increased participation in paid work has also been accompanied by an increase in men's unpaid work in the home.[1]

These figures suggest something of a convergence now in the work and family lives of women and men. But change is happening faster, and more clearly, in workplaces than in family life. Using data from the time use diaries collected as part of the 1992 and 1998 Canadian General Social Survey, Beaujot and Liu (2005) found that, regardless of the presence of children, the dominant model for the division of paid and unpaid work—involving about half of all couples—was what they called the "complementary-traditional" approach, in which wives did less paid and more unpaid work than their husbands. The next largest category, comprising about 23 per cent of all couples, was the category they called "women's double burden," in which wives did as much (or more) paid work as their husbands and also more unpaid work. The authors note that children increased the unpaid work of both men and women, but especially of women. Indeed, they point out that "the largest gender differentiation" in time use occurred for couples with young children and that "[t]his is the stage in the life course where specialization is most visible in family and work strategies" (Beaujot and Liu 2005:941). The 2005 Canadian General Social Survey confirmed these general trends. On average, married men with children spent the most time in paid work; married women with children spent the most time on housework. These differences in practice are also reflected in cultural representations. Researchers who analyzed a year-long series of articles dedicated to family issues published in a Canadian national newspaper between 1999 and 2000 found that the representations of mothers and fathers in the series were "in line with the reality of mothers as primary caregivers" (Wall and Arnold 2007:522).

These findings reflect, on a large scale, what Fox (2001) found in her study of 40 heterosexual couples living in Toronto, who were making the transition to parenthood. From individual and couple interviews conducted through the first year after their child's birth, Fox showed how most of the caring and household work gradually devolved to the mothers. She commented: "On average, the couples in this study probably entered parenthood with a stronger commitment to sharing the work and the responsibilities than is usual. Nevertheless, most of them developed the gendered patterns typical in Canadian families" (Fox 2001:388). Canadian family scholar Kerry Daly notes that, "although most couples aspire to achieve a 50/50 division of labour in the home," they seldom reach this goal (Daly 2004:12).

Why is this so? One explanation might be that mothers' assumption of more of the family responsibilities and fathers' greater focus on paid work are pragmatic reflections of an institutional context in which men, on average, earn more than women (making the man's job more likely to be the privileged job in the family); in which workplaces are slow to recognize that men, as well as women, may have family responsibilities they need to balance against work demands; and in which (as Fox and others have also pointed out) social supports to new parents are limited. Another possibility, as Daly goes on to suggest, is that women do more household work because they want to preserve for themselves the control over the household — or because men have been reluctant to give up the power and privilege associated with paid work.

But these are only partial explanations. They fail to get to what I believe is the heart of the matter. As I will argue in more detail in the chapter to follow, gender relations in individual Canadian families are shaped by the cultural context in which they unfold. An important dimension of this context is the persistence of traditional beliefs and expectations about mothering and fathering, which position mothers as ultimately responsible for children (even if they are in paid employment) and fathers as ultimately responsible for financial provision (even if they are involved with hands-on caregiving as well). In other words, the mother continues to be seen as the "primary parent," nurturer, and childcare expert, responsible above all for the family's well-being. The father continues to be positioned as the breadwinner, whose family responsibilities are seen to be primarily discharged through his financial contribution to the household. The persistence of these traditional expectations about mothers and fathers has two overall effects: 1) a division of unpaid family work (reflected in the statistics cited earlier) that, though changing, remains inequitable and 2) a clear distinction between "mothering" and "fathering" work. This is a puzzle, in light of the facts of contemporary work and family life in Canada, where the vast majority of families are dual-earner families and where partners' *working* lives are now much more similar than different. It is a puzzle, too, given the structural changes at the level of public policy and individual workplaces that might be expected to open doors to greater gender equity than currently seems to exist. And it is a problem for anyone concerned about gender equity both at work and at home.

Scholars who take up this problem tend to focus on the persistence of the old patterns and on the apparent absence of change. This is an important contribution—where inequities exist, we need to be reminded that they exist. But a focus on what has not changed overlooks what *has* changed. If we concentrate exclusively on the majority of Canadian families who appear to be conforming to traditional expectations about mothering and fathering and who do *not* share family work equitably, our attention gets distracted from the small but growing minority that does not conform. Yet these are the families who might have most to teach us about new ways of organizing family life, in circumstances in which the old ideologies no longer make sense.

In these families, the ones this book is about, women and men for many reasons are working against conventional understandings of what mothers and fathers are supposed to do (and what most of them seem to do in practice). These are not families in which primary responsibility for breadwinning or caregiving is allocated along gender lines. In these families, it may be fathers who are primary caregivers and mothers who are primary earners. Or it may be that there is a genuinely equitable division of earning and caring, with both partners sharing the earning and similarly invested in the caring. These arrangements may have come about because both partners are strongly committed to equity in their relationship and want earning and caring responsibilities to be more evenly shared. Sometimes, life circumstances (such as illness or unemployment) get in the way at critical moments, making conventional arrangements impractical or impossible. Sometimes, it's a combination of the two: particular life circumstances confront two people who are willing to challenge conventional expectations about mothers, fathers, and family life. Conventional expectations are further challenged by same-sex couples, who, by virtue of their family structure, also reframe understandings of mothering and fathering.

This book is based on my interviews with 32 couples, living in cities across Canada, who—to introduce the metaphor I have used for the book's title—were going *against the grain* of dominant understandings about mothering and fathering in all the ways I have indicated. I made them the focus of my study because I wanted to draw attention to situations where change in family gender relations was actually taking place. It seemed to me that, in all their differing circumstances, these were the families in which traditional ideas were most likely to be challenged and mothering and fathering were most likely to be transformed.

The potential for transformative change is illustrated by Lois and George, one of the couples who participated in the study.[3] When I interviewed them, they had been together for 16 years. They were the parents of Elizabeth (nearly 13) and David (10). Elizabeth was born when they were both students. At the time, neither Lois nor George had a "proper" job to be privileged, and both were equally inexperienced in childcare. So they entered parenthood as joint partners. They learned together what they had to do for Elizabeth, organizing her care around their class schedules and part-time work. With no family support close by, they made occasional use of a drop-in day care centre and accepted the help of neighbours. Mostly, though, with very little money, they managed alone. Things changed when Lois finished her degree program. She was able to find a full-time job, which she held (while George continued to combine childcare and school work) until she gave birth to David. This was the point when it made sense to begin to take a longer view of work and career. The family moved to a province with better long-term employment prospects, and Lois found the kind of professional job she was looking for. George recalled that, though he too was looking for work, it was clear that Lois's prospects were much better. And both had agreed that they wanted one parent at home during their children's preschool years. So for the ensuing six or so years, George was a full-time stay-at-home caregiver, and Lois was the family's sole financial provider. Along the way, they moved from the bedroom community where they had initially settled to a much livelier and more progressive inner-city neighbourhood. This made a big difference to George. Through community volunteer work in a field in which he had an interest, he established a network that helped him find a full-time professional job when David entered Grade 2. When they were interviewed, Lois and George were in a new phase in their family lives. Now they were organizing the requirements of two careers around the needs of two children who were, however, well into school and much more independent.

Lois and George had gone from evenly sharing all the earning and all the childcare, as poor working students, to a neat reversal of the traditional mother-caregiver/father-breadwinner pattern when George stayed home and Lois went to work. These early experiences clearly shaped what followed. When George went back to paid work, they resumed their even-handed sharing of household work. But they had become very different kinds of parents from most other dual-career couples. Lois was an unconventional mother in that, though she had plenty of devoted hands-on

equal –▷ f = bread
        m = home –▷ equal

5

experience and the enormous maternal bonding advantage produced by pregnancy, childbirth, and breastfeeding, she had never considered herself the "expert" on the children and had never positioned herself as the primary parent. Much of the work conventionally done by mothers she had been willing to have George assume. George was an unconventional father by virtue of his ongoing, hands-on involvement in childcare and domestic labour — mother's work, in most other Canadian households. And he had been willing to delegate the family's financial support — a defining feature of responsible fatherhood — to Lois. The outcome, at the time I interviewed them, was that they viewed themselves as more or less interchangeable as far as their children were concerned, as parents rather than mother and father, differentiated by the quirks and foibles of their individual personalities but not along conventional gender lines.

I came to see the interchangeability Lois and George seemed to have achieved, in practices that did not appear to fit conventional "mothering" and "fathering" labels, as the kind of leading-edge change that going against the grain could represent, and I will have much more to say about it in the course of the book. Here, though, it is important to specify what I think change like this might mean, what a small group of families, like those of Lois and George, can tell us about the future of family life. From one perspective, the answer is, not much. According to this view, these families are anomalies, statistical outliers to the dominant pattern that is, by many scholarly accounts, stubbornly resistant to change. This interpretation, however, also implies a particular view of change — change as dramatic, decisive, revolutionary. This is the view of change implicit in US sociologist Arlie Hochschild's now well-known metaphor of the "stalled revolution" to describe the inequitable division of unpaid work that accompanied the much more equitable sharing of paid work during the 1980s (Hochschild 1989). In the wake of the women's movement and other social movements of the 1960s and 1970s, revolutionary change was the kind that was expected. Anything less was not always acknowledged as change at all.

Another view of the families in my study, families going against the grain of conventional expectations of family life, is that they represent the change that gets missed when the focus is on the big picture of demographic patterns and dominant social trends. This change, the change that is happening in individual families, one by one by one, is not dramatic or revolutionary. This change is slow, but it is persistent, and it builds incrementally, family by family. Oriel Sullivan (2004, 2006), a sociologist interested in understanding how change in household gender relations happens, describes it as "a slow dripping of change," change that may perhaps be "unnoticeable from year to year" but that "in the end is persistent enough to lead to the slow dissolution of previously existing structures" (Sullivan 2006:15–16). This view of change switches the focus to what is taking place on the ground, in individual households. It calls for a close examination of what is going on at the interactional rather than the broader structural level, to help us see the contours of change that might lie ahead.

Seen in this light, the couples in this study are the forerunners, the trailblazers. They may be visible partly because their challenge to conventional ideals is more explicit and overt, but, in practice, they may not be so different from legions of Canadian families for whom the realities of daily life make conformity to old ideals unworkable. As they challenge these old ideals, either from choice or necessity, they raise important questions. How do parents get to go "against the grain" in the first place? (In other words, what makes them trailblazers?) What is it like for a mother, traditionally the undisputed expert on her children, when the other parent is as well placed to be the primary parent? What is it like for a father whose involvement with his children's care compromises his career aspirations and ability to provide for his family financially? How do parental expectations and arrangements play out in families with two mothers, or two fathers? Above all, what happens to "mothering" and "fathering" when couples, as parents, go "against the grain"? These and other questions are addressed in the chapters to follow.

Outline of the Book

Part I contains two chapters that continue the work of setting the scene for the research described in the book:

- Chapter 1 locates the study in the broad institutional and cultural context critical to the theoretical framework that underpins it, a framework that is also described in the chapter.
- Chapter 2 provides details about the study itself. It describes the process of recruiting participants, the study methodology, and information about the way study materials were analyzed.

Part II introduces the parents of preschool children who participated in the study. It is organized around the two main groupings of caregiving arrangements in place when I interviewed these parents, and it examines the implications of each arrangement for the work mothers and fathers were doing:

- Chapter 3 focuses on the first of these groupings: couples in which mothers were primary breadwinners and partners (usually fathers) were home-based primary caregivers.
- Chapter 4 focuses on the second grouping: couples who were sharing both the earning and the caring in their families.

Part III introduces the parents of school-age children and examines the way earning and caring arrangements—and mothering and fathering— may have changed over time, especially following children's important transition to school:

- Chapter 5 describes the challenges to shared earning and caring encountered by some of the parents of older children.
- Chapter 6 explores the experiences of parents whose sharing of all the earning and caring work, over time, transformed their practices as mothers and fathers.

Part IV consists of a brief review and a reflection on the implications of the study:

- Chapter 7 returns to the theoretical argument formulated in the book's early chapters and examines the potential for shifts in family gender patterns by families like those in the study, those going "against the grain."

Chapter One

Establishing the Context

In this chapter, I take up some of the ideas raised in the introduction to Part I, as I outline the context for my study of couples going against the grain of conventional family life. These couples, as I suggested earlier, are at the forefront of change — change that has been taking place slowly and incrementally towards a reduction in the gendered allocation of responsibility for earning and caring work. As I also noted, they represent the change that can get missed when the focus is on the big picture of macro-level events and demographic trends. But they are also part of that big picture. They are living their family lives in a particular time and place, in a particular social, economic, and political climate that both enables and constrains the possibility of equitable gender relations at home.

So how does big-picture change link to the "slow dripping" change that scholars such as Sullivan (2004, 2006) describe as happening in individual households similar to those I introduce in this study? What is the connection between the broader structural level of institutions, public policy, and cultural expectations about gender and the actual practices of individual mothers and fathers? The theoretical answer I offer here, and will explain in more detail later in the chapter, builds on a view of gender relations as constructed through every level of social life. From this perspective, individual practices are shaped by institutional forces and cultural beliefs, but they may, in turn (incrementally and over time), produce changes in both. In other words, "macro" and "micro" are recursively, interactively linked to produce "cycles of change" in gender relations (Risman 2004:435). Sometimes, major institutional shifts open up windows of opportunity for

institutional change → individual change → cultural change

individuals to make changes in household gender relations — changes that, over time, may lead to change also in cultural expectations and beliefs. Sometimes, it is the aggregated action of individuals and of grassroots groups pushing for change that produces the shifts at the institutional or policy level — shifts that, in turn, may lead to future change at the individual, interactional level, and so on.

In the Canadian context, these cycles can be explored through attention to some of the major institutional and structural changes that have affected the way women and men have divided earning and caring work over time. Historical researchers have also examined the discursive environment of cultural beliefs and expectations about mothering, fathering, and the needs of children to which individual parents have, over time, been held accountable. Finally, empirical research on household gender relations and the division of labour shows how individual families, enabled or constrained by the institutional and cultural resources available to them, have actually been dividing up paid work and family responsibilities at different points in time. Change over time weaves cyclically though all these domains, and there is considerable overlap between them. In what follows, however, I will take up each (more or less) separately, in a necessarily selective overview. Its aim is to unpack some of the structural and interactional linkages, and to show the historical and social context into which the couples in this study fit.

The next section considers some of the broad institutional shifts linked to women's and men's participation in paid employment and family work in Canada. The second section deals, at the level of popular discourse, with the way beliefs and expectations about mothering and fathering have been articulated over time. Closely linked to expectations about parents are expectations about children and their needs. These expectations have also changed over time and are the focus of the third section of the chapter. The fourth section looks at empirical studies of household gender relations and the division of labour at different time periods. Finally, I return to the theoretical perspective that underpins the study and to the study participants who will help me elaborate it.

The Institutional Context

Historically, family life in Canada and elsewhere has always been shaped by opportunities for earning a living. The origins of the *ideological* connection between mothers and nurture and between fathers and breadwinning are usually located in the period of early industrialization. As this economic form gradually replaced agricultural economies in Europe and North America from the early nineteenth century onwards, so the basis of family financial support for most families shifted to wages earned by work in industrial workplaces.[1] The notion of "separate spheres" of responsibility and influence, organized exclusively on the basis of gender, corresponded to middle-class social reformers' fears, at the end of the nineteenth century, about the stability of working-class families in the wake of major social and economic change (Bradbury 2005; Chunn 2003). These fears were the basis of major legislative and public policy shifts as well.

Many of these public policy shifts and their connections to family life in Canada over the twentieth century have been documented by sociologist Jane Ursel (1992). Ursel begins her historical analysis with the legislative changes of the late nineteenth century (such as the Ontario Factories Act of 1884), legislative changes aimed at regulating conditions in the new industrial workplaces. These legislative changes, often building on federal and provincial inquiries into employment conditions, imposed special conditions on the labour of women and children—ostensibly to protect them but with the latent consequence of constructing women's labour as different, and women as a subordinate class of worker. Ursel notes:

> [T]he very first steps taken by the state to mediate in the productive process, not only reflected a nineteenth-century patriarchal model of womanhood, but also through its recommendations served to ensure that this model with its procreative assumptions would not be abandoned in the face of a major economic transformation. (Ursel 1992:91)

These early actions cast long shadows. For most of the early decades of the twentieth century, women's participation in the formal paid labour force was limited to a narrow range of occupations, segregated from men's employment, and generally much lower paid. Usually, though not invariably, paid employment was restricted to single women. Marriage and childbirth commonly meant withdrawal (or expulsion) from paid employment. For example, in 1931, only 3.5 per cent of all married women were in the paid labour force (Duffy, Mandell, and Pupo 1989:10). This clear, state-sanctioned relegation of women to the "private sphere" of home and children had the corresponding effect of privileging men's labour and men as workers.[2] Ursel notes that changes in family welfare legislation during the early years of the twentieth century also contributed to making men's responsibilities as breadwinners more explicit (Ursel 1992:123).

The advent of World War II opened doors for women that had previously been firmly shut. With war came a suddenly booming economy and a rapidly increased need for labour in war manufacturing as well as other industries caused by men's absence on military service. An estimated 600,000 women entered the paid labour force in the years between 1939 and 1944, working in jobs previously held only by men and producing changes at the institutional level, such as the establishment of childcare facilities to accommodate the needs of working mothers.

The end of the war saw a stark withdrawal of state support for working women. The federal Re-Instatement in Civil Employment Act of 1942, guaranteeing that ex-service personnel would get back the jobs they had held before joining up, meant that women had to leave their non-traditional war-time work; federal assessments at the time of future demand for women's labour concentrated on traditional women's trades, for example, clerical work and hairdressing. In 1945, the government began again to enforce the civil service regulations banning married women from working for the federal government (Ursel 1992). A variety of policy documents at the time clearly assumed women would voluntarily withdraw from paid employment and take up their "domestic roles." One such document, produced in 1946 in the Department of Labour, noted that "women are encouraged only to enter the labour market when economic activity is at such a level that their employment will not prevent men from taking positions" (Porter 1993:115). Income tax changes that acted as a disincentive to married women working and special regulations limiting women's access to unemployment insurance (partly by channelling them into low-paid work) imposed further structural limitations on change in the distribution of paid work and family work. The postwar years also saw the start of the 15-year "baby boom," and a period of economic prosperity that, briefly, made it possible for many households, even working-class ones, to survive on one income. The 1950s produced a demographic reflection of the caregiver mother/breadwinner father model that, though temporary, far from universal, and historically anomalous, has had enormous cultural influence.

However, other transitions had been set in motion by the labour force shifts of the war years. A model of women as workers, even if they were still secondary and paid less, had been introduced and would prove difficult to dislodge completely. The postwar economic boom, the growth of the service economy, and the expansion of the public sector with the emergence of the welfare state created many jobs considered suitable for women, and women flocked to fill them. Slowly, women's organizations and trade unions became concerned with equality rights for women workers, as attitudes about women's roles began to shift (Porter 1993). Other structural changes followed, in the 1960s and beyond. Increased educational opportunities for women accompanied a growing recognition of the economic need for women's labour. Women's labour force participation was also shaped during this period by the development of effective birth control — and, significantly, its decriminalization. The birth control pill was available in Canada by 1961, but it wasn't until 1969 that the Liberal government, as part of an overhaul of the Criminal Code, repealed the legislation making the advertisement and sale of contraceptives technically illegal; the new legislation also allowed hospitals to perform therapeutic abortions (McLaren and McLaren 1997).[3] Effective contraception reduced the chance that women would need to forego or curtail educational and employment opportunities because of unplanned pregnancies. It allowed married women to continue their paid employment at a time when the rising cost of living made it difficult for families to manage on one salary. The 1960s was the start of a decades-long increase in the participation of married women and, increasingly, women with young children in the labour force.

A cohort of better-educated women, as labour force participants, was also well placed to observe the inequities that shaped that participation: lower salaries in a labour market that continued to segregate them in a narrow band of occupations and an unchanged division of family labour that left them still doing a "second shift" of household and childcare work as well (Hochschild 1989). In Ursel's words, women joined the "ranks of the rebellious" in the student and labour movements of the 1960s, challenging the structural forces that limited their freedom and joining, in the process, what came to be known as the "second wave" of the women's movement. The federal government's response was to appoint, in 1970, the Royal Commission on the Status of Women. Its mandate was "to inquire into legislation, regulations and policies that concern or affect the rights of women" (Ursel 1992:283–84). The commission's report was a landmark document. As Ursel notes,

> For the first time in Canadian history the patriarchal structures and assumptions of our society were examined and presented for public scrutiny. The

indictment was powerful. The commission revealed the inequities upon which traditional institutions were built, acknowledged the irreversibility of women's extended role in production and gave clear warning that the consequences of women's new role would be far reaching and fundamental to the structures of our families, our work and our society. (Ursel 1992:284)

The findings of the royal commission, and the structural changes that followed its recommendations, have helped produce the social and political environment shaping family life today. While 100 years ago the solution to the problem of balancing work and family was to allocate each to "separate spheres" of gendered responsibility, the last three decades of Canadian history have seen changes recognizing women as workers, as well as (actual or potential) mothers. Examples of these changes include the institution, in 1971, of provisions for maternity leave in the federal Unemployment Insurance Act, extended in 1990 to include 10 weeks of parental benefits (available to either parent).[4] Further recognition of the needs of working families was evident in the 1972 provision in the federal Income Tax Act for childcare expenses related to work to be allowed as deductions from taxable income. Following one of the key recommendations of the Royal Commission on the Status of Women, the years between 1984 and 1995 also saw three (unsuccessful) federal initiatives, in the form of task forces or special committees, to develop a national childcare policy (Friendly 2001).

Mothers and fathers in Canada today raise children in a neo-liberal political environment that offers mixed support for families. At its most progressive, the Canadian state since 2005 has allowed same-sex marriage; same-sex adoption, which comes under provincial not federal jurisdiction, is now legal in most provinces. But, although there is a willingness at the policy level to be more inclusive in terms of family forms, there is limited help, in a practical sense, for working families, especially in comparison to the resources available to families in many Scandinavian and European countries. Parental leave is a good example. With the aim of allowing working parents to spend a longer time caring for their babies, while still ensuring their secure re-entry to employment, the federal Employment Insurance Act was amended (effective December 31, 2000) to provide eligible Canadian parents with access to up to a year's leave at 55 per cent of average insured earnings; the leave can be taken by one parent or shared by both (Marshall 2003). But eligibility criteria still prevent a sizeable minority of working parents from making use of the leave. And although extended leaves may be feasible in large organizations, they may be more difficult to accommodate in the small enterprises where large numbers of Canadians work. It should also be noted that uptake of parental leave by Canadian fathers has been slow; in 2001, only 10 per cent of eligible fathers had taken it up (Marshall 2003). By 2006, the proportion had increased significantly in Quebec in response to the province's takeover of parental leave provisions in March 2005.[5] In the rest of Canada, however, fathers' take-up rate remained at around 10 per cent (Marshall 2008).

The provision of quality childcare is a more contentious public policy issue. The majority of young Canadian families in all regions, as well as in all economic, ethnic, and language groups, have both parents either in the paid labour force or in education or training programs (Friendly 2004). Yet, in spite of widespread need, public provision of childcare is minimal. The one exception is the province of Quebec, where a 1997 Early Childhood and Childcare Strategy instituted by the Parti Québécois greatly extended regulated childcare. Over several years, through centres or licensed family providers, the program was designed to provide care for all children from infancy to 12 years (Tougas 2001). As of 2007 the official cost was $7 per day per child.[6] Still, a major concern of researchers in the area of early childhood education and care in Canada is the absence of a national childcare policy (in spite of the federal government initiatives noted earlier). The policy proposed by the federal Liberal government under the leadership of Prime Minister Paul Martin was overturned by the minority Conservative government elected in 2006 and replaced with a system of annual allowances for parents (of $1,200 per preschool child). The effect of this policy change has been to entrench childcare even more solidly as the responsibility of parents and not the state. A recent review of early childhood education and care by the Organisation for Economic Cooperation and Development found Canadian national and provincial policy to be "in its initial stages." The review commented on the small number of Canadian children in regulated childcare spaces (less than 20 per cent of those aged under six years, compared to 78 per cent in Denmark, 69 per cent in France, and 60 per cent in the UK). It also noted long waiting lists in community centres, a stagnation of quality across the board, and "generalized underfunding" in the childcare sector (Friendly 2006).

Pocock (2005) suggests that countries can be considered as "work-care regimes" reflecting the broad social, cultural, and institutional contexts that, nationally, represent the dominant ways in which work and family responsibilities are balanced. Writing about Australia, she notes a shift from an earlier regime characterized by male breadwinner/female caregiver families to a current model that she describes as a "modified breadwinner" regime. Pocock characterizes the future (with an accompanying question mark) as ushering in a "shared work, shared care" regime. From Pocock's description of the cultural and institutional factors associated with the current Australian model (for example, women working mainly in part-time paid employment and men contributing to childcare only mini-mally), Canada has moved beyond Australia's "modified breadwinner" regime but has not yet reached the progressive future in which there is state support for women and men to share earning and caring equally and in which diverse arrangements are "supported, not judged" (Pocock 2005:44).

At the level of the workplace also, support for families is limited in Canada. The social concerns created by the preponderance of dual-earner families in the workforce have generally not been matched by appropriate policies or programs. After 10 years of research on organizations and "work-family balance" in Canada, Higgins and Duxbury comment that "employ-ers' sensitivity to work-family issues tends to lag behind these concerns as an issue for employees" (Higgins and Duxbury 2002:11). The authors' sur-vey data, in 1991 and 2001, indicate that most respondents at both time points had little or no flexibility in terms of when or where they worked — even though, according to the most recent Work and Employment Survey conducted by Statistics Canada in 1999, flexible work schedules remained the most common "family-friendly" work arrangement.

Even where they are available, however, family-friendly policies are not unproblematic. Framed usually in gender-neutral terms and proposed as equally available to women and men, they are implicitly "gender-coded" (Connell 2005). To the extent that it is women, rather than men, who take them up for family reasons, they come to be seen as special benefits or concessions *for* women (Jones and Causer 1995; Lewis 1997) rather than as rights to which all workers are entitled.[7] One consequence is that work-place assumptions that men have no family responsibilities are further entrenched, making it difficult for men who *do* want more family involve-ment to ask for any accommodation at work (Levine and Pittinsky 1997; Ranson 2001). At the same time, failures to enact policies to help people balance work and family responsibilities continue to disadvantage women and may explain the tendency among Canadian women to delay child-bearing until their careers are established (Drolet 2003). This tendency may apply particularly to women in professional, technical, and managerial occupations—some of whom, indeed, may see careers and motherhood as being incompatible (Higgins and Duxbury 2002; Jorgenson 2002).

In part, the general failure of workplaces to accommodate the needs of working families links to global changes in the organization of work in an economy now much changed from the old industrial order, in Canada and elsewhere. Organizational restructuring, "downsizing," and the shift to contingent, non-permanent work does not create an environment in which workers—either women or men—are encouraged to ask for family support, even if employers were willing to provide it. The picture at the start of the twenty-first century is of workplaces, and workers, crossing a "great divide" (Smith 2001) to a "New Economy." The emerging world of work is characterized by an increasingly diverse workforce and the proliferation of non-standard employment contracts requiring people to work longer hours in a "24/7" economy (Wharton 2006). Old protections and entitlements—only ever available to a privileged proportion of workers anyway—are vanishing. The risks and also the opportunities ensuing from these new work arrangements come to be experienced by individual families in highly individual ways.[8] However the bottom line, in Canada as in many other industrialized countries, is that the responsibilities of parenthood continue to be "gendered and privatized" (Fox 2001:388)—with mothers continuing to face greater demands than fathers.

family support not encouraged by work

The Discursive Environment

Parents, in Canada as elsewhere, live in an institutional context in which certain *material* supports for family life are—or are not—provided. They also live in a discursive environment in which *ideas* about mothering, fathering, and family life circulate freely. These are resources of another kind that parents draw on as they negotiate earning and caring responsibilities in their own families. As in the institutional context just described, change seems to be occurring in the discursive environment as well. For example, Sullivan notes the scholarship on attitudes and values that suggests an increasing rejection of traditional gender ideologies. She points to changes in language—for example, the "fading from prominence of overtly sexist or racist language" (Sullivan 2006:32). Finally, she highlights changing symbolic representations of masculinities and of fatherhood. Sullivan considers that "the overall picture suggests shifts in attitudes, language, and symbolic representations occurring both within and between successive generations and interplaying with slow changes in other practices, such as changes in fatherhood behaviors" (Sullivan 2006:39).

This change has emerged from a starting point a century or so ago when traditional ideas about mothering and fathering as "separate spheres" of responsibility seemed not to have been contested at all. Historical studies in Canada (e.g., Arnup 1994; Ursel 1992) show clearly how women's organizations and public policymakers of the late nineteenth and early twentieth centuries contributed, through public pronouncements, government reports, and civic activism, to uphold mothers as responsible for their children's health and well-being. Through the early decades of the twentieth century, fathers' responsibility for breadwinning was also clearly articulated. Comacchio (1997) notes that the widely disseminated advice literature, though purported to be for parents, was explicitly directed to mothers. Advice to fathers was more along the lines of remembering to spend *some* time with their children; Comacchio cites a 1938 letter in *Maclean's* magazine exhorting fathers to allow at least one hour per week to "give entirely" to their sons. "An hour a week does not seem much," the letter writer noted, "but how many fathers there are who have imperceptibly become so involved in the web of their daily occupations that even this hour is forgotten or put off, or in some way neglected" (Comacchio 1997:396). Writing of the years between 1945 and 1960 in Canada, Gleason (1997) notes the contribution of popular psychological discourse to the construction of the "normal" family — an institution widely believed to be at risk after years of economic depression and war. Gleason cites Dr. William Blatz, a prominent psychologist and child development expert, who wrote in *Chatelaine* magazine in 1955 that "in every human relationship there is always a dominant and a submissive party." Blatz's point was that couples could agree to negotiate areas of dominance and submission — "they could agree that the husband will dominate in certain fields such as the handling of the family's finances while the wife will dominate in the handling of the children" (Gleason 1997:457–58). Gleason notes that the rhetoric of "separate spheres" dominated popular discourse of the period.

More recent cultural representations of mothering, fathering, and family life have moved beyond this unproblematically and explicitly gendered division of labour, notably through the changing images of fathers that the growing numbers of mothers in paid employment seemed to call for. Beginning in the 1980s, the "New Father" as an emotionally involved and capable caregiver acquired prominence in television, film, advertising, and other media accounts (Wall and Arnold 2007). Critics challenged the extent to which the _culture_ of "new fatherhood" was actually matched by changes in the _conduct_ of fatherhood on a day-to-day level (LaRossa 1988). But Wall and Arnold (2007) point to a "growing body of research" questioning the extent to which cultural representations of fatherhood really have changed as much as was once assumed:

> When media portrayals and advice literature are subject to content and discourse analysis, superficial references to "new fathers" and "parents" are often undermined by images and text that position fathers as part-time, secondary, less competent parents with fewer parenting responsibilities and greater breadwinning responsibilities than mothers. (Wall and Arnold 2007:511)

This was exactly what Wall and Arnold found in their own analysis of a year-long series of 54 articles on "Family Matters" running from September 1999 to June 2000 in the Canadian national daily newspaper _The Globe and Mail_. The authors found that fathers in the series received much less attention overall and were indeed represented as secondary rather than primary parents. Sunderland (2006) found a similar diminution of the father role. She analyzed the November 2002 editions of three US magazines devoted to the care of infants and young children — _Parents_, _Parenting_, and _Baby Years_. (_Parents_ is widely available in Canada too.[9]) Sunderland makes the point that, although the magazines' very titles suggest a wish to appeal to both mothers and fathers, it is mothers who are primarily addressed and represented in the text.[10] These more recent analyses highlight the extent of change in the broader cultural environment in which Canadian parents are raising children. At one level, fathers are assumed to be involved and sharing caregivers. Craig (2006:261) suggests that "we are moving toward a social ideal of father as co-parent" — a far remove from the remote and weary breadwinner image of the mid-twentieth century. But at another level, below the surface, old assumptions about mothers as primary parents are powerfully present.

One of the most striking contemporary challenges to conventional images of family life, in Canada and elsewhere, is the increase in the numbers of same-sex couples raising children. The ideological challenge here is to the assumption firmly underpinning any representation of mothering or fathering — that the parenting couple is heterosexual. Smith's (1993) description of the "Standard North American Family" — a conception of family based on a married couple with children in which primary responsibility for paid and unpaid work is divided along gendered lines — clearly excludes gay and lesbian parents, whose claims to parenting rights are widely perceived as illegitimate (Weeks, Heaphy, and Donovan 2001). Same-sex parents disrupt the image of homosexuality as non-procreative (Dunne 2000). At the same time, they call for the construction of dual-mother or dual-father relationships in a heteronormative context in which biological parenthood is privileged (Hequembourg and Farrell 1999; Patterson 2000; Stacey and Biblarz 2001).

Children and Their Needs

Perceptions of the needs of children and how these perceptions shape what parents believe their responsibilities to be have always been critical elements in the family division of labour — they have been part of the transition to, and through, industrial society. The same broad economic changes in the industrialized world that entrenched the separation of homes and workplaces and that symbolically positioned mothers as responsible for the domestic sphere of children and household signalled a shift in thinking about children too. From being economic contributors in a pre-industrial economy and wage earners among the working class after the shift to an industrial economy, children came to be regarded in the early decades of the twentieth century as "sacred" beings, to be cared for not for their future economic contributions but for their sentimental value as objects to be loved and cherished for their own sake (Mintz 2004; Zelizer 1985). The practical, institutional actions that underpinned this change — protective legislation that barred children from employment in most industrial workplaces and the gradual implementation of mandatory schooling (Bradbury 2005; Chunn 2003; Gaffield 1990) — also served to extend and enshrine childhood as a special state, one removed from adult concerns and obligations. Children as objects to be cherished imposed new obligations on parents, who were bound now to give children a "good childhood" (Arendell 2001) and "the best start in life" (Beck-Gernsheim 2002). What constituted a good childhood became increasingly the domain of experts: physicians, social workers, educators, and, most recently, developmental psychologists. In Canada, for example, this expertise was first mobilized in the late nineteenth and early twentieth centuries to deal with high infant mortality rates in the major urban centres. Arnup (1994) describes how, over the decades of the twentieth century, the advice changed with the change in medical views about children's needs—from a preoccupation with feeding and a focus on schedules and regimentation to a new maturational development approach best exemplified in the advice manual *Baby and Child Care*, first published by Dr. Benjamin Spock in 1946.

The 1950s was an era characterized by Spock's permissive, relaxed, and child-centred approach to child rearing. It was (perhaps as a consequence) also an era of autonomous child culture. The presence in many middle-class families of a mother at home, available to children but occupied also in meeting the heavy social expectations of good housewifery, created the social environment in which children had considerable freedom. Frønes (1997) describes this period, experienced in many industrialized countries, as the era of "the child at play." However, in subsequent decades, the increased participation of mothers in the paid labour force and the shift to a "New Economy" required that children move into "a more organized landscape" (Frønes 1997:22). This new landscape was shaped not only by their parents' working lives but also by increasing levels of parental education and growing demands on parents to be involved not only with their children's physical and emotional well-being and safety but also with their cognitive development. In Canada, Wall (2004) points to research and theories in developmental psychology that underlie this shift, and she cites a variety of developmental psychology known as "new brain research" as an example. Advice literature informed by this research tells parents that children need early and appropriate stimulation—before they turn six—to ensure optimal brain development. If they don't get it, parents are told, children will experience a deficit that can't easily be made up.[11] Quirke's (2006) analysis of Canadian parenting magazine articles found a similar emphasis on children's cognitive development and schooling. In short, as Fox (2006) has noted, "expectations about the work needed to raise a child successfully have escalated at a dizzying rate: the bar is now sky-high" (Fox 2006:236).

These contemporary expectations are being applied to parents who are better educated than those of previous generations; today's parents have also, on average, come to parenthood later, and they have had fewer children. So children have become, especially for middle- and upper-class parents, something "planned and wanted," their "fundamental projects" (Frønes 1997:25). Parental efforts to shape their children's future are intended, at least in part, to increase their cultural capital and to equip them for optimal achievement and happiness as adults (Beck and Beck-Gernsheim 1995; Beck-Gernsheim 2002). Inevitably, class differences are reproduced in the process. Lareau (2002) contrasts the "concerted cultivation" of middle-class children (mainly through expensive and labour-intensive extracurricular activities) with the emphasis by working-class parents on "the accomplishment of natural growth"—a style that involves giving children more orders but leaving their time more free, conforming more to the image of the child at play than to the postindustrial era's "organized child." That said, class-based differences in education and access to resources do not diminish the hegemony of (middle-class) expectations and beliefs about child development to which all families— and particularly mothers—are now held accountable.

Empirical Studies of Household Gender Relations and the Division of Labour

The earlier sections of this chapter have presented an overview of the broad institutional context and the changing discursive environment in which Canadian mothers and fathers over the past century or so have raised their children. I turn now to studies whose focus is on the detail of that family life—to the ways earning and caring responsibilities have been shared in individual families at different time periods. Here, the historical research is more scant; studies have tended to focus more on the public world of paid work than on the private world of caregiving and family life. In the decades leading to World War II, there were certainly examples of women's paid employment encroaching on traditional male turf (e.g., Parr 1990; Tillotson 1996); but there is little to suggest that caring work during these years was ever seen as anything other than the responsibility of women (Strong-Boag 1988).[12] This accompanied a dominant belief that breadwinning was the man's responsibility (Sager 1996). In the immediate postwar period, Rutherdale's (1996) study of fathers in Prince George suggested a strong commitment to male breadwinning accompanying the belief that mothers should work only at home and a sense that paid work and family work did indeed take place in "separate spheres."

However, more recent qualitative studies tend to reflect the large-scale Canadian survey findings on gender relations and the household division of labour cited in the introduction, which show that change, though slow, was clearly taking place. Luxton's study of "three generations of women's work in the home"—the subtitle of her 1980 book—examined domestic work through a 1976–1977 case study of 100 working-class households in Flin Flon, Manitoba. She found that just over half of the 52 women in the youngest group, who had set up households in the 1960s and 1970s, had paid employment at some time after their marriage, but none had worked outside the home when their children were young. Five years later, in a follow-up study of 49 of the women, she found a decided shift from the committed domesticity of the earlier study. Though all had children under 12 (more than half had preschoolers), most of the women were working outside the home. And, while in the original study all the women considered themselves responsible for the domestic and family work, five years later husbands were more involved.

Luxton estimated that, in the 1981 follow-up, just over half the families were moving in the direction of what she called "shared spheres and changing relations." In these families, women "unanimously insisted that husbands help out and all said their husbands did some domestic labour on a regular basis" (Luxton 1990:45). But the women's accounts suggested that the shift from the traditional male breadwinner–female caregiver model to greater sharing of both earning and caregiving was not easy. It often involved men profoundly reluctant to share the household work and made for tension and unhappiness in many families. Men's help also only extended so far; for example, Luxton reported that, even though men were more involved with their children, women were still responsible for overall childcare:

> Furthermore, men "babysat" their own children — something women never did. The implication of this typical reference was that the children were the responsibility of the mother, and the father "helped out." This attitudinal difference was often carried out in behaviour as well. Women repeatedly described situations where men would agree to watch the children, but would then get involved in some other activity and would ignore the children. (Luxton 1990:49)

A decade or so later, Luxton and Corman found similar shifts — and stalls — in gender relations in their study of working-class steelworker families in Hamilton, Ontario between 1984 and 1994. Here, too, there were some changes over time in the direction of more equally shared household work, as more women entered paying jobs. But traditional ideas about men, women, and family life also persisted. Perhaps more to the point, the nature of the working-class jobs that sustained the families in the study—low-paying for women, higher-paying but inflexible for men—meant that "the economic deck [was] still stacked against an egalitarian redistribution of responsibilities within families and among the larger community" (Luxton and Corman 2001:51).

Fox's (2001) study of 40 Toronto couples also focused on the division of caring work, in this case, among couples during their first year as parents. As I noted in the introduction, Fox found that, over the course of the year and partly in response to the kind of intensive mothering the mothers wanted to do, the bulk of the childcare—along with the housework—gradually became the mothers' responsibility. Most of the couples became much more traditional in their orientations as parents than they thought would be the case before their children were born.[13]

More compelling evidence of *change* comes from Canadian researchers who have opted, as I did, to look at gender relations in families explicitly contravening conventional expectations about mothering and fathering. For example, Fox and Fumia (2001) conducted a small study of eight non-traditional Toronto couples as part of a larger study of diversity in family life. The couples' strategies for dividing earning and caring work included an exchange of traditional caregiving and breadwinner responsibilities, taking turns at caregiving and homemaking over a longer term, "egalitarian co-parenting," and raising children in "decidedly non-nuclear" households (Fox and Fumia 2001:359–61). Nelson (1996) explored the creation of family in the households of 30 lesbian mothers in Alberta and described many ways in which they disrupted conventional understandings of mothering and family life. Dienhart (1998) studied 18 heterosexual couples, who were negotiating a relationship in which caregiving was shared. The couples in the study represented a variety of models for dividing earning and caring work, but all were committed to a more balanced sharing of their work as parents. The title of Dienhart's book, *Reshaping Fatherhood*, speaks to its implicit focus on getting men more involved in caregiving. Finally, the most comprehensive Canadian work on the gendered division of caregiving labour is that of Doucet (2000, 2004a, 2004b, 2006a, 2006b). Doucet's research, by far the most extensive as well as the most recent, involved men who were primary caregivers to their children. Her project included 118 fathers, whose participation variously involved in-depth interviews, surveys, telephone interviews, Internet correspondence, and focus groups. Fourteen mothers (partners of participating fathers) were also interviewed. Doucet's wide-ranging, theoretically and methodologically rigorous discussion addresses a central question that is also the title of her 2006 book: *Do Men Mother?* These projects, though different in scale, are oriented, as mine is, to sites of potential change in mothering and fathering relationships and will be cited in more detail in later chapters.[14]

The change these studies describe, in the Canadian context, is on a very small scale; currently, the implicit assumption underlying all such research is that the phenomenon under study is unusual. But it corresponds to change evident on a global scale. Sullivan (2006) cites cross-national time use studies to make this point and to note that all this change, however slow and slight, is in the direction of more egalitarian relationships in the home. That said, the fact that families like those studied by Fox, Doucet, Dienhart, and Nelson represent what is still considered unconventional is a telling reminder that a transformation of gender relations in Canadian homes is still far from widespread.

Theorizing Change: The "Doing" — and "Undoing" — of Gender in Family Life

At the start of the chapter, I offered a general outline of a theoretical perspective on changing gender relations in families, one that linked broad institutional forces and cultural beliefs to individual practices and interactions. In this view, change occurs in cycles, through feedback loops linking the "macro" structural level with the "micro" interactional level. In what followed, I painted, with broad brush strokes, the cycles of change over the past century or so in policy, beliefs, and individual practices relating to gender relations in families, ending with the context in which the Canadian parents of today organize the earning and caring responsibilities that will support and nurture their families.

The theoretical argument these cycles of past change illuminate is that people's practices as women and men, mothers and fathers are shaped by the broader context but also constitute it. To the extent that people conform to cultural expectations and stereotypes about how women and men should behave, those expectations become further entrenched. But expectations may change over time (and institutions, as well) as the practices of individuals change. This argument is grounded in the social constructionist gender theorizing recognized as deriving mainly from the foundational work of scholars such as West and Zimmerman (1987), Berk (1985), and

Connell (1987, 1995, 2000, 2002). From this perspective, gender is "an achieved property of social conduct" — not something that we *are*, or something that we *have*, but something that we *do*. It is, furthermore, a situated accomplishment, done at the interactional level by people with an awareness of the expectations of others — others who may hold the "doers" to account for its performance (West and Zimmerman 1987:126). People "do gender" as they engage in practices that do — or do not — conform to broader social expectations about masculinity and femininity. From here, the connection to mothering and fathering is clear. "Doing" mothering or fathering, in conventional or unconventional ways, is also doing gender — over time and in a couple context.

The critical reciprocal linkage between the "doing" of gender at the interactional level and the institutional context in which the doing takes place is key to understanding how *change* in gender relations and practices in households might occur. Much of the earlier discussion in this chapter leads to the conclusion that contemporary change in women's and men's working lives — change that has made these lives much more similar than different — has moved ahead of change in ideas and expectations about mothering and fathering. As I noted in the introduction, large-scale survey findings in Canada continue to show most employed mothers carrying a heavier load of family work than employed fathers. Risman (2004) attributes inequity of this kind to "the differential expectations attached to being a mother and father, a husband and wife" (Risman 2004:436). In other words, in the face of considerable institutional change, what have not changed — or not changed fast or far enough — are cultural beliefs about parents. As Ridgeway and Correll (2004) note, these beliefs have "a remarkable ability to persist in the face of social change that might undermine them" (Ridgeway and Correll 2004:527).

Yet, over time, as we have seen, beliefs and expectations *do* change, partly as a consequence of people who, at the level of individual interaction, either refuse or are unable to be governed by them. These are the people Deutsch (2007) thinks should be of much more interest to gender scholars. Deutsch, too, is concerned about the "inequality that persists in the face of ... structural change" (Deutsch 2007:114). But she is also concerned to recognize the "revolutionary potential of human agency" that she views as the major contribution of the "doing gender" approach (Deutsch 2007:108). Deutsch points out that much work based on this approach has focused on the way individual interactions in a wide variety of settings have tended to conform to and hence reproduce the dominant beliefs and expectations about gender. She wants to remind us that, at the interactional level, people's actions have the potential to change expectations, as well as to entrench them. So, she argues, research from this perspective needs to expand beyond its present concentration on the persistence of gender inequality to ask a new set of questions, to explore what *has* (rather than has not) changed. "Doing gender," she suggests, has come to be understood as describing social interactions that reproduce social difference, so this is how the term should be used. "*Undoing* gender"[15] should be used to refer to social interactions that reduce gender difference. A study like this one, of couples contravening normative expectations about mothering and fathering, fits well with Deutsch's suggested approach.

Deutsch's work also provides an opening for me to extend the theoretical discussion of change into an exploration of what "undoing gender" might look like in such a study. Her own research, from which her theoretical argument derives, has included a sample of family nonconformists similar in many ways to my own. Deutsch's study couples equally shared all the parental work in their families. This focus was explicit; she wanted to counter prior research that concentrated on the persistence of inequality in order to show that "mother" and "father" need not inevitably be taken up as intractable gender roles (Deutsch 1999). From this research, Deutsch notes the multiple ways that couples "created equality with varying degrees of gendered behavior":

> Some created a genderless model by taking turns and equalizing all aspects of parenting. Others, however, divided the work equally overall but specialized in aspects of parenting that were more or less gendered (Deutsch 1999). She cooked and he cleaned; she comforted and he helped with homework. (Deutsch 2007:117)

Research like this, Deutsch argues, shows that, contrary to dominant expectations, "parenting need not be gendered" (Deutsch 2007:121). She cites it as an example of the alternative way of thinking about gender she wants to introduce. The couples in her study were clearly "undoing gender."

The couples I interviewed were those I thought would also be "undoing gender" in their interactions and practices as parents. They were redistributing the responsibilities generally associated with mothering and fathering, and challenging old expectations in the process. In that sense, they seemed well placed to (continue to) "undo" the kinds of mothering and fathering most widely supported and represented in the current institutional and cultural context and to give us a glimpse of the change that might become more widespread in future. I will argue, on the basis of my work with these couples, that in some — though not all — cases, mothering and fathering can indeed become degendered through practices that, over time, see fathers doing work conventionally associated with mothers and vice versa. This was the case with Lois and George, whom I described in the introduction to Part I. I noted there that, over time, they came to see themselves as interchangeable, as *parents* rather than mother and father. Deutsch, as I have just noted, suggests that "parenting need not be gendered." However, the argument I will make, based on the experiences of the couples I will introduce in the chapters to follow, is that the "degendering" of mothering and fathering *produces* "parenting." How this happens and what this version of parenting actually looks like will be major themes of the closing chapter.[16]

Chapter Two

The Study

The couples who participated in this study were those who were "going against the grain" of dominant expectations about mothering and fathering. In the last chapter, I described them as couples whom I thought would be "undoing gender" because of the way they organized earning and caring responsibilities in their families. What distinguishes this study from other Canadian research is its specific focus on an unconventional division of labour, across a variety of family forms and specific household arrangements.[1]

The Participants

Decisions about who to include in the research were made, and remade, at several points during the four years (from 2003 to 2007) I was gathering data. I knew I wanted to work with couples. But which couples, specifically? I decided to exclude step-parents, on the assumption that they would probably be dealing with issues (often involving another non-resident parent) that could complicate couple negotiations about caregiving and family finances. My selection criteria were further refined after an early set of interviews with a couple who had equitably shared the care of their young son and then continued to share caregiving through a joint custody arrangement after they separated. The heavy freight of relationship issues that emerged in these interviews persuaded me that the questions of interest to me were best explored in the "pure" case: two people in an intact relationship who were caring for their own children.

One group easily met my general criteria: heterosexual couples who had explicitly overturned conventional earning and caring arrangements by positioning fathers as full-time, home-based primary caregivers and mothers as primary breadwinners. (To introduce the term I define more precisely in coming chapters, I called these couples "crossovers.") Of the 32 couples in the study, 10 had this arrangement at the time they were interviewed, and 6 other couples with older children had had this arrangement some time in the past. Couples in this group were the most easily recognizable and unproblematic in terms of recruitment.

I was also interested in dual-earner couples who were managing an equitable split between *both* earning *and* caring responsibilities. I was clear enough about my criteria, even in the early stages of the project, that I knew I did not want to include dual-earner couples in which fathers "helped" with a caring load for which mothers continued to take the major responsibility. As with the crossover couples, some dual-earner couples who met this more rigorous requirement were also easy to identify — notably the parents of preschool children who organized their work in shifts to ensure full-time parental care of their children. Four couples were "shift workers" caring for preschool children; two had been shift workers some time in their older children's past.

Others in the dual-earner category — those who had more conventional, full-time jobs and depended on outside childcare at least some of the time — were more difficult to identify as going against the grain because the ways they contravened broader gender patterns were less visible and less tangible. Sometimes, they themselves were not sure they met my criteria. Dennis and Penny formed one such couple; I interviewed them at an early stage in my research. The parents of nearly nine-year-old Jamie and three-year-old Fergus, they were both working full time, using after-school care and day care for their children, and sharing childcare and household responsibilities outside of work hours. Dennis commented:

> To some extent we chose this kind of relationship, but to some extent it's not that unusual either. Like, we're working parents who have kids … and are taking care of them together, you know. And so some of it is just, like, if you are two adults who are working full time, you have to share.

Dennis's perspective on the division of family labour he and Penny had established discounted the fact that, for most of the first three years of Jamie's life, he had been the primary caregiver. He had also taken four of the nine months' parental leave on Fergus's arrival, becoming one of only

10 per cent or so of Canadian fathers to take up the parental leave option. And the nature of his caregiving, elaborated more in Penny's account than his own, clearly positioned him as an equal partner, deeply invested in his children's well-being and, significantly, unwilling to cede any ultimate responsibility to Penny when it came to family decision making. The distinction between father as "helper" (Coltrane 1989) and father as (more or less) equal partner was critical in my recruitment process when it came to couples like Penny and Dennis. Although dual-earner families are now the dominant form in Canada and fathers are taking on more of the caregiving load, as I noted earlier, they seldom share to the extent that Dennis was doing. This was why, in my terms, Penny and Dennis were going "against the grain."

Making the distinction was not always easy, and it contributed to the broader challenge of finding couples who fit the study's criteria. As others before me, notably Haas (1980, 1982) and Risman (1998), also noted, the unconventional is more difficult to locate than the conventional. With Schwartz, I could say, "There was an element of 'I can't define it, but I know it when I see it' to my initial search" (1994:4). This meant, on several occasions, talking to couples who, though they considered themselves to be eligible study participants, did not meet my more exacting requirements. For example, one man volunteered for the study on the basis that he and his partner shared caregiving equally. When I met them, I discovered that he had certainly accommodated his college teaching schedule in order to be home with his preschool daughter every morning while her mother worked part time. But he compensated for the later start to his working day by working many evenings. His partner, as well as doing all the household domestic work, also carried all the decision-making responsibility for their daughter. His mornings watching over her represented the full extent of his share. In contrast, when Sam volunteered himself and his partner Jessica for the study, I was at first inclined to think that they too might have been another dual-earner couple featuring a "helper" father and a mother doing most of the work. Sam actually persuaded me to follow up, and I discovered how right he was to do so. As later chapters will indicate, Sam and Jessica turned out to provide a model of egalitarian family life, and they made a significant contribution to the study.

In the first wave of interviewing, my focus was on heterosexual couples, and my theoretical interest was in the ways mothering and fathering played out in tandem and in interaction within the same family. I recruited couples meeting the criteria I have just described by activating my own personal and professional networks; making use of e-mail listservs at two universities, one college, and a parent resource centre; attending childbirth education classes at a hospital; and contacting other community organizations I thought might provide links to "eligible" couples. But any student of change in family gender relations needs to take account of same-sex parents as well. Although their numbers are still very small (less than one per cent of the total of all couples in families according to the 2006 Census of Canada), they are increasing, and their theoretical contribution to any analysis of mothering and fathering is obvious. In the second phase of interviewing, I sought out same-sex couples as well. This introduced another recruiting dilemma. At one level, all same-sex couples are going "against the grain" in the sense of challenging dominant, implicitly hetero-sexual understandings of mothering and fathering. However, some same-sex couples are decidedly traditional in their division of earning and caring responsibilities. One such couple, referred by a university contact, was a good example. The biological mother of their baby was a full-time, home-based caregiver and intended to work only part time if and when she resumed work. Her partner participated in childcare when she could. But she had a busy, highly paid professional career, and, more significantly, she was not "out" as a lesbian at work. It was hard to find two mothers in this family.

It became clear to me that my original criteria still needed to apply; same-sex couples, like heterosexual couples, would be included in the study only if they, too, were egalitarian in sharing both earning and caring responsibilities or if they transgressed conventional expectations about mothering and fathering in other ways. Kendra and Janice comprised one such couple. Kendra, the birth mother, was planning to be the primary breadwinner, and Janice, the co-mother, would be the primary caregiver. In that sense, they were the same-sex equivalent of the heterosexual crossover parents described earlier.

In my sample of same-sex couples, I wanted to include men as well. But gay men caring for their own children in arrangements other than step-parenting ones are still *very* hard to find. My early decision to exclude step-parenting arrangements neatly eliminated from consideration the significant majority of gay fathers, whose children were the product of prior heterosexual relationships and whose gay partners were thus *de facto* step-parents. However, one of my recruiting strategies—an appeal for

study participants on the listserv of a national gay and lesbian organization—produced a response from Mitchell and Tony, who were adoptive
parents. Obviously, gay fathers with adopted children were the ones I
needed to find.

My search for an adoption agency offering services to gay parents led to
a serendipitous conversation with the executive director of one such
agency. This conversation pushed me to think also about the theoretically
interesting position of heterosexual adoptive parents negotiating mothering and fathering arrangements uncomplicated by the biological privilege—
and often, the subsequent default "primary parent" status—usually enjoyed
by birth mothers. Through this adoption agency, I found the final group of
couples included in the study: two more gay couples whose earning and
caring arrangements, actual or anticipated, fit my criteria for going
"against the grain," as well as three heterosexual couples who were raising
adopted children in the unconventional ways that were my research focus.

Having outlined my study selection criteria as they developed, I should
also note that these criteria were flexible. I was inclined to bend them to
include, rather than exclude, couples I felt would make a contribution to
the study. For example, two of the same-sex couples were fairly new parents, with children less than a year old. But same-sex couples who fit my
criteria were very difficult to locate. I weighed their limited parental experience against the considerable interest and relevance for the study of their
thinking and planning for the future. Another example of my selection
flexibility was my decision to include Christine and James, "shift workers"
organizing their work schedules to ensure full-time parental care for their
two preschoolers. In fact, they were not quite able to pull off the 50–50
split that strict adherence to the criteria would have dictated; Christine
was at home three weekdays to James's two, and he earned more of the
family income. But each saw their current arrangements as a stage on the
way to an equal balance that would probably involve each partner working
less than full time. As it was, their passionate commitment to equality, the
way they were sharing the challenges of their current family circumstances, and James's unusually family-oriented work arrangements easily
justified their inclusion, from my perspective.

Altogether, I included 32 couples, with children ranging in age from
newborn to 17 years, who participated in the study between 2003 and
2007. Of these, 13 couples (40 per cent of the total) were referred by someone who knew them; and 19 couples voluntarily responded to one of my

appeals for participants. All the couples were living in major urban centres: 8 in British Columbia, 17 in Alberta, and 7 in Ontario. A more complete description of the participants is available in the appendix. Here is a summary of some of the relevant details, however:

- 27 couples were heterosexual, 3 were gay, and 2 were lesbian; the 3 gay couples had adopted children, as had 3 of the heterosexual couples;
- the mothers' ages ranged from 30 to 50, and the fathers' from 30 to 64;
- the mothers' education level was generally higher, with 26 of the 31 mothers and 18 of the 33 fathers possessing at least an undergraduate university degree;
- estimated annual family incomes ranged from $14,000 to more than $200,000, with almost half of the couples earning a family income of $90,000 or more;
- only 2 participants, both fathers, were from racial or ethnic backgrounds other than White.

Though a range of education and income levels and occupations was represented in the group, there was certainly a preponderance of well-educated White professionals, especially among the mothers. However, my intention was not to generalize to a broader population but to map a phenomenon — the contravention of dominant gender patterns in paid and family work. For such an exercise, what matters much more than the frequency of any descriptive category is the range — of education, income, ethnic background, and so on — that is represented. In that sense, the participants in this study contributed many points to the map.

Interviews and Analysis

The project's data came from semi-structured interviews. I met with each partner in a couple separately, for a time usually ranging from about 45 minutes to an hour and a half. Interviewing partners separately was a conscious decision: like Hertz (1995), I was interested in individual accounts, not in one "couple" account jointly constructed. For all but three of the couples, at least one partner was interviewed at home, and, in most cases both were. (Other interviews were done either in the partner's workplace or in a coffee shop close to home. In two cases, time constraints meant that telephone interviews were used to follow up brief in-person meetings.)

Each interview began with a focus on the couple's earning and caring arrangements — how they came about, how they had changed over time, how well they worked, and for whom. In choosing individual rather than couple interviews, I was also encouraging an individual perspective on these arrangements. So, from a common initial focus, the interviews ranged widely over topics linked to each couple's circumstances and each individual's "take" on them. Field notes were made after all interviews, most of which were fully transcribed.[2]

Though this was an interview study, my approach to the interviews can best be described as ethnographic. I was exploring a particular social phenomenon — earning and caring "against the grain" — that did not occur in a single setting but was more like the "amorphous social experiences" described by Lofland et al. (2006:19). In that sense, like most phenomena associated with family life, it did not lend itself to observation; interviewing thus needed to stand in for observation as a way to explore all the dimensions of the phenomenon. This meant making interviews work in a different way — making them, figuratively at least, what Matthews (2005:801) describes as "episodes of participant observation" in which interviewees are encouraged through questions and probes to "create fieldnotes about the research topic that record the world through the informant's eyes."

One of the clearest ways participating couples could be differentiated was in terms of the age of their children. As it turned out, children's ages covered almost the entire span of official dependency. At one end was 10-week-old Alexia, whose parents Andrew and David had adopted her at birth. She was present during our interviews as a wide-eyed babe in arms in a pink sleeper. At the other end was 17-year-old Leah, the daughter of Laura and Ian, interested in art and music and about to start Grade 12. Children's ages significantly shaped the arrangements that couples made to provide care and financial support, and arrangements changed over time, as the experiences of Laura and Ian, described in a later chapter, will show. Preschool children generally are in a different category from school-age children in terms of the kind of care they need and the institutional arrangements available for its provision. Once children reach school age, responsibility for their supervision during the day shifts to the education system. So the transition to school was often also a significant transition point for the couples in the study, in terms of the way they organized earning and caring responsibilities.

Within these two general groupings—parents of preschoolers and parents of school-age children—there were also differences in earning and caring arrangements. It became clear, for example, that families in which the father was the home-based primary caregiver to preschoolers faced different issues from those in which there were two earners working hard to share caring work equitably as well. It made sense, especially among preschooler parents, to group them according to their distinctive work and family arrangements. These analytic decisions meant that I was considering the couples in small, discrete groupings, based first on the ages of their children and then on the earning and caring arrangements they had made. In other words, the couples did not for me constitute a "sample" in which all the interview material was pooled and then examined systematically for cross-cutting themes. Conforming, at least in intention, to Zussman's view of what "works best" in qualitative research, my approach was more opportunistic than systematic, geared to specify rather than generalize, and working from cases not samples (Zussman 2004:352).

My analysis was also informed by the work of Gubrium and Holstein (1997; see also Holstein and Gubrium 1994, 1997), who call for a "new language" to talk about the social world, a language that can balance naturalistic "descriptions of reality" with attention to the way such descriptions are constructed. This is analysis at the "lived border of reality and representation" (Gubrium and Holstein 1997:101; see also May 2001 and Mason 2002a, 2002b). My strategy was to read the interviews literally and naturalistically, for descriptions of what people were doing, but also to read them as accounts or particular framings of those doings. This is a delicate balancing act. To give interviews only a literal reading is to miss many of the nuances in accounts framed by interviewees with a particular purpose or audience in mind. But to read them only as accounts, as carefully crafted stories detached from the "real world," is to ironicize what people say in a way I find disrespectful; in research, as in life, we do sometimes have to be able to take people "at their word." I did, however, always bear in mind that the interviews were also accounts, stories told to me that could have been told differently under different circumstances and to a different audience.[3]

As the audience for all these interviews (more, as an active participant in their construction), I bear considerable responsibility. My person, my background, my biases, and my questions all shaped the accounts that were produced, as well as my interpretations of those accounts (Holstein and Gubrium 1997; Coffey 2002). Research participants who sat down with me, in homes or offices or over coffee, saw an older middle-aged White woman whose middle-class background they had probably already deduced from my university affiliation, among other cues. In conversation, they soon learned other things: that I was also a mother, that I too had spent time at home as a primary caregiver to preschoolers, that I too had juggled earning and caring work when my children were older. Some also learned that, as a single working mother and, before that, a much more traditional one, I had a family history that was different from theirs. I'm sure I communicated my sense that what they were trying to do in their families was a worthy enterprise. All, I think, would have sensed in me someone who was deeply interested in what they had to say.

Commitment to the principle of reflexivity in research of this kind compels researchers to acknowledge their role, both as co-creators of the interview accounts that constitute their data and as interpreters of those accounts in the distinctive narrative that is the written-up end product. But there is a fine line between acknowledging our presence and its likely effects and "overemphasizing our potential to change things" (Atkinson and Coffey 2002:812). Too much attention to the researcher drowns out the voices of the participants, who are the main focus, and diminishes their role as experts on the phenomenon under study. Judith Stacey comments:

> A thoroughly reflexive and dialogic narrative strategy can become too relativistic or solipsistic. Moreover, such a strategy encumbers the writing process beyond the limits of my patience or agility, just as it might unduly strain the forbearance of readers. (Stacey 1998:36)

I agree with Stacey. In the same vein, I have appreciated Barbara Katz Rothman's distinction between research and "me-search" (Rothman 2005:ix). The chapters that follow are about the 32 couples who participated in the research—but without going into the sort of detail that overwhelms this focus, I must make it clear that what follows is my story of their stories, told mostly in the kind of everyday language that seemed to fit the accounts and the individual circumstances I was discussing.[4]

Part II

Getting Started: Caring for Children in the Preschool Years

Introduction

Organizing family life with preschoolers poses many challenges. The demands of at least one job have to be negotiated around children needing care that somebody has to provide around the clock. What will work best depends on a wide array of circumstances, including parents' earning power and interests, their perception of children's needs, the number of children in the family, and other family and community resources. Here and in the two chapters to follow, I introduce the couples in the study who were in these early years of caregiving. The nature of their earning and caring arrangements and how they came about will set the scene for an exploration of mothering and fathering as shaped by these arrangements.

For the 19 couples involved, an early question was whether their children would have exclusively parental care or whether parental care would be supplemented by outside childcare. For those who wanted only parental care, one option was to designate one parent as primary caregiver and the other as primary breadwinner. For heterosexual couples, the traditional choice would have been to designate the mother as the primary caregiver and the father as the primary breadwinner. The heterosexual couples in my study who went with this option instead designated the father as the primary caregiver. Adapting Sweet and Moen (2006), I called this group the *crossovers*.[1] The other choice for couples wanting round-the-clock parental care was to organize their paid work in staggered shifts so that one parent was always available at home. Couples who chose this option, whom I designated the *shift-workers*, were going against the grain in the sense that both family and employment responsibilities had generally equal status for each parent; importantly, both took more or less equal shares of the caring. A third category of parents supplemented parental care with outside childcare. They were, on the face of it, like more conventional dual-earning couples, juggling two paying jobs around the needs of their children. Unlike these more conventional couples, however, the preschooler parents in this study who were dual earners went against the grain of conventional arrangements by virtue of their family structure (*who* was doing the juggling and for whom) and also in the way they privileged and allocated work and family responsibilities. I called them *dual-dividers* to indicate their combination of full-time earning with shared caregiving.[2]

Nine of the couples with preschool children were *crossovers*. Of these, six heterosexual couples had had this arrangement from the beginning of their lives as parents, with the father usually assuming stay-at-home caregiver responsibilities when the mother returned to work after her first maternity (or, in one case, adoption) leave. One lesbian couple I interviewed when their first child was seven months old were planning an equivalent crossover: the birth mother intended to return to full-time paid work at the end of her year's maternity leave, when the co-mother would become the home-based primary caregiver. Two couples came later to their crossover arrangements from earlier, more conventional divisions of earning and caring work. In one case, the mother's growing private professional practice — and the expected birth of a second child — coincided with the father's wish to quit his paying job and develop home-based work. In the other, the very complicated childcare arrangements needed as a result of an unexpected third pregnancy was the push for a father, already working from home, to take on all the caregiving.

Given the demographic trend towards later age at first childbirth (Altrucher and Williams 2003; Beaujot 2004; Grindstaff 1984), it is not too surprising that all but one of the birth mothers were in their 30s when they had their first baby — and the ticking biological clock was a factor in many discussions about the timing of the pregnancy. Another factor, and the common thread in all the mothers' accounts, was their employment status. All were professionally employed, in secure, well-paying jobs, or were on track to obtain such employment. All were highly motivated to continue working. All had partners who could not match their professional training or their earning potential and who were much less firmly attached to paid employment or career paths of any kind. But beyond these bare demographic descriptors lay parents' individual assessments of their own and their partners' interests, aspirations, and capacities, as well as a sense of the arrangements that would work best for the family as a whole. Like the couples interviewed by Dienhart (1998), they shared the belief that parental care surpassed any other kind. Although ticking biological clocks may have dictated the timing of parenthood and career potential may have made the designation of primary earner and primary caregiver responsibilities seem straightforward, parents' accounts suggested other elements of this unconventional division of labour that also played in to the arrangement. In almost every case, there was a comfortable convergence of goals and interests, in which the demographic factors noted above linked to individual circumstances that made the crossover arrangement the obvious choice and one that, in several cases, was extended beyond the birth of the first child. In these cases, the arrangement seemed destined to last as long as there were preschool children at home.

Four of the study couples with preschool children were *shift-workers*. Like the crossover parents, the shift-workers had strong views about the superiority of parental care. But, for a variety of reasons, they wanted or needed to organize it in a way that did not position one parent exclusively at home and the other exclusively at work. For all the shift-workers, children arrived at a time in both partners' lives when sharing was possible. These couples, considered as cases, illuminated the different circumstances and motivations that may lead to the shift-work arrangement. One couple, like the shift-worker couples described by Hochschild (1989) and Deutsch and Saxon (1998), came to their even-handed sharing of childcare and paid work through financial necessity not philosophical commitment: the need for two incomes was the chief motivator for a classic shift-work arrangement in which the mother worked days and the father worked nights. In another case, it was philosophical commitment to sharing both the earning and the caring that led parents to alternate days of paid work and caregiving. The third couple alternated morning and afternoon work shifts; in this case, an older and more experienced father was cutting back on work hours to accommodate a younger professional mother's resumption of her career. The morning-afternoon alternation was the temporary and early choice in the fourth case, a gay couple that had recently adopted a newborn.

The *dual-dividers* were couples who, like the shift-workers just described, were dual earners. However, at the time I interviewed them, they were using paid childcare or workplace-supported parental leave to help them balance two more or less full-time paying jobs and the care of preschool children. What set this group apart from other, more representative dual-earner couples can best be understood by a closer look at that more representative pair: statistically, it would involve a heterosexual couple in which the father's income would typically be greater than the mother's; she would be more likely to take parental leave; and it would be her job, rather than his, that would be more likely to be modified to accommodate family responsibilities.[3] The six couples I describe here possessed few if any of these characteristics. Men, as well as women, took parental leave; women frequently earned the higher incomes; and women's as well as men's jobs were privileged in the family. Moreover, for the same-sex couples in this category, the family comparisons were not between mothers and fathers in the first place.

In terms of timing, all the babies that turned these couples into parents were planned. For two couples — biological mothers in their 30s with younger partners — joint readiness was partly a matter of the fathers' willingness to accommodate the mothers' more urgent sense of timing. For the other couples, both partners' intentions were necessarily equal and strong: three couples had to go through the rigorous approval process required of adoptive parents, and one lesbian couple achieved a pregnancy through in vitro fertilization. In all these cases, a strong commitment to being parents was combined with little control over when children arrived.

All the babies also entered dual-earner families that, with some gaps and digressions, continued to manage around two paying jobs. But what particularly distinguished this group of parents was the flexibility of their paid work. Sometimes flexible work arrangements preceded — and so helped determine — childcare arrangements. For these parents also, arrangements were very fluid. Changes came as children moved out of maternal or parental leave coverage and into the age range of institutional childcare arrangements. Changes were also cyclical, as the sequence of arrangements established for the first baby were repeated for the second baby. These cycles also had consequences for older children, who might be withdrawn from outside daycare to spend time at home again with a parent on leave and an infant sibling.

All of the foregoing makes clear that, for most partners with preschool children, the paths leading to unconventional divisions of earning and caring work had their starting point in complex sets of relationships — to paid work, to domestic work, to community resources and institutions, and, above all, to one another. Choices about paid work and childcare involved both partners, and early choices affected later outcomes for both, as well. These choices and their outcomes during the preschool years are the basis of the next two chapters.

In Chapter 3, I introduce in more detail the *crossover* couples—those with breadwinner mothers and partners (in most cases fathers) at home caring for preschoolers. This arrangement raises important questions about mothering and fathering when conventional gender boundaries are crossed as mothers and fathers, in one sense at least, change places.

Chapter 4 moves to the couples in the study whose division of labour involved both partners sharing both earning and caring—the *shift-workers* and the *dual-dividers*. For these couples, it was their even-handed sharing of *family* responsibilities, as well as financial provision, that distinguished them from dual-earner couples in general. These couples raised questions about work-family balance between partners, as well as between individuals and work(places), and about the nature of mothering and fathering when the sharing of *all* responsibilities causes conventional gender boundaries to blur.

Chapter Three

The "Crossovers": Breadwinner Mothers with Partners at Home

Tanya and Adam were the classic crossover couple. When I met them, Tanya was 42 and an established university professor. Adam was 36 and the full-time stay-at-home caregiver to their two children, Joel, aged five, and Lucy, aged eight months. Tanya and Adam first met when she was finishing her undergraduate degree. He had a technical college diploma and was working at a sales job. From early in their relationship, with Tanya's decision to pursue graduate training and an academic appointment, her career path was clearly delineated, and she followed it without interruption. Adam's situation was different. He interspersed periods of employment with travel, both on his own and later, in order to be with Tanya as she completed her graduate program in another province. After they married, he supported them both through other sales jobs until, towards the end of her PhD work, Tanya gave birth to Joel. Tanya recalled that they put Joel in a day care centre to start with, while Adam worked and she finished her PhD dissertation. "He got sick constantly, and so we were up all night with him anyway," she said. Adam, with little commitment to his current job, had always been willing in principle to take on the caregiver role. So they inaugurated the unconventional sharing of paid and family work that had characterized their family ever since. They replaced his income with student loans to tide them over. Tanya, in due course, finished her PhD and started a full-time university job. When I met them, Tanya had just returned to work after a six-month maternity leave following the birth of their daughter, Lucy. Adam had been the home-based caregiver for about five years.

Mothering and Fathering in "Crossover" Families

The experiences of Tanya and Adam clearly illuminate the way conventional expectations about mothering and fathering are challenged when the mother is the primary (in Tanya's case the sole) breadwinner and the father is the primary caregiver, based full time at home. On the face of it, Tanya and Adam, like the other heterosexual crossover couples, had simply reversed the traditional family roles. In her workplace, Tanya could assume the privileges of those of her male colleagues who had stay-at-home wives, and she could see that she was actually better off than the male colleagues whose partners were also employed full time. "Their life is way more complicated than mine," she commented. For Tanya, work-related travel was no problem, and she acknowledged that she could spend full days in her office without thinking too much about what was happening at home. She was free to concentrate on the workplace demands that would make her job secure and ensure her promotion. Adam, for his part, did all the day-to-day care of very young children that is much more often the domain of mothers. He changed diapers and also entertained, soothed, and fed a preschooler and an infant. He was the parent who located and participated in the weekday community play group and the evening class for parents. He did all of the cooking and most of the cleaning. He considered his personality to be well suited for the caregiver role, and he was not craving a return to paid employment. "I'm not career driven," he said.

But, at another level, this apparent "role reversal" was not nearly so straightforward. Tanya was still breastfeeding Lucy, so her day started and ended with a quintessentially embodied mothering practice that no working father could perform. She was the parent Joel turned to when he was sick or woke up in the night. She took great pains to compensate him in other ways for her absence at work—phone calls during the day, special adventure outings on the weekend. "It's more being responsive to what the kids are *not* telling you," she said. "As a woman I'm probably more sensitive to that than a dad would be." When possible, she also organized some of her work-related travel so that the whole family could accompany her. She managed the household calendar, keeping track of such diverse events as garbage collection days and family birthdays. She organized all the birthday parties too, as well as performing the "kin work" of staying in touch with extended family members.

Adam as the stay-at-home parent earned no income. But he had done extensive renovations to their first home and all the landscaping for the new house to which they moved when Tanya started her present job. At the time we met, he was finishing the basement. This work was something he enjoyed and also a way, as he phrased it, to "earn his keep" financially, rather than getting a job to cover the cost of having someone else do the work. "I have the sense that, it may not be accurate but, that I actually do take on more than some stay-at-home moms," he said. "You know, house renovation stuff—many moms may not be comfortable doing something like that." Adam's expertise and enjoyment with respect to this more typically masculine activity perhaps compensated for another dimension of home-based caring that also distinguished him from stay-at-home mothers—the work of negotiating social networks and community resources established with mothers, not fathers, in mind. Adam found some of his community encounters "a little bit awkward at times."

Statistically, Tanya and Adam were anomalies:[1] Adam as a man at home and Tanya (relaying a friend's comment) as a working woman with "a wife." Adam was emphatic about the rewards of being close to his children, being their "coach and mentor." But he was aware that his time as their primary caregiver was at the expense of a more conventional place in the working world:

> I've been able to sort of keep pushing this off into the future, and I haven't devoted a lot of time or energy towards what I want to do.... I guess I take solace from the fact that I just want to be a good parent and be able to be there.... And [I'm] uncertain about how to make myself fit into the rest of the world, and, say, working society when the—when the time comes.

Tanya was aware of the benefits she reaped, in terms of her career, because of Adam's assumption of so much of the childcare and domestic burden. But she also realized that Adam's time at home with their children put him in a privileged position when it came to forming close attachments with them:

In a way that's frightening to me because I think, "Am I not going to have that? Am I going to be just like those men who don't know their kids?" And you know, I think that no, I'm the mom.... The mom kind of knows these things. But that's something that I'm very aware of... Am I just going to be a man in a skirt? Is that what it's going to end up like?

Tanya's questions are an echo of those raised by Barbara Katz Rothman in her discussion of "managerial mothers." Rothman cites Gloria Steinem's comment about such women: "We've become the men we wanted to marry" (Rothman 1989). Adam, like other men facilitating their partners' professional work, was acutely conscious of being outside that world, and not sure how he would "fit back in."

The concerns voiced by Tanya and Adam go to the heart of the matter: the critical issues for mothers and fathers built in to this particular version of earning and caring against the grain. For mothers, it is the need to delegate to the other parent some, if not all, of the authority conventionally ascribed to mothers on the presumption of their greater expertise and knowledge of their children. I have labelled this "executive responsibility." Closely related is the question of attachment. The reward for this authority and responsibility is the mantle of primary parent—the privilege of being "it" not only in terms of ultimate, executive responsibility for family life but also in terms of emotional attachment to children. If ultimate responsibility for children is delegated to or shared by the other parent, this emotional connection might also have to go—and, with it, a core ideological underpinning of motherhood and femininity. For fathers, the issue is the delegation of the breadwinner responsibilities traditionally considered the core paternal contribution to family life. The breadwinner role derives from men's longstanding attachment to paid work and the intricate connection, for most men, between work and masculinity. Men giving up paying jobs in order to run homes and care for children— "women's work" in most social circles—is a radical shift in the gender order. In the remainder of this chapter, I explore how these issues were addressed, first by the mothers and then by the fathers who were living with preschool children in "crossover" arrangements.

Mothers, Executive Responsibility, and Attachment

The allocation of responsibility for children links to the dominant understandings of mothering described in Chapter 1. In contemporary North

America, these understandings have become encapsulated, and widely cited in research, as "intensive mothering" (Arendell 2001; Hays 1996). Ideologically, at least, intensive mothering sets up the mother as the child's primary caregiver, in an approach to child rearing that is "child-centred, expert-guided, emotionally absorbing, labor-intensive and financially expensive" (Hays 1996:8). Mothers' actual practices, as Fox (2006) points out, do not—indeed they often *cannot*—conform to such middle-class expectations, but the expectations continue to dominate. So mothers who have full-time paid employment face what Hays calls "cultural contradictions" as they attempt to reconcile expectations about "good mothering" with the demands of employers in workplaces where family responsibilities are usually downplayed or ignored.

In practice, inevitably, employed mothers must delegate much of the daily caring work once considered the exclusive domain of mothers to other caregivers during the hours they spend away from home. Studies such as those by Garey (1995, 1999), Macdonald (1998), and Uttal (1996) have examined how mothers reconcile the contradictory identities of "mother" and "worker" under such circumstances. This research points to the variety of ways they reframe the caregiving work of others, in most cases retaining executive responsibility (as employers of the caregivers). It also highlights the ways mothers may discursively rearrange and re-evaluate mothering practices so that those practices they retain for themselves are also those seen as the core of "good mothering."

What may also be re-evaluated is the attachment that develops between children and their caregivers. Nelson (1994) and Uttal (2002) note the work that caregivers do, by practising "detached attachment," to uphold the supremacy of the mother-child bond for the children in their care. Nelson writes of the "genuine struggle" this work involves. Macdonald's (1998) study provides another angle on this issue through examples of the ways mothers diminished the strength and importance of the bonds their children forged with nannies or au pair workers. Macdonald also describes the "shadow work" performed by those caregivers to maintain the dominance of the mother.

The ground shifts, however, when most of the daily care of children is delegated not to a paid caregiver but to the other parent. This links to Dienhart's (1998) discussion of "acculturation holdovers" for mothers— the feeling that, even when fathers are involved and competent, they as mothers *should* be their children's first point of contact, the primary parent.[2] Under those circumstances, do mothers retain ultimate, executive responsibility for their children? Does the mother-child attachment change as mothers relinquish primary caregiver status? These are the questions to be addressed in the next two sections.

Mothers and Executive Responsibility: Who's (Really) in Charge?
Sheila, a physician, was coming to the end of maternity leave after the birth of her second baby when I interviewed her. Her husband Keith, who had been the at-home caregiver to their first child, was planning to carry on in the full-time caregiver role when Sheila returned to work. In Sheila's mind, there was no question of who had ultimate responsibility for the children. She acknowledged my suggestion that she played CEO to Keith's executive assistant, joking, "I've trained him well." She explained that her time at home on maternity leave was important because "I'm establishing how we're going to do things." Sheila named herself as the person who picked up the book on discipline, who bought all the children's clothes and decorated their rooms, who did "pretty much everything," in fact. Though Keith "had a say in it," Sheila commented, "I still think it's the typical husband-wife thing where the wife thinks the little things are important, that micromanagement is important, and I still micromanage." Sheila, as a family physician, brought professional expertise to the family that Keith did not have. She had also put in plenty of hands-on caregiving time—through two maternity leaves and a flexible schedule that allowed considerable time at home during the day. Beside that, Keith's daily and ongoing care of the children did not, in Sheila's eyes, authorize him to take charge.

Mothers managing from a distance, as office supervisors of fathers doing the fieldwork of childcare, was an image that occurred in other interviews as well. In the same way that perceptions of a "competence gap" between women and men are considered to disadvantage women in paid employment (Ridgeway and Correll 2000), men's competence as caregivers and family managers was also sometimes seen to fall short. The management activities Tanya engaged in (organizing the calendar, for example) have already been noted. Echoes of Tanya's management strategies and Sheila's combination of maternal expertise and authority also emerged in Ruth's account. Ruth brought a university degree, research skills, and an interest in the global varieties of caregiving styles to the care of her three-year-old son Connor. When he was born, Ruth took seven months of maternity leave. But, like Sheila, she had the higher paying, much more secure job. So when she returned to work, her husband Warren became Connor's full-time caregiver. Warren's background was quite different from Ruth's. With no formal post-secondary training, he had been working in a sporting goods store before Connor's birth. He had no experience of babies. Meanwhile, Ruth, on the basis of her research, had decided that they would practise "attachment parenting," a style of caregiving involving constant, close contact between parent and child and, frequently, the baby sleeping with parents in a "family bed."[3] Ruth's expertise, like Sheila's, established the ground rules. It continued to influence Connor's care in the form of approaches to discipline, which engaged Ruth and Warren in the same kinds of conversations as those Tanya and Adam had as well. Warren, according to Ruth, was "a little bit too hard" on Connor. "He thinks you have to draw the line with children at times, and let them know that you are the boss," she said. "I'd like to take a different approach to disciplining Connor, but I'm not there enough to do it, to fulfil it."

Ruth's alternative strategy, as she reported it to me, was to sit down with Warren and talk about "a whole list of things, about all the things that happened to us during the day" in order to establish a less tense and non-judgemental context in which approaches to Connor's care could be aired. In this context,

> [H]e'll say, "Yeah, I think I'm too hard on Connor, and I have to ease off a little." And so I feel like, OK, he's been hearing me.… And I do, I have some books, a discipline book by William Sears [see note 3, above] and some things I've printed off the Internet about successful disciplining techniques that build esteem, and he's taken the initiative to read those. I just leave them lying round the house [laughs].

Though she attributed their differences more to their personalities and learning styles (hers more intellectual and research based, his learning by doing), Ruth's account contained many elements of the mother "training" the father. But this training, in Ruth's account, was also training to take over. Though she could see that doing the research on issues such as Connor's health or school choices would be her responsibility, "I'm trying to push them off and put them on to Warren, because I don't have enough time in my life, to do that. And as he's going to be the primary caregiver, he's got to take responsibility for those things as well." She foresaw a slow transition though. "There are some things, if he takes over, I'm going to have to help him.... He'll want to do it, but he won't know how."

From Ruth's account, Warren was not always a compliant student or caregiving partner. In his case, micromanagement would not work. Ruth commented that, in non-essentials, such as the clothes Connor wore or the way meals were organized, she had to "let go of trying to impose my values of how a child should be reared." She spoke of having to let go of trying to "control Warren and the situation." Instead, as she put it, she was working to acknowledge Warren as "a smart man" who cared about Connor's health and welfare, even if his approach was more laid back.

The accounts of the "manager" mothers shed light on the issue of maternal gatekeeping—frequently referred to in the scholarly literature as the means by which women may limit men's involvement in family life.[4] Allen and Hawkins (1999) conceptualize maternal gatekeeping in terms of three dimensions: the setting of rigid standards, the need for external validation of a maternal identity, and the belief in differentiated gender roles. Sheila, Tanya, and Ruth, as breadwinners, were clearly not committed to conventional gender roles, and the fact that their partners did more of the caregiving than they did made it hard to argue that, in these families, fathers' involvement was limited. But their managing work spoke to the standards they set for caregiving, and the mother identity was also clearly important to all three.

Among other crossover couples, however, executive responsibility seemed to be less contested and more evenly shared. Several possible reasons emerged from the interview accounts. One was that, unlike Ruth and Warren, these couples held in common a bigger share of the implicit assumptions and expectations about children's needs and caregiver responsibilities that constitute background and baggage for all new parents, so there was less to be contested in daily practice.[5] One was that mothers, however expert they may have been, were explicitly committed to the sharing of responsibility. One was that this group contained stay-at-home caregivers who, from their partners' accounts, were experts in their own right and therefore not in any need of management or control.

For Julia and Matt, all these possible explanations seemed to converge. After seven months of maternity leave, Julia, a lawyer, returned to full-time work, and Matt took over the care of their son Tim, who was four months past his second birthday at the time of the interviews. Like all the other couples described so far, the couple's division of caring and earning labour was at one level a purely pragmatic choice: Julia's was the secure, high-paying job; Matt was leaving much less secure work in construction to become a stay-at-home father. Matt's work background and career aspirations were different from Julia's. But they were also at odds with his university education. Though it was a practical decision that positioned her at work and him at home, there was not the divergence of skills and intellectual interests that shaped the experience of Ruth and Warren. Julia's account contained repeated references to the similarity of their approach to child rearing and of their views about Tim's needs. In one especially telling comment, she observed, "Our style of parenting is quite similar, so we don't have a lot of disagreement about *how he's raising [Tim]*" (my emphasis). Julia framed herself and Matt as equal partners in a team approach to Tim's care, an approach in which individual roles and responsibilities were neither lost nor arranged in a status hierarchy but instead contributed to an organic whole. Julia's account was unusual in that it also contained a recognition of the relationship between Tim and his father going on at home in Julia's absence. Rather than acting as a distant CEO, Julia acknowledged that "they have this whole little world that I don't always feel completely a part of." Rather than enforcing ground rules when she was at home, Julia's focus seemed rather on the need, after working hours, to "re-establish myself in [Tim's] life every day."

The image of equal partners emerged in Paula's account too, even though her expertise as a child psychologist could well have overwhelmed her partner's inexperience and positioned her as the ultimate, executive authority. Paula's partner Alan had been a home-based caregiver to their three-year-old son Mark for the six months prior to the interviews. Before that, both had paid employment: Paula developing her private practice, Alan as a graphic designer. Even at that time, though, Paula commented,

> I still always felt like we were a team with the parenting and didn't feel the division that I hear from either clients or people who come to my classes or just friends of mine… "Well, he kind of leaves the parenting stuff up to me."… I always felt like, when he was home, he was home, and that we still made those decisions together.

Alan's commitment to participate may have been facilitated by Paula's commitment not to allow her formal credentials and expertise to trump his growing sense of himself as a caregiver:

I figured I would probably be a very difficult person to be married to, given all my experience in parenting and the work that I did, that it could be slightly intimidating to be trying to co-parent with me.... And so I really tried to let him find his own path and not say, "Here's the way I think we should do things." And he ploughed ahead with his own path. He didn't ever say, "Was this right?" Or he didn't show any kind of lack of confidence, which I was really impressed with. And it just really flourished that way, and so now ... sometimes I'm amazed that he'll remind me or he'll say, "No, I don't think we should do things that way" ... and I think, "Well, of course we shouldn't! That's what I've been telling everyone else out there!"

Alan became an expert in his own right. In their own ways, so did all the caregivers described so far. Even those positioned as executive assistants to the mother as CEO were acknowledged by those mothers for their patience, competence, and care. But, in some of those cases, there was a sense from the mothers' accounts that the fathers needed to get up to speed, to learn what the mothers already knew. Measuring fathers by the standards of mothers contains a hint of what Hawkins and Dollahite (1997) call the "deficit model" of fathering and may overlook the extra or different contributions fathers bring to caregiving (Doucet 2004b, 2006a). But, on the basis that mothers' retention of executive responsibility is closely linked to their perceptions of the knowledge and competence of their caregiving partners, Julia's willingness to share the responsibility and Paula's determination not to assume control by default signal a shift in family dynamics.

Kendra and Janice were also committed to equal partnership in the raising of their seven-month-old daughter Hannah. As lesbian parents, they needed to confront in their own circle the dominant social understandings about which one of them was the "real" mother, understandings that several research studies have documented (e.g., Gabb 2005; Reimann 1997). At the time they were interviewed, they had yet to complete the process by which Janice (as the non-biological mother) would formally adopt Hannah. Legally, Janice had no status with respect to Hannah's care and welfare. But, in every other way and even though it would have been easy for Kendra, as Hannah's biological mother, to assume ultimate responsibility, Kendra's account resonated with her commitment to equal sharing. Hannah was bottle fed, so Kendra did not retain for herself the exclusive bonds that breastfeeding a baby can forge. She was also planning to return to full-time employment after a year of maternity leave, leaving Janice as the home-based caregiver. In one way, she was framing this division of labour in highly traditional terms, describing Janice as a more traditional mother. In another way, though, this positioning could also work better to strengthen Janice's position as Hannah's second mother.

Sharing of responsibility with another person means that the time and emotional energy involved in being the executive in charge is also shared. Someone else, in Julia's words, is taking on a share of "all of that kind of worry and emotional responsibility that you have for your children and whether all their needs are being met in every respect." Donna's account contained a heartfelt message about this liberation. With three children under the age of six, both Donna (the primary earner) and her home-based partner Scott felt the pressure of family demands. But, as Donna commented, "I don't like the feeling…if they always want me." Asked whether she had any regrets or sadness about stepping away from primary parent status, she commented,

> Part of my whole premise for marrying Scott [was] to have someone that's a great father because I missed that when I was growing up…. So does it make me sad at all? Instead it just makes me really proud that that he is so good to them. And, in a way, I have the philosophy that they're our kids, so why should it be a mother's responsibility to feel more like she's the one that needs to take care of them?

Mothers and Attachment: Keeping in Touch

The question asked at the beginning of this chapter was whether the mother-child attachment changed as mothers relinquished primary caregiver status — the presumption being that primary caregiver status carries primary attachment status with it. For the mothers included in this section, who all had very young children, this was a particularly complex question. Aside from the fact that, in an interview study, "attachment" is an abstract and difficult concept to address, there were other challenges. Though all the mothers had children under six years of age, their individual circumstances varied greatly. The children's ages ranged from infancy to nearly school age, and family size ranged from one child to three. This range is best understood by considering Kendra, at one end, and Donna, at the other. Kendra was still on maternity leave with her first child, seven-month-old Hannah; Donna had three children ranging in age from nearly two to five years. Two mothers in this group, Patricia and Kendra's partner Janice, were not biological mothers. This diversity in individual circumstances actually illuminated, in microcosm, the fluctuations in maternal involvement with children and the way practices — and attachments — change over time as children grow. If the mothers' sense of their emotional *status* with their children was difficult to assess, the interview accounts showed clearly the work women did to maintain and foster the emotional connection over time.

The biological mothers, because of their connection to their children through pregnancy, birth, and breastfeeding, might be considered to have an advantage that working fathers (and non-biological mothers) did not have. These intensely embodied experiences were a foundation on which all of them built, at least to some extent. And "keeping in touch" (with the emphasis on *touch*) turns out to be an apt metaphor for the practices many mothers employed when they were back at work. For example, most mothers continued to breastfeed for at least a short period after returning to work, as a way to extend as long as possible the intimate mother-child connection nursing provides.

Patricia's story was an interesting counterpoint. She was the mother of five-year-old Jonathan, adopted as a newborn. For Patricia, a physician, and her caregiver partner Graham, adoption was a deliberate choice not a consequence of infertility. From their accounts, it was, rather, an outcome of their shared belief that they could be as fulfilled raising an adopted child (who needed a family) as a biological child. In Fisher's (2003) terms, they were altruistic or preferential adopters. Patricia commented:

> It's a matter of "love is love," right? You give it freely. For us, that was never an issue.... Even when I think about my relationship with Jonathan, and could that have been different in any way [had he been Patricia's biological child], again I think the answer is no. The moment I held him — yeah, I hadn't had that number of months of feeling him move and developing that bond. So a bond was slower to develop. But it happened very quickly when I held him. You know, that was that.

Most mothers explicitly named themselves as the prime comforter, the person to whom children turned when they were sick or distressed at night. For very young children, night hours are not always hours lost to sleep, and mothers capitalized on the caregiving opportunities that occurred then. For example, Ruth and her husband Warren, as noted earlier, practised attachment parenting. This parenting approach not only involved close physical connection between parents and child during waking hours but also "co-sleeping." Three-year-old Connor had slept in his parents' bed, at his mother's side, from birth. He nursed there through the night as a baby. His physical presence during the night, an extension of the "supper time and bath time and reading books in bed time" that Ruth described as her evening routines with Connor, was, in Ruth's view, an important means of maintaining her close relationship with Connor.

Other mothers described scaled-down versions of this night-time closeness, along with other aspects of their after-hours care. Tanya acknowledged her active participation in an array of such activities:

> The kids come to me when they're sick. I foster that. I want them to do that.... It feeds my need to know that I'm still needed. If you want Mom when you're sick, fine, I'll crawl into bed with you.... I'll give you a snuggle if you have a bad dream.... [Joel] is going through a phase now, he goes through this about every year to eighteen months, where he starts to have nightmares...And so we have what we call a little nest in our bedroom, that he can just come up and climb up into...but it's on my side of the bed. He doesn't want it on Dad's side of the bed; he wants it on my side of the bed. Fine, if that's what it takes to keep you happy, to give you comfort. You know, he sometimes wants to fall asleep on my pillow. Fine, if that's all it takes to give you the comfort that you need.... We're very sensitive to the need for him to have that connection because I'm just not physically there all day.

Physical connectedness was often accompanied, in mothers of very young children, by an ongoing attentiveness to the details of the child's day unfolding in another place and under another's care. Though they were not physically present, the mothers of very young children practised the kind of "attentive love" that Ruddick (1982) considers central to maternal thinking. Paula, on work days when she was separated from three-year-old Mark, spoke of being more consumed than Mark's father Alan would be with "what's going on with him when I'm away from him." Julia, whose awareness of the "whole little world" her son Tim shared with his caregiver father was noted earlier, spoke of a similar need to know—and of her husband Matt's attentiveness in ensuring that she did. "He catches me up as soon as I go home," she said. "We spend the first half hour going over the whole day."

Paula and Julia had only one child on whom to lavish this interest and attention and with whom a close emotional bond could be forged. The addition of one or more extra children had the potential to change both needs and allegiances in a fluid economy of time and other parental resources. Wendy laughingly recalled that she had probably asked more questions about the day with her first child. Now, with three, "I don't need every detail!" Wendy also noted the shift in the children's own allegiances as her periods of employment alternated with times at home on maternity leave. Interviewed within days of the end of her third such leave, Wendy noted that "now, they want Mom." But very soon, Dad would be the parent to whom they turned first. "Their loyalties change very quickly when you go back to work," she said.

Wendy could take a longer view than Sheila, who was coming to the end of her second maternity leave. Sheila's retention of executive responsibility for Kevin, aged two and a half, and six-month-old Brent has already been described. She was also in no doubt of her current status as Kevin's primary parent. "When I get home, it's still Daddy is Daddy and Mommy is best," she said. Sheila noted that an illness during her second pregnancy reduced her ability to interact with Kevin, so he directed more attention to Keith, his father. However, she said, "Until that point, for those two whole years, when I got home, Kevin followed me everywhere":

> When he got hurt, he called for his mommy. When he needed something, he called for Mommy, even though I'm the one at work. And when I got sick, that did change. But now I've been home for six months, and, well, it's back [laughs]. So, if Keith and I are home together and I'm upstairs, Kevin's upstairs with me; he still follows me round like a little duckling.

But she also noted that, over time, as Keith continued in the primary caregiver role, Kevin might become "a bit more partial" to Keith:

> I can see that. I suppose that would be a bit heart-wrenching, but I wouldn't want to do anything to sabotage it because, you know what? If Keith's the one at home, then that's the role he plays.

Donna could tell her that this outcome is not inevitable. As children grow, their needs change. Their time with the primary caregiver is reduced as they enter the institutional world of playgroups and drop-in day care.

Physical connectedness, the only satisfactory means of bonding with a baby, becomes less central for a child who can talk and wants to be listened to as well as cuddled. The development of intellect and personality accompanies a growing ability to make choices; children's own agency begins to influence parent-child relationships. In Donna's case, there were distinct parental preferences among her three children. Nadine, the middle child, had been an extremely demanding baby, who was acutely distressed when Donna returned to work after a six-month leave. Of the three children, Nadine continued to be the most dependent on her mother. As Donna commented, "She slept on top of me until she was eight months old, and she just still has that strong need for being so close." On the other hand, Everett, at nearly two, was showing a preference for Scott, his father. The dynamics of the family were resolving along gender lines, with Nadine and Isabel, the eldest, aligning with their mother and Everett with his father.

But preferences and allegiances were not the substance of most of the maternal talk about relationships with children. Mothers were generous in their recognition of the close connections children formed with the parent at home. Rather than reckoning up parental winners and losers, they were more inclined to speak in terms of the value to their children of two individuals unconditionally committed to them and in tune with their needs. Julia articulated this perspective most clearly. She spoke of worrying that, on her return to work from maternity leave, she would be "less bonded" with her son Tim. "I think it was a little hard to let go of initially," she said. "But once I did let go of it, it was great." The change, for Julia, had brought new understanding about the linkages between herself, Tim, and Tim's caregiver father Matt:

> It's not as if there's this much in the pot and [Matt]'s got eighty and now I've only got twenty. It doesn't seem to work like that.... There's so much of it there that, in a way, the more he's taken on, I think it hasn't meant that I've lost any of it. I'm still as much of a mother as I would be if I was home all the time or if [Tim] was going to day care, or whatever.... We have our own sort of relationship. I have things that are particular to our relationship.... I think he has his own relationship with each of us, and it's been really great because I think [Matt] and I really understand what it is to be parents in an equal way.... It actually makes me feel a lot more comfortable about my own life. About the fact that [Tim]'s so bonded with him, so if, god forbid, anything ever did happen to me... at least he has somebody who he is really, truly connected with.

Fathers, Work, and Domesticity

In the same way that dominant expectations about mothering and motherhood shape not only maternal practice but also the way women make sense of their experiences as mothers, so expectations about fathering and fatherhood influence men. In a sense, these expectations are reciprocal: as mothers are expected to have ultimate responsibility for children, so fathers are expected to have ultimate responsibility for the family's financial support. This, as I discussed in Chapter 1, is the cultural backdrop against which the experiences of the home-based caregiver fathers in this study must be viewed. Though their numbers are growing, they still comprise a tiny proportion of Canadian fathers overall (see note 1, above).

Fathers' designation as breadwinners is often reckoned to date from the industrial revolution. Over time, the workplaces away from the home, which arrived with industrialization, came to be perceived as men's turf, as did the wages paid for work conducted there. The concept of the "family wage" reinforced the dominant view of fathers as sole providers. The apparently inextricable link between fathers and paid employment builds on cultural expectations about work as a fundamental component of contemporary masculinity. Research suggests that fathers see breadwinning as something they must do to fulfil their responsibilities not only as fathers but also as men. As I noted in Chapter 1, men's caregiving has gradually increased over time. But studies in Canada (e.g., Luxton and Corman 2001) and in the United States (e.g., Roy 2004; Townsend 2002) indicate that a man who is not a breadwinner may feel that his masculinity is being judged and found wanting. Townsend, in a 2002 ethnographic study of a fathers in a northern California town, found that they tended to view economic provision as part of what he called a "package deal," in which having children, being married, holding down a steady job, and owning a home were interconnected elements. Daly and Palkovitz (2004) note that work and family issues for women have been framed in a discourse of *choice*, the assumption being that women were "choosing" paid employment after decades of either being deliberately excluded from such work or being told their place was at home. By contrast, "it is culturally assumed that men will work and pay attention to their families (in that order)" (Daly and Palkovitz 2004:212). Griswold (1993) comments: "Despite men's differences, breadwinning has remained the great unifying element in men's lives. Its obligations bind men across the boundaries of color and class, and shape their sense of self, manhood, and gender" (quoted in McGraw and Walker 2004:183).

If fathers are expected to be breadwinners first, it is not surprising that the involvement they do have with their children might be different from that of mothers. Pleck and Stueve (2001) note the now classic statement by Lamb, Pleck, Charnov, and Levine (1985) proposing three dimensions, which, in later iterations, came to be known as *engagement* or direct paternal interaction with the child, *accessibility* or availability to the child, and *responsibility* or "the role [the] father takes in making sure the child is taken care of and arranging for resources to be available for the child" (Pleck and Stueve 2001:211). Pleck and Stueve, along with other collaborators (e.g., Pleck and Masciadrelli 2004; Marsiglio and Pleck 2005) draw attention to the criticisms of the paternal involvement construct and, in particular, to the dearth of research on the "responsibility" domain. With these caveats in mind, however, studies have tended to indicate that it is in the area of taking responsibility that fathers are least involved. Fathers are characterized as "helpers" rather than full co-parents (Coltrane 1996:54).

Men who are full-time caregivers to preschool children may challenge these assumptions, especially if (as was the case with the full-time caregiver fathers in this study) they are voluntarily unemployed. For such men, the discourse of choice frames a decision *not* to engage in paid work. As primary caregivers, they are "new fathers" par excellence. But they challenge convention in that their exceptional involvement in caregiving is not the overlay to a foundation of financial provision. For these fathers, caregiving is, in most cases, the total package.

This package comes with many challenges. How do men manage the transition from paid work to home-based caregiving, and how do they experience caregiving and other domestic work? In particular, do they take responsibility for their children in the sense specified by Lamb et al. (1985)? How do they function, at home and in their communities, in physical and social space more often occupied by women? These questions are considered in the next two sections.

Working but Not Earning

The transition from paid employment to home-based caregiving did not involve immediate career sacrifices for any of the men in the group. All were partnered with women whose paid work at the time they had children was more stable and at a higher professional level than their own. In fact, the women had careers and career aspirations; most of the men did not. Alan had been working under stressful conditions in a graphic design firm. Peter had been doing customer service work. Keith had a contract position as an accountant. Matt had been working in construction, Adam in technical sales, Graham in a non-profit organization. None of them was unhappy to move home. Providing care for their very young children was framed by all of them as more valuable and enjoyable than the paid work that they had been doing. They resembled the men in Gerson's study, whose turn towards family involvement was often propelled by a lack of interest in the "fast track" and commitment to what Gerson called "non-domestic women" (Gerson 1993). Time at home, at this stage of their children's lives, was also time away from the working worlds of most men. It could also be construed as time out, a reprieve from the demands of the conventional workplace and an opportunity to reflect on what might come next. *When* that time out occurred in the course of the father's working life could be of some consequence, as Warren's situation illustrated.

Warren, at 30 the youngest of the fathers in the group, had been working as a repair mechanic in a sporting goods store when his son Connor was born. From Warren's account, his wife Ruth was the one with "the plan." She was three years older and more ready to have a baby than Warren was. "Being a dad was last on my list of things to do," he said.

> Even now, I don't feel like I'm ready.... I tell Ruth that, I think I should have waited, you know? And the timing, the timing seemed kind of out of balance because...I wanted to have a career...I wanted to have something.

Although Warren's ambivalence about fatherhood was quickly replaced by a passionate devotion to Connor and a commitment to his care, the "something" that he wanted also began to emerge. He had always had an interest in art and a talent for building things. He began by building furniture for their own house and then conceived the plan of designing and producing furniture pieces for sale. He was doing some of this furniture building work late at night because there were few daytime spaces available away from three-year-old Connor. This absence of child-free time was largely a consequence of the "attachment" style of parental care, already mentioned, that both Warren and Ruth practised. This close engagement with Connor made Warren increasingly unwilling to leave him with anyone else, even grandparents and even for a short period. During his interview, the tension between his commitment to being Connor's sole caregiver and his frustration about not having the time to "get his thing going" as a builder of original furniture was almost palpable.

Scott also confronted time constraints on home-based work. But, in his case, becoming the full-time caregiver to three small children was a smoother transition. Scott was a designer who had always worked from home, and he had already established himself in a specialized field. The transition in his case involved dispensing with the paid caregiving, both in the home and outside it, that the couple had used before Scott's wife Donna took her last maternity leave. In terms of his work, it involved a significant scaling back, from a daily eight or so hours to just an hour or two if things worked out well on any given day. But he did keep up the work, even though the scale changed, through ongoing contracts. Scott noted the availability of grandparents as back-up childcare if "things were getting really tight" and Donna's sensitivity to his work time constraints and her ability to help find solutions. Unlike most of the other fathers in the group, Scott did have career aspirations, though not of a corporate, career-ladder kind.

> I did aspire, I still do aspire to be as good as I can be.... I'm getting good reviews from people, and people are saying nice things, and I sort of sometimes think, "Well, I probably could be a little better if I didn't have kids." So I guess, if [there's] a downside, that's it. But... it's just the way it is. It's just the way I've chosen to live.

For Scott, like legions of women in his situation, it was a question of putting a viable and absorbing career on the back-burner rather than thinking about starting from scratch when the children reached school age. This time in the course of his working life was, in his words, "a blip."

Scott's home-based design practice was exactly what Alan was hoping to establish too. This was the work connection he hoped to maintain during his time as a home-based caregiver. But he felt called to account by the lower work priority his stay-at-home status seemed to imply:

> Sometimes I feel I'm supposed to be working more than I am or devoting a whole bunch of time to setting up this [home office]. I do have, I guess, a hard time dealing with expectations of being a careerist type.... It's not something that I enjoy trying to put into words, talking to other people and saying, "I'm

a stay-at-home dad" or whatever. That's I guess the hard part for me, ... framing it, what I really like to do versus what people understand I do.... You know, when you are just doing this because it seems natural to you and it's much more rewarding than what you would otherwise be doing... it's almost like you feel you have to justify it ... which you don't think should be the case.

Scott, with ongoing home-based work, and even Alan, with a clear plan for the next stage of his working life, were in a different position from Matt, Adam, and Keith, for whom the "starting from scratch" scenario was a closer fit. For all of them, "time out" was a better description of this stage of their relationship to paid work. Keith spoke of his earlier accounting job as "not doing much for the soul." Adam spoke of still not being sure "what I want to be when I grow up." Matt spoke of his time at home with son Tim as "an opportunity to recreate myself." All were aware of the social expectations about men and paid work against which their own private choices would be weighed. They were aware, in the terms of West and Zimmerman (1987), that others would hold them accountable for those choices. As Keith said,

> I think probably one of the biggest things is just what I see as being societal pressures. You know, people asking, "Well, why don't you ... go back to work, or go part-time?" And I don't know how much of it is actual or how much of it is self-imposed.

Just how much of this pressure to work outside the home might be self-imposed is evident in the following comment from Matt, reproduced here at length to illustrate the contradictions he was struggling with:

> Looking back, I was a little naïve about what it would be like, and I had no problem with the untraditional part of it being untraditional for a man to stay at home.... But it's a little difficult because ... whenever I see other men stay at home, I have the same kind of reaction ... that it doesn't look right and that it [laughs] is somewhat unnatural. And even though I really like it, and it's good for me ... I can't help, you know, thinking that in a way.... I have to confess that it always, for me, feels that there has to be some reason I'm home or some kind of justification ... there has to be some kind of reason that I'm not able to [laughs] be the breadwinner, or something.... I think for a man that feels like a little bit of a failure in a way.... But not really for me [laughs].

A recurring theme in some stay-at-home fathers' accounts was the anticipation of a future flexible work arrangement that would still leave them free to continue to care for their children outside school hours. As Keith commented,

> Yes, they might be going to school during the day, but, you know, school hours are pretty short and kids have a lot of time off school and when they're sick they have to be home. So the idea is that I go back to something that's flexible.

For Keith, as for several other fathers, self-employment of some kind was a possibility. Warren's furniture making was just such an example. Alan, the designer, was in the process of setting himself up, like Scott, to work on home-based contracts. But even Scott was anticipating a workday the length of a school day. Alan and his wife Paula were hoping to reach the point at which each worked part time while sharing the caregiving of three-year-old Mark and the baby due in three months. In other words, there would be no easy resumption of breadwinner status for these fathers once their children were in school. The job switch that transgressed gender conventions by privileging their partners' careers during the early years was likely to be maintained at the next stage too. Though all would likely be in paid employment of some kind, it would probably not be of a kind that would challenge the status and earning power of their partners' jobs. The strategy of "scaling back" — having one partner (often the woman) working reduced hours to help meet family demands (Becker and Moen 1999; Sweet and Moen 2006) — seemed, in contrast, likely to define the working lives of many of the fathers in this group.

One of Keith's future work scenarios was "fixing up homes": buying them, doing some work on them, and then selling them. Home renovation on their own homes, especially for men who had no current connection to paid employment, was the home-based work that, as Adam's comment (cited earlier) suggests, distinguished them from most home-based women. In principle, what they were doing was not so different from what many home-based women have often done, namely convert more stereotypically feminine domestic skills like cooking or sewing into money-saving (or occasionally money-making) enterprises. All three men had turned to quintessentially masculine activities that were also significant in-kind household financial contributions. Adam's landscaping and basement renovations have already been noted. Keith and Matt were home renovators too, and, in the case of Matt, the former home construction worker, the renovation was major. The interview accounts do not reveal whether these activities were a direct response to their discomfort about being men at home or whether, like home-based mothers, they turned to what they knew best in order to help out. But the fact that all three turned to home-based work that, in someone else's home, would be paid work most often done by a man reflects the pattern also noted in other research on home-based male caregivers. (See, for example, Doucet 2004a, 2006a).

Of all the fathers' accounts of being home-based and away from the regular workforce, 41-year-old Graham's stood out for the contentedness that permeated it. Graham had been a full-time caregiver for five years, ever since his partner Patricia returned to work after a six-month leave with their adopted son Jonathan. They had agreed that they wanted the home-based parental care for Jonathan that they had both experienced from their own mothers, and, because Patricia, as a specialist physician, was able to earn an extremely high income (one far higher than Graham could make), the pragmatic choice was for Graham to become the care-giver. Graham described himself as "ecstatic" to be able to be home with his son during the "magical time" when he was very young. But both part-ners agreed that he had the skills and the personality for the job—he was a nurturer, with lots of patience. And, unlike all the other fathers in the group, he did not foresee a return to paid employment, even when Jonathan started school. The fact that there was no financial need opened the door to other possibilities for fulfilment:

> I'll be the stay-at-home dad whose child brings his friends home for lunch, at school. I'll be driving field trips, volunteering in the school, whatever.... I could be involved in some service group in the community.... I feel very lucky that I'll be able to dabble in some things like that without worrying about pay-ing the bills. So I can do things that help.

In their own homes, no matter what else they were doing, fathers were also doing the traditional women's work of caring for children and man-aging a household, two separate categories of unpaid work that are often conflated for stay-at-home caregivers. As generations of women before them have recognized and as extensive feminist scholarship has pointed out, all this unpaid work is still work. One strategy emerging from the men's accounts was to frame this work, and to speak of it, as a job. Warren's account contained several examples of this "job" perspective, though he was at pains to distance himself from what he suspected was his father-in-law's view of the job—"traipsing around wearing an apron all day, you know, baking cakes and cookies." Warren commented, "Basically I still do guy things, you know, but I take care of a boy."

Warren's careful distinction between the caregiving and other domestic work was not sustained in his account of a regular day, in which getting Connor's meals and spending time with him were interspersed with "doing my dishes," sweeping, and cleaning. Then, "if it's nice, we head outside, and I can do whatever I do outside"—perhaps gardening in the summer, chipping ice from the sidewalk in the winter. In the course of these days of activity in the constant company of a child for whom he was solely responsible, other competencies began to develop. Warren described the outcome:

> I'm into such a routine, and I know him. I can read him. It makes it easier to predict his next—well, I can't predict his next move, but I know what's going to work to discipline him...and, you know, what isn't, and it just feels like a relief.

Other fathers described a similar unfolding of awareness and confidence. For example, Alan, having spent a lot of time with his son Mark before he was at home with him full time, said he "had a home routine and could spend a whole day taking care of [him] and feeling positive about that and feeling competent with it." As he said, "I could do what needed to be done pretty intuitively." Adam, a full-time caregiver for five years, experienced some challenges with his first child: "I had a difficult time sort of getting to know his different... moods and cries and when he was hungry whereas with our second one, it's much more instinctive and seems to come fairly naturally... I guess it's a combination of practice and learning to pick up on those subtle cues."

Adam's explanation—"practice and learning"—to account for "what seems to come fairly naturally" or (in Alan's terms) "pretty intuitively" neatly paraphrases an extensive body of feminist literature (e.g., Glenn et al. 1994; Ruddick 1982) that seeks to explode the notion that mothers are naturally (read biologically) better equipped to care for children. From this constructionist perspective, "mothering" is framed as something that is learned on the job and, therefore, something that fathers, if they have a mind to, can learn as well. As Scott said, "It's a skill that you acquire from just doing it."

What was also apparent, in some of the accounts, was the extent to which individual men, such as Keith, actually relished both the caregiving and the household management. Overall, he commented, it had gone "very, very well." Keith acknowledged that, with the end of his partner Sheila's maternity leave in sight, he was "kind of excited about getting back to just being me at home again." Matt felt the same way. He described the maternity leave period when his partner Julia had been home with their son Tim as "a difficult time" for her. "As much as she loved Tim, I don't think she could stay home for herself," he said. He recalled her early ambivalence about having him replace her at home — her sense, he thought, of its unfairness — and how, in the course of the leave, "it became pretty obvious to her that she would really only trust me to look after [Tim]." He had no qualms about stepping in. Having had some child care experience with a much younger sibling, Matt was confident: "I knew I would like it, and be good at it."

> I was looking forward to taking over in a way.... I like things done a certain way, and it was nice to have the house to myself... and also have, you know, a little more power over how [Tim] was.... It definitely went smoothly, more smoothly for me.

This proficiency and confidence illuminates another dimension of gender at work. In the same way that women have demonstrated their competence on the more public turf of male-dominated occupations and workplaces, in some individual homes, including some of the ones included here, men may do a better job at work women have traditionally done. Men's competence as caregivers reveals the other side of the executive responsibility issue discussed in connection with the mothers. If, as with Keith or Warren, their partners' accounts appeared to downplay the men's authority and expertise, the fact remained that, for most of their children's waking hours, fathers were "it." In some cases, the fathers clearly knew this, but they also recognized the challenge this situation might be for mothers who were both less available and more concerned to be central in their children's lives. Matt, acknowledged by his partner Julia as an equal in terms of caregiving, spoke explicitly about these concerns. Asked if his time with Tim meant he knew Tim better than Julia did, he answered:

I don't think I know him any better than Julia. And in part … because I think Julia is somewhat envious of what I get to do … that kind of advantage I have over her with Tim … It would be easy for me to exploit that and even develop that, in Tim's mind, so I'm kind of conscious not to, conscious to make sure that doesn't happen.

Keith spoke of how things went when Sheila, the self-confessed "micro-manager," was home on maternity leave with their second baby:

I want to make sure Sheila gets her fill. You know … she's staying at home too, and, to a certain degree … you know, I kind of set my pattern out as, "This is my turf," right? And then all of a sudden she's infringing on it, and I have to be able to make sure that that door is open so that she can come in.

Matt and Keith were in one sense in the same situation as the caregivers described in the study cited by Macdonald (1998). The time they spent with their children positioned them strategically to develop close relationships with them — potentially closer than the mother-child relationship might be. Both Matt and Keith were doing careful "shadow work" to ensure the mothers did not feel displaced.

Negotiating Domestic and Community Space

The second major question to be addressed concerns the caregiver fathers' presence at home and in their communities — both spaces more conventionally associated with women. For these men, their homes were places *where* they worked as caregivers but also spaces *requiring* work, in the form of cleaning and routine upkeep. Those homes were also nodes in a network that included the immediate neighbourhood and the wider city spaces that were points on the geographic map of small children's lives.

Men's accounts — and in some cases those of their partners — suggested a certain transformation of domesticity once men took over the work. While Tanya and Ruth, for example, spoke of partners needing to learn how to keep up with housecleaning and laundry on an ongoing basis, other men made it clear they needed no such instruction. "It's never clean enough for me," said Matt. "I'll be trying to tidy up as I go throughout the day," said Keith. "Sheila is a little bit more relaxed, I think, about things at home." Keith was one of the fathers who, as noted earlier, viewed the combination of caregiving and domestic work as a job, and one in which he wanted to show he was competent:

Every Monday was cleaning day. I had to make sure that the house was clean by the end of the day. You know, part of it is because I like to have [tidiness] and the other part is that, in the back of my mind this is now my responsibility and in every job you have paperwork or whatever it might be that you don't necessarily like to do but something that you have to do, so you just do it.

Keith had another reason for cleaning up — "in case somebody comes by, they don't come and say, 'Oh, yeah, he's the stay-at-home dad that can't take care of everything.'"

As the earlier house renovation discussion also indicates, men's labour transformed homes in other ways as well. Landscaping and gardening were further examples. "Homemaker" is a term most commonly associated with women, used to describe the broader sense in which their work made living spaces comfortable and inviting for family members. From their partners' accounts, not all the men qualified as homemakers in this sense. (And not all partners liked the experience of having someone else managing the home space. Tanya commented, "My home is not my home … There's always somebody else in my house.") But for other fathers, such as Keith, Matt, and Peter, "homemaking" was a fair description of their accumulated domestic work at home.

Much of this work was solitary, or at least solitary in the sense of requiring no other adult. And, for all the men in this group of at-home caregivers, it was carried out in single-family homes in city residential neighbourhoods where men at home were rare. This links to another dimension of workplaces: the sociability which most provide. For some of the stay-at-home fathers, flexible work hours meant that partners were also around for part of the time during the day. But, in general, there was little sociability available beyond that provided by very young children. Unless they actively sought it, adult contact was in very short supply. The possibility of "hiding out," particularly for men who were uneasy about being classified as stay-at-home fathers, was real. As Alan commented, "There is certainly a social aspect to being at the office each day. And the longer you are away from people it's almost like … the less likely you are to reach out and contact them."

Alan's wife Paula was one of the flexible-hours partners at home occasionally during the work week. He had also taken on a short-term evening teaching job. However, Warren seemed to have fewer defences against an isolation that clearly resonated in his account. Two influences seemed to be at work in Warren's case. First, he was, as noted earlier, deeply committed to an "attachment" style of caregiving, which assumed the more or less constant presence of a parent on the job. Second, he expressed considerable discomfort about the strongly gendered social settings available to preschool children outside the home. Warren was aware that Connor would benefit from involvement in a play group where he could "learn to interact" with other children. But Warren wanted to be around, "to have some control…so I can intervene if it's something that I don't like." And he felt excluded from the world of "moms and tots" groups where both he and Connor might have had some social contact during the day.

> It's always moms and tots, moms and this, moms and that, right? And it's just like, can I go to this? And I'm thinking, no, because…it's something that these women have set up…[so] that they can get together and socialize between themselves, right? I think they would be put off by having a guy there.

Instead, Warren and Connor would head for public places such as the zoo or the library "because it's neutral." When Warren felt he needed a break ("if I know I'm going to snap"), he would visit his parents ("somewhere where I can just breathe"). He commented, "I find in the winter I head over there a lot." Such resources, however, were not available to most of the fathers in the group. To give themselves a break, especially if their partners worked regular daytime hours away from home, fathers turned to the more institutionalized world of playgroups and classes for preschoolers. For those uneasy about their status as stay-at-home fathers, this required them to break cover in a way that Warren, for example, seemed unwilling to do. It put an end to "hiding out."

The world of preschool playgroups and early childhood classes has emerged from social expectations about children's needs, which I discussed in Chapter 1. In particular, current trends in developmental psychology, requiring parents to provide children with appropriate stimulation before they turn six or risk less than optimal cognitive development (Wall 2004), are likely to be a powerful incentive, especially for well-educated middle-class parents. Fathers in the study who might not have ventured into this world on their own account were willing to do so for the sake of their children. Those who did make the effort to break through the "moms and tots" gender barrier were well aware of their token status. Matt joined a play group with Tim and commented: "In terms of the isolation, being the only male in a room full of fourteen or fifteen women and their kids doesn't really do a lot for me." Of his play-group experience with his son Joel, Adam said, "I think it was better for Joel than it was for myself."

Of the full-time caregiver group, Peter, Scott, and Graham expressed much less ambivalence about the social context of their children's activities outside the home. Peter spoke of doing some research to check out the options and to avoid what he called "chit-chatty" groups in favour of those with an educational component, groups in which he might learn something about child development or get practical child-rearing advice while his children socialized. With three children each, Peter and Scott maintained a steady schedule of activities to keep everybody occupied. "I'll always say the worst days... are the days we just stay [home]," Scott commented. For both fathers, the schedule also included some drop-in day care at the gym or local Y where they could fit in a workout on their own.

The interview accounts indicated that, outside of the institutional context, fathers on rare occasions were able, over time, to establish some social connections with individual women — neighbours or mothers of their children's friends or classmates — who were also home-based caregivers. In these cases, common needs for support and sociability overcame gender barriers. For example, Keith and a home-based neighbour mother were planning a babysitting exchange to give each of them some child-free space in the day. Scott spoke about the group of nursery school mothers with whom he met weekly towards the end of the nursery school term; they socialized while they awaited the end-of-class pick-up of children. Graham, having worked in elementary schools, had had some experience of female-dominated groups before he became a stay-at-home father and was not put off. He consciously, and ironically, called them the "*other* mothers," positioning himself as a "mother" too. Of their talk, he said, "This is not male conversation! This is not how guys get together and hang out!" Then he added, "I'm not a beer-swilling, football-cheering, cigar-smoking guy. I guess I do all right in those situations too... I can talk the talk with 'other moms.'"

Scott's and Graham's easy acceptance of this gender imbalance and their ability and willingness to fit in were remarkable. The "estrogen-filled worlds" identified by the caregiver fathers in Doucet's research (Doucet 2006a, 2006b) were a concern for these fathers too. What most of the men would have appreciated (and some actively sought) was some contact with other men doing what they were doing. As Adam said,

I get a chance to sometimes socialize with the other moms but it's not that often, and I don't like to push too hard for that because I don't want to wear out my welcome. And, at the same time ... it would be nice to have more contact with other dads.

A comparison of all the men's accounts shows that Adam seemed to be one of the men most committed to both the job and the designation of "stay-at-home father." (He noted, "That's how I refer to myself: 'I'm a full-time stay-at-home dad.'") Although other fathers also spoke of their caregiving work as a job, Adam wanted to take the further step of formalizing, even professionalizing it. He had been to a conference put on by a US organization for stay-at-home fathers, he was part of a fathers' group, and he conscientiously networked with any other stay-at-home fathers who crossed his path. But, as he also commented, his life was very busy; there was a limit to the amount of time he had available for community building with other fathers. This was also Scott's problem. He, in fact, had been approached to join a fathers' group, but caring for three children under six took all the time he had available. Peter and Keith also tried to establish connections with other home-based fathers, though neither had had much success. Peter commented that he would organize a group if "someone would help," but he too was caring for three children and was too busy to do the organizing on his own. What seemed to be missing, for all the men, was a critical mass of caregiver fathers in their own neighbourhoods to make the networking a little easier.

The connections that did get made seemed more likely to be the result of casual playground encounters or meetings in spaces that were, to use Warren's term, more "neutral." It is hard to say whether this was because other caregiver fathers shared Warren's discomfort with the more institutionalized, mother-dominated settings of playgroups and classes and avoided them or because the interactional opportunities in such settings did not lend themselves to men getting together. What did seem likely was that, if more men participated, those less comfortable with their stay-at-home status might feel less conspicuous and, therefore, more inclined to participate in a social setting from which they knew their children would benefit. This was certainly Warren's position. Getting together with other fathers, he thought, would provide some new experiences for his son and, "just like a coincidence," the opportunity for him to talk to other men:

Like, you know, not necessarily about guy things or staying at home or being a stay-at-home dad or anything, not to vent, but just to talk about whatever, just anything.

Implicit in Warren's formulation was a wish to normalize what he and the other stay-at-home fathers were doing, to degender at an institutional level the work of caring for children. The increased public visibility of fathers as caregivers would also, at a broader societal level, signal that the phenomenon of "full-time stay-at-home fathers," to use Adam's designation, was becoming (more) mainstream.

Summing Up

The accounts of all the women in this group, breadwinners with caregiver partners at home, showed clearly how remote was the possibility that any of them would become, in Tanya's words, "men in skirts," at least as far as their caregiving was concerned. As the foregoing discussion has shown, they worked hard to retain the emotional connection with their young children that male breadwinners, in more traditional family gender regimes, might have been prepared to cede to caregiver mothers. So if "men in skirts" are, as Tanya feared, fathers disguised as mothers, these women did not become fathers. The difference, as the mothers perceived it, was that they came home from work, and, unless the exhaustion of the working day overwhelmed them (and sometimes it did), they moved right into the family circle. Occasionally, this freed the partner who had been home all day to disappear for a while. More often, and especially in families with more than one child, it was a matter of joining in and sharing the evening round of dinner, clean-up, baths, stories, and other evening rituals before the children went to sleep. There were references in several interviews to the narrow window of time at the end of the day when this (re)connection work had to happen.

This key feature of the work of these mothers is worth stressing. Had they been fathers with caregiver partners at home, they might have been able to expect and would socially have been allowed some of the off-duty leisure time to which male breadwinners can lay claim. (That they do claim it is evident in the leisure-time differences that large-scale surveys invariably find.[6]) Breadwinners with the jobs that are privileged in their families can also legitimately spend more time at work than the acceptable minimum either to increase earnings or to ensure future job security. None of the mothers in this group were breadwinners like that. They were aware of the importance of their income to their family's well-being, but, though like the breadwinner fathers described by Ranson (2001) they had the discretion to extend their work hours if the need arose, generally all put limits on the time their paid employment could take. In this sense, they benefitted less than breadwinner fathers might from the caregiver parent at home. As the discussion above also indicated, some of the mothers in this group viewed themselves as retaining executive responsibility for the children — a role few contemporary breadwinner fathers would dream of assuming.

Their after-hours work at home was hard work. But it was mainly the emotional work of reconnecting with children. These mothers generally did not have to take on the accumulation of other domestic work, such as housecleaning and laundry, that also contributes to what Hochschild (1989) called the "second shift" of work waiting at home for most employed mothers. For the breadwinner mothers, the housework part of the second shift was generally handled — more or less competently, in their eyes — by the partner at home. In this sense, they were exactly like breadwinners with "a wife." Although delegation of responsibility for children was much more contentious or problematic, delegation of household responsibilities was generally not contested at all. These women — and in particular the ones with partners highly competent in household management, for example, Julia and Sheila — could focus on children after work because most other household responsibilities had been taken care of.

I have argued that the breadwinner mothers did not become fathers, though they did share some of the privileges available to men in their situation. Similarly, the caregiver fathers did not become mothers, though they were doing work usually associated with mothering.[7] In some though not all cases, caregiver fathers described themselves as responding differently to their children than their partners did. Most spoke of their partners as gentler, more comforting, and more nurturing — positioning them as "mothers" in the traditional sense. For themselves, they generally claimed many of the practices more traditionally associated with fathers, such as play, especially rough play, and other physical pursuits. Sometimes, they claimed to be firmer disciplinarians and stricter with routines. They were also fathers rather than mothers in their navigation of the social settings available to infants and preschoolers in their communities.

The stay-at-home fathers as a group confronted costs associated with their withdrawal from the world of full-time paid employment. These costs were partly social; their unconventional family division of labour meant they were held accountable for or felt themselves held accountable for transgressing traditional expectations about masculinity and father-hood. They were also likely to experience the career costs common to care-giver mothers, for whom career interruptions are documented sources of disadvantage (see, for example, Spivey 2005). For most of the fathers in the group, their time as caregivers marked a watershed between a working life that had failed to take long-term hold and a future that was an open ques-tion. Most of them worried, at least a little, about how that future would unfold. Yet their willingness to break away from the dominant masculine model of identity with paid work, their sense of themselves as open to other commitments, and their close and growing bonds with their chil-dren suggested that any future engagement with paid work would not be on the old terms.

All these characteristics also ensured that they would not be traditional fathers. Extended practice in the intimate, hands-on work of infant and child care saw to that. Though they could not share the most obvious embodied experiences of mothering—pregnancy, birth, and breastfeeding—the fact that they provided *hands-on* care is a clue to the extent to which they were drawn in to bodily engagement with their children, through feeding, diapering, bathing, and soothing. Like many of the caregiver fathers described in Coltrane's (1989) study, they had done everything but breastfeeding, from their children's birth onwards. Like the fathers Coltrane observed, they too, over the course of caregiving, came to learn the ways of the child in their care—"maternal thinking," as Ruddick (1982) described it (Coltrane 1996:83). There was now much more com-mon ground with mothers. Lupton and Barclay note that the "blurring of body/self boundaries" commonly associated with new mothering "may be experienced as more confronting by men because it challenges specifically dominant ideals of masculinity" (Lupton and Barclay 1997:32). But these fathers seemed equal to the challenge. The reasons that such physical care-giving by men is important, not just for their own children but for "their elderly fathers" or "their own sick wives," are argued eloquently by Barbara Katz Rothman (1989), in a moving testimony to her husband's caring labour for their children and for her. Many of the men in this group appeared to me to be the kind of caring fathers Rothman was describing.

Although they did not care for their children in exactly the same way that their partners might have done, they were able to attend to children's needs on a daily and ongoing basis. A mother's occasional extended absence, on a business trip, for example, did not leave a space that could not be filled. As Keith commented, "I can get up in the middle of the night and feed Brent just like Sheila can, but in a bottle. I can change a diaper just as well; I can go shopping just as well as she can." (Sheila commented that, if anyone had to be away for a few days, Keith's absence, rather than hers, would present problems.) Like the couples striving for shared parental care in Dienhart's (1998) study, both partners were, in many important ways, interchangeable as caregivers. Without duplicating the contributions and style of the missing parent, each could generally substitute for the other in a way that ensured children's needs were well met.

There was also, in these families, a shared understanding of what those needs were. Parental practice conformed to many of the criteria of the "intensive mothering" described by Hays (1996). The fact that fathers rather than mothers were providing much of the requisite labour did not detract from the shared commitment to giving children the optimal "start in life" that, as noted in Chapter 1, has come to be seen as a contemporary child-rearing requirement. This shared understanding was also the practical outcome of a view of parental care as superior and worth the foregone paternal income. On this issue, though, two separate rationales prevailed: the lost income was viewed either as not needed or as inadequate to cover the cost of alternate care.

As the accounts of the mothers and the fathers have shown, the question of who had ultimate responsibility for the children was not always clear. It was, in any case, a matter of individual perception. Fathers, in some cases, were also careful to position mothers as central, even though the time they themselves spent with children meant they assumed much more responsibility on a daily basis. As Matt commented, "I have so many decisions I get to make every day unilaterally, without [Julia's] input at all." But whether or not they took more responsibility or knew their children better than the mothers did, the fathers in this group were, unequivocally, extremely involved. Because their children were very young, that involvement brought them closer to the recent and occasionally ongoing intense physical engagement and attention that characterized the caregiving provided by the mothers. This involvement had the effect of providing children with, in Tanya's terms, "two in-tune parents, as opposed to one tuned-in parent and one, kind of, peripheral." As Julia commented,

It's very bonding, because … as parents, we have very much to talk about because he definitely knows what it is to be a parent, and I think I do too.… In one sense, we have a common job that we can talk a lot about. And I think that, in the more traditional situation, oftentimes the man isn't as in touch with that stuff; he just can't discuss it. Like Matt and I can discuss Tim the way I would discuss Tim with a girlfriend who has a child of a similar age. We can discuss, and he's interested to discuss, all of those things … what kind of juice is best, you know, all of the little minute sort of things that you discuss about parenting.… We're both very much interested in that and we're very much a team in that respect.

In Chapter 1, I introduced the work of Deutsch (2007) and others to suggest the possibility that couples going against the grain of conventional understandings of mothering and fathering might be "undoing" gender. Julia's comment speaks to that possibility. She articulates a phenomenon that is critical to an understanding of how mothering and fathering, in these most unconventional of earning and caring arrangements, *could* be "undone." Though it didn't happen for every crossover couple, some, for example, Julia and Matt, were able to share caring work *on equal terms*. I use this phrase advisedly, to suggest a sharing not only of work but also of language — two key elements in a model of future change.

Chapter Four

"Shift-Workers" and "Dual-Dividers": Sharing Earning, Sharing Caring

The couples described in the previous chapter were unusual not only in terms of their unconventional positioning of fathers at home and mothers as breadwinners but also because single-earner households are a diminishing minority of Canadian families. What does "going against the grain" look like in families when both partners are also sharing the earning work? Among the parents of preschool children in the study, ten couples were in this category: dual-earner pairs trying for a fairly shared division of labour across the whole range of earning and caring activities. There was one key difference between them: the extent to which they supplemented their own childcare activities with outside, non-parental care. Four couples were "shift-workers," coordinating their paid employment so that one parent was available to care for the children almost all the time. Six couples were "dual-dividers," using outside childcare during their own more or less standard work hours but sharing care after work, and sharing responsibility all the time. Three of the dual-divider couples were also same-sex couples, whose family lives posed additional challenges to conventional understandings of mothering and fathering.

The sort of across-the-board sharing these couples achieved might seem like an inevitable and not especially surprising outcome for any dual-earner household with two busy, well-intentioned parents trying to divide the load. Yet research suggests that, even among couples aspiring to share equally, differences and divisions can still occur. Coltrane (1989) discovered, in a study of 20 couples in which fathers assumed "significant responsibility for routine child care" (Coltrane 1989:474), that only 12 couples seemed to be taking joint *responsibility* for housework and childcare, as well as sharing the actual work involved. The remaining 8 couples conformed more to a "manager-helper" model (with mothers as managers). Later work by Risman and her colleagues (Risman 1998, Risman and Johnson-Sumerford 1998) offers an even more nuanced distinction. Like Coltrane, Risman was looking for "fair families" who "share[d] the responsibilities of paid work and family work without regard for gender prescriptions" (Risman and Johnson-Sumerford 1998:23). Among the 15 married couples who participated in this project, conducted over a four-year period, the researchers found no differences between partners in their participation in paid work, and there was a gender-free division of family work as well. Partners were differentiated by gender only in the management of emotion. In 6 of the families, the mother was described as the "emotion expert," who monitored the emotional tenor of the marital relationship and was acknowledged by both partners to have a closer relationship to the children. Other mothers in the study, who shared the emotion work more equally, did also experience some of the pain involved in sharing a child's primary attachment as well. In Dienhart's (1998) terms, these mothers, too, were subject to "acculturation holdovers" — having to reconcile themselves to displacement from primary parent status.

Similar "acculturation holdovers" appeared to be at work in Potuchek's (1992) study of the orientation to breadwinning among women in dual-earner couples. Potuchek found that, based on their assessment of the importance of their job to the family and their belief that earning should be a shared responsibility, only 15 per cent were true "co-breadwinners." The largest proportion of the women (21 per cent), while employed full time, clearly positioned their husbands' jobs as more important and their husbands as primary providers. The divergence of behaviour and ideology was also demonstrated in Deutsch's research on blue-collar workers who alternated shifts in order to ensure one parent could be home with the children (Deutsch 1999, 2002; Deutsch and Saxon 1998). Deutsch concluded that, unlike many middle-class couples who talk the egalitarian talk without necessarily putting it into practice, the working-class couples in her study did the opposite. They retained traditional understandings of mothering and fathering while enacting a clearly non-traditional division of earning and caring work.

A different set of issues confronts same-sex couples. Research suggests that these couples may have more egalitarian relationships (Dunne 2000; Kurdek 2007; Nelson 1996; Sullivan 1996; but see Carrington 2002). However, though liberated from the heavily gendered expectations that can, by default, shape the sharing of paid work and family responsibilities in heterosexual couples, same-sex couples are not outside the cultural expectations about mothering and fathering. The privileging of biological over other forms of motherhood (Miall and March 2003) may complicate for lesbian mothers the negotiating of "mother" identities between biological and "social" mothers (Dalton and Bielby 2000; Reimann 1997). Gay men who wish to become fathers outside of heterosexual relationships (for example, by adopting or fostering children) face structural and institutional constraints quite different from anything faced by heterosexual fathers, to say nothing of homophobic social stereotypes of gay men as paedophiles and a danger to children (Berkowitz and Marsiglio 2007; Stacey 2006). As Stacey notes, "Raised as males, most gay men do not receive direct cultural socialization in the feminine labors of 'love and ritual'—kin work, emotion work, domestic labor, childcare, nurturing. Yet unlike heterosexual men, they cannot rely on women to perform these services for them" (Stacey 2006:30).

The question, then, is how the couples I introduce in this chapter, who *do* manage to share equitably both earning and caring responsibilities, also manage to surmount "acculturation holdovers," such as those facing heterosexual couples, and the special challenges facing same-sex couples. How are questions of maternal responsibility and attachment affected when mothers are sharing with, not delegating to, their partners? How do fathers fare when their combination of paid work and family responsibilities is more characteristic of that experienced by employed mothers? What happens when the family must accommodate two jobs and two invested caregiver parents—and sometimes two mothers or two fathers as well? These are the questions to be addressed in the remainder of the chapter.

Shift Work: Two Employed Parents Giving Full-Time Parental Care

Denise and Gary provided one version of the "shift-work" model that allowed for more or less exclusive parental care. Denise, a school guidance counsellor, worked a regular school day while her airline pilot partner Gary cared for their son Daniel. When she got home from her work shift, Gary, assigned to night and weekend flights, left for his. Three other couples coordinated their work hours with the same goal.[1] Christine and James, both college instructors and the parents of two young children, organized their teaching schedules on alternating days so that one of them was always at home. Diane and Geoff, the parents of three-year-old Kelly, each worked slightly less than full-time hours, which were scheduled around the half-day shifts of caregiving that they divided between them. Andrew and David, the adoptive parents of 10-week-old Alexia, had been catapulted by her unexpected arrival into split morning and afternoon shift arrangements as they figured out how they would manage her care over the longer term.

Compared to the families discussed in the previous chapter, with breadwinner mothers and caregiver partners, the three heterosexual couples described here faced challenges that were not so stark. The mothers were sharing rather than delegating the ongoing daily care; in other words, they were doing more of the "mothering" work. So questions of executive responsibility and attachment might be expected to be less pressing. The fathers, though sharing the caregiving, were also in full-time paid employment. As well as being "involved fathers," they also fit the more conventional image of breadwinner (even though they were not winning all the bread). That said, considered *as cases*, each couple illuminates the critical questions of responsibility, attachment, and relationships to paid work introduced in the previous chapter.

Mothering in Shift-Work Families

Denise, interviewed when she was at home on her second maternity leave, had returned to work when her first child, Daniel, was a year old. Daniel was cared for during Denise's working day by his father, Gary. This might have positioned Gary, for practical purposes, as the primary parent. But, from her account, Denise (possessing what she described as a "Type A personality") was another CEO mother, managing from a distance the caregiving work that Gary did. And although she answered "yes and no" to a direct question about wanting to be a stay-at-home mother, the "no" part — relating to her love of her job and the adult interaction that her job also gave her — was trumped in her account by the "yes":

When I say yes and no, I want to be home now. I would like to go back into counselling when the kids are in school, and then have my career continue. I am very thankful that my career was established and that I got in 13 years [in my profession] and that I experienced all that I did because I'm happy to let that go right now to be home.

As a school board employee and a member of an occupation that was both female dominated and unionized, Denise was able to take advantage of generous leave provisions that, in her case, would have allowed her up to two years away from work without compromise to her job status (Ranson 1998). Extended leave, plus extended breaks during the summer, did give her more time at home than many other mothers in full-time jobs. Like Sheila, introduced in the previous chapter, she made use of both her time at home and her professional expertise to establish ground rules. (In his interview, Gary joked that, when she left for work in the morning, she would leave behind a list of instructions about Daniel's care for the day.)

Yet Gary was the person providing most of the daytime care. Denise acknowledged that he was "a fabulous father," but she struggled with the possibility that, on the basis of his own extended caregiving experience, he might occasionally know best. "That's a tough one for me," she said. "I need to really improve in running with the 'Yeah, Daddy knows too.' That's been a painful glitch too because Gary would be like, 'Oh, yeah, right, I'm not the mommy.'" Denise's high standards for childcare and her strong maternal identity—key elements of maternal gatekeeping, as I noted in Chapter 3—made the sharing of responsibility and authority with Gary very difficult. For Denise, both were closely linked to a struggle over attachment and primary parent status. Ideologically, she wanted to be a more traditional mother. Separation—from her child and from her mothering ideal—produced "lots of tears":

There'd be a time…where Gary would have to take him to the doctor, and I wasn't there. Well, I'm the mom: I should be there, you know…. A lot of the times, though, were just the everyday, like doing arts and crafts, reading with him. Those kinds of things I would try to squish in when I came home, and sometimes it would just backfire and blow up in my face…. I was able to do [things] with him on weekends and after school, like going to the park and stuff. I just felt like I was missing out. And I guess that was kind of a selfish thing because I knew he was doing it with Gary. He was doing it with Dad. He was doing all those things; it just wasn't with me.... I wanted that time, I wanted to be the one to be there with him.

Denise spoke from her experience of her first child. Her new baby was an unknown quantity. Though the caregiving workload was bound to increase, she had yet to encounter the changing family dynamics produced by another child. Christine would have had a great deal to tell her. At the time of our interview, her children were a year older than Denise's — and it had been a very difficult year. Like Ruth and Warren, whose situation was described in the previous chapter, Christine and her husband James also practised an attachment style of caregiving, involving extended breastfeeding and the nursing child sleeping in the parents' bed. In the early stages, the breastfeeding component clearly positions the mother to be the primary parent. However, their second child had gastric problems and allergies so severe that they registered even through minute traces of allergens in breast milk. The result was a baby who was distressed for much of his first six months or so. In that kind of situation, questions of executive responsibility and attachment are overwhelmed by the much more immediate and practical concerns of getting through each day. It often resolves to a one-parent-per-child division of labour, and that was a common management strategy for Christine and James. Christine described a typical evening, when things started to get "very difficult" around 7 or 8 p.m.:

> I'd stay down and nurse Myles. James would take Cameron upstairs ... do bath time ... read stories and get him to sleep [if] possible. Although, for the longest time, he wouldn't sleep without Mommy, so then James and I would trade off. He would come down and take the baby. When he was a bit younger and really fussy, that meant wearing him [carrying him in arms or a baby sling]. And then I would go up and get Cameron down [to sleep].... I would come back down and nurse [the baby] again. By this time, it's like 10 o'clock; then I would go up to bed and leave James with the baby, and he would stay up until 12 or whatever and then he would come up and bring the baby to me.

The general arrangement was that Christine would tend to the baby during what remained of the night — unless he was particularly restless, in which case, James would help. James then took over the (very) early morning shift. In short, neither parent got much sleep.

During the working week, Christine spent more time with the children than James did: three days to his two. Because of the intensely child-centred caregiving they practised, with breastfeeding on demand as its centrepiece, she pointed out that their experiences of childcare were quite different:

> When I'm with the children, they're basically on me physically.... They don't hang off him like they hang off me. And when we're both here they're hanging off me and not him, and I call, "James, James, come and take [one or other child]!"

In that sense, Christine seemed to be the primary parent, and she acknowledged that James deferred to her as the mother. She was, she suggested, "the comforter" and perhaps more patient with Cameron, the four-year-old. At the same time, she commented that, on the days when James was in charge, the children did not appear to miss her. He had his own routine of activities with them, and he was also able to get more household and other work done.

Christine's caregiving shifts were much more social than James's: on two of her weekdays at home, she participated in a moms and tots group, and, on the third day, she had an informal version of it in her house. Christine reported that, when both she and James were at home, she tended to be fully occupied, physically, with the children, while James was "busy sort of keeping things running." In other words, he provided solid, ongoing support for her caregiving, as well as relieving her from that caregiving to enable her to work outside the home. Christine viewed their approach to their children as part of a broader vision of family life she described as "holistic," informed by a wish to live more simply in a material sense in order to have more time for things that might matter more than financial prosperity. Because of this philosophy and their current stage of child rearing, questions of whether Christine had ultimate responsibility for the children or whether they were more attached to her did not loom large. "Neither of us [is] getting more whatever it is, more respect or knowledge career-wise versus home-wise," she said. "I think we're both on a pretty even footing."

Diane's experience was different again. Coming new to motherhood, with a partner (Geoff) who had cared for the children of his first marriage, she could not assume the default position of mother as expert. She was careful to explain, though, that Geoff didn't hold his experience over her head. "He doesn't usually say, 'Well, in my experience before blah blah

blah,' but, in his actions, he conveys expertise," she said. He was also, she said, endlessly patient, and she was not:

> Geoff said he's going to open a school one day and have Kelly [their three-year-old] and myself as his students, so we can learn some patience.... I have none, none at all. Between Kelly and Geoff, Kelly testing, Geoff teaching, I'm learning.

Geoff's support was critical because it was all she had. Both Diane and Geoff were immigrants to Canada. Neither had family members at hand to help out, and Diane, as a more recent newcomer, also lacked a support network of friends. Her account suggested a slow and sometimes painful process of reaching out to other mothers (through Kelly's play group, for example), a dependence on Geoff's more established circle of friends, and some relief (after nearly two years at home and "a bit of cabin fever") to be employed again. "It made me human," she said. Throughout Diane's account, Geoff was present behind the scenes, deeply involved in his own second chance at fathering and doing, in her estimation, about 60 per cent of the household work as well as putting in slightly longer hours at his job. The effect of his contribution seemed to be to give her space to enjoy her time with Kelly, who was going to be "my one and only." Geoff, she said, was "great." But, if in some things she was in need of teaching, his expertise didn't appear to get in the way of her own relationship with Kelly. She recognized that she and Geoff were different people, with different styles and strengths. Her account, like Julia's, which was introduced in the previous chapter, suggested an awareness that parental attachment was not a zero-sum game. Two could have it, equally if differently.

Fathering in Shift-Work Families

Like the stay-at-home fathers discussed in the previous chapter, Gary, James, and Geoff, as the partners of the mothers discussed above, were deeply involved in the care of their children. Although the caregiving split was not always 50–50 and perceptions about their authority and expertise may have varied, in terms of hands-on time spent, they were doing about as much of the hands-on caregiving work as the mothers were. The striking difference between these fathers and the full-time father caregivers, however, was that they also had full-time paid employment.

Given the time they spent in caregiving, it is clear that their jobs occupied a different place in the ranking of priorities than fathers' jobs conventionally do. Each job had to be bent significantly to accommodate family demands. As with the stay-at-home fathers, however, these accommodations were happening in the context of interwoven life trajectories within the family. All the babies requiring care were born to parents at different stages in their personal and working lives. Those parents had different strategies for balancing work and family needs and different plans for sustaining the balance over time.

Gary, at 38, was a pilot, and he was the one father of the three who really loved his job. Going to work, he said, was like going out to play. In the ten years between his marriage to Denise and the arrival of their first child, Daniel, he had made rapid progress up the ranks of the regional airline for which he worked. So when the time arrived for Denise to go back to her teaching job after Daniel's birth, he had enough seniority to be scheduled for what are known as "stand-up" flights. These leave late in the evening; the pilot stays over at the destination and then flies home early the next morning. These stand-up flights were a means for Gary to keep working full time while still being (with occasional backup from grandparents) the primary daytime caregiver.

A schedule made up exclusively of stand-up flights is recognized to be physically punishing. But, as Gary commented, "You do what you have to do." He shared Denise's commitment to parental care, and he deeply appreciated the opportunity to have the input into his son's life that his working arrangement with Denise provided. But this arrangement, although going against the grain of conventional family practice, was also somewhat against the grain of his own gender ideology. In his eyes, the mother is the most important parent for very young children, and he knew how very much Denise wanted to be the home-based primary caregiver. The year-long parental leave she had just started, after their second child's birth, would allow them to return to a more traditional division of labour — traditional, at least, in the sense that he would be working more standard hours. If finances allowed her to fulfil her wish to be at home until the children were in school, he would support her, partly because of his views on the primacy of the mother but mainly because he knew how much she wanted it. He was anticipating becoming a more conventional breadwinner. But he was also thinking seriously about how to maintain the high level of involvement he had had with his son, and how to establish it with his daughter, while working regular hours. These relationships continued to be priorities.

James was an instructor at a post-secondary institution. Having worked on contract as a sessional instructor, never knowing from term to term whether or what he would be teaching, he was appointed to a permanent full-time position right at the time of his first child's birth. From James's account, this job was significant for several reasons: it vindicated his decision to focus on teaching and not to pursue a more research-oriented and (he suspected) more stressful university position, it resolved his worries about finances as parenthood loomed, and it enabled him to negotiate his schedule to free up two days a week for caregiving. In doing so, James was not running any great risk. His department, he said, was "pretty accommodating":

> There's quite a few people in the department actually that have kids and are trying to do something similar. Maybe not as extreme as us but, you know, they often try to tweak their schedules a bit to spend more time at home with the kids.

Though working in a supportive, family-friendly environment enabled James to provide substantial caregiving, he did still have to meet job demands as well. And with two young children, the family was not in a position to forego his full-time salary just yet. Life for James was very busy. But it might not remain so in the future. James said that both he and Christine wanted to do work they enjoyed, but they didn't want to derive their identity from work. Work took time, to make money to meet needs. The fewer the needs, the less time would be taken up with work:

> It comes back to needs and wants.... I guess ideally for me the set-up would be like if we were both just teaching a couple of courses per term.... I wouldn't find that to be any sort of imposition on my time at all, and it would be sort of welcome. I think the two would complement each other, the work and the home.... I think it would be easy to coordinate everything, so that'd be the ideal situation and maybe a few years down the road we might do that, and go half-time.

Geoff, the 45-year-old autobody mechanic, was older than Gary and James, and his age factored into his vision of how his working life would unfold as his son Kelly reached school age. He was also older (by nine years) than his partner Diane. She would be ready to (re)launch at the time he could be thinking about gearing down or, at any rate, moving to something that was easier on his body. (He jokingly described the pay-off for spending more time at home to care for Kelly as "less time on my knees.") Geoff's situation was a good example of the way lives are linked in families: he was, in fact, planning to let Diane's future employment choices guide his own. Diane was currently working as an industrial chemist, a job with high earning potential. But she had also trained as a teacher and was undecided about which track she might pursue. If she worked full time as a chemist, her substantial earnings would take some financial pressure off Geoff, who thought he would get some training as an automobile insurance appraiser—a natural white-collar follow-on from his long experience working with damaged cars. If Diane chose to return to teaching (a tempting option for her because her schedule would mesh so well with Kelly's), then Geoff thought he would probably stay with the better-paying autobody work.

For all three men, as noted earlier, paid work was bent to accommodate their caregiving responsibilities, but it was not surrendered. However they managed it, all three fathers were also securely attached to the world of paid work. So their unusually strong commitment to caregiving—and their social evaluation as "involved fathers"—was not at the expense of their status as financial providers. Unlike the stay-at-home caregiver fathers described in the previous chapter, Gary, James, and Geoff, as well as gay fathers Andrew and David, would not feel themselves called to account as men by their absence from the paid workforce. (In fact, as Coltrane [1989] and Deutsch [1999] suggest, they might earn disproportionately more kudos for upholding both sides of the fatherhood bargain.)

But the commitment to share both the earning and the caring with their partners posed other challenges. For Gary and James, in particular, life was perhaps even busier and more stressful than it was for their partners. Gary worked a physically demanding night-shift schedule compared to Denise's regular school hours, and James fitted a full-time job into three days compared to Christine's more conventional part-time schedule. At the same time, though, they were sharing a close to equal load of the hands-on caregiving, in other words, close to half of the total childcare.

Of the three, Gary's situation was closer to that of the stay-at-home caregiver fathers already described. He was at home with his son Daniel all day during every working day and, in the process, achieved what he described as a very close relationship with him. Having participated in almost every aspect of Daniel's care before his partner Denise returned to work (he was another father who had done everything but breastfeed), Gary spoke of the particular fulfilment of being able to feed him too, with the switch to midday formula required by Denise's absence. ("Finally I had breasts!" he joked.)

Gary's caregiving was constrained by Denise's intense need to be the primary parent: the lists she left to organize his days at home with Daniel positioned him clearly, in Coltrane's (1989) terms, as helper to her manager. He did not always accept her directives, and both Gary and Denise spoke of occasional conflict over how particular situations should be handled. Gary commented that sometimes, "I just shake my head." But usually, he said, his position was, "OK, if that's what Mommy wants, that's what we'll do." As noted earlier, Gary spoke of himself as something of a traditionalist, who believed that the mother was the more important parent, especially for young children. He also noted that Denise brought professional expertise to her caregiving that he lacked. He attributed Daniel's advanced developmental status to Denise's insights, so he was generally willing to defer to her in the childcare arena. However, Gary's interview did suggest that a certain amount of "shadow work" on his part might have been required to sustain the mother-as-primary-parent image.

James was caring for two very young children in an environment in which extended breastfeeding and, by extension, the role of the mother were central. At the same time, as Christine's situation, described earlier, makes clear, this type of mothering requires a solidly supportive second parent (Fox 2001). In this case, too, both James and Christine were learning to care for a baby who was frequently in distress. James was providing this support, either caring for one child while Christine cared for the other or "keeping things running" in the background when Christine was with both children. James, however, was also a solo caregiver in his own right for two full days a week. Especially in the first few months of baby Myles's life, it was very hard work. "It's far, far more gruelling than any job I've ever had," he commented. "Even summer jobs working on construction sites doesn't compare!" Things got easier as the baby's digestive problems were resolved; asked to assess his caregiving, James said, "I would say I'm pretty good at it."

His style as a caregiver was different from Christine's intensely embodied approach—partly because he wasn't the one doing the breastfeeding but also because, as both his and Christine's accounts suggested, his personality was different. In Doucet's (2004b, 2006a) terms, he brought a different background to the job. Understandably, the children reacted differently to him than they did to their mother. On more than one occasion during his interview, he observed that they were "less clingy" when he was in charge and more inclined to play independently, which, occasionally, freed up some time for him to grade papers or do some housework. In James's account, it was he rather than Christine who could do the multi-tasking more commonly attributed to women. He also contrasted the social dimension of his caregiving with Christine's:

> Christine's more of a social butterfly than I am. She's always going out and about. She's the one that's met lots of people in the neighbourhood and so Cameron has met lots of friends through that.

As was the case with some of the stay-at-home fathers, James's caregiving was more solitary. In part, this was because he was so busy and because it was on his days at home that more of the housework got done, to say nothing of his own class preparation. His routines included activities such as breakfast at a neighbourhood family restaurant followed by a visit to the library; walks in the ravine near their house; or trips to the playground. On his own account (and in terms of Christine's description of him as more reserved and quiet), he had no personal need of social interaction on his days at home. And his children got plenty of it on their mother's shift.

James too, like Gary, downplayed a little the extent to which he might defer to his partner, framing it as being willing to give way on small matters but wanting to have input into anything major. "I don't think we have any major conflicts," he said. "Generally speaking, we're on the same page." The difference in styles did not necessarily cause James to diminish the quality of his own caregiving of his sons compared to Christine's. "It seems like things are just a bit calmer when they're just with me than when Christine has them," he commented with a laugh. In terms of their attachment to him, he noted,

> I think they both are a lot closer to me than they would be otherwise.... They probably still would go to their mother first, but they're both pretty close to me too. You know, the days that Christine's working all day, I have no trouble with them. They're not whining... or missing Mommy or anything like that, so it's nice.

Thus, the difference in caregiving styles and in what each parent had to offer did not preclude the possibility that, in terms of their overall ability to care for their children, James and Christine were interchangeable; in different ways, both were able to meet their children's needs.

Life was perhaps less hectic for Geoff than for Gary and James because he had reduced his hours of work to accommodate caregiving, and there was also only one child — three-year-old Kelly — needing care. Geoff's extensive involvement with Kelly emerged, as noted earlier, through his partner Diane's account as well. She was a somewhat isolated newcomer to Canada, a first-time mother, and herself an only child. He was a much more established immigrant and much more accustomed also (as one of five siblings) to family life with children, and he had plenty of caregiving experience, gained through raising two children from a former marriage. He commented with a laugh, "I felt I knew a lot. You know, really."

Geoff had been hands on from the beginning: giving Kelly his first bath at home (with Diane watching — nervously, he thought), taking the lead on toilet training, sitting in on playschool sessions when they were choosing a play group for Kelly, and giving him little jobs in the kitchen as he cooked or cleaned up. Unlike James (and perhaps also unlike Diane), Geoff actually relished the social dimension of preschooler caregiving. He was the parent who took him swimming ("I *love* going swimming with him on Saturday mornings") and to other preschooler activity groups ("just the two of us").

Geoff's involvement had increased significantly in the year before his interview, when Diane's return to paid work initiated their shared caregiving arrangement. It was starting to register with Kelly:

> I think Diane knows him better because of the time she spent around him at the beginning. But since I've been at home more, I find we're a lot closer, whereas before he'd always go to Diane. He'd come to me, but Diane was always the main parent.... But now I think Diane's feeling the opposite, you know. "He's always with you."

Diane's account painted Geoff as a gentle and supportive nurturer, both to Kelly and to her. On his own account, Geoff said,

> I will always try and have the most time with him [that I can]. Because, in the back of my mind, I still haven't, I've still lost out on my other two children, and that's something...I don't want that to happen. I get involved.

Special, unanticipated circumstances prompted Andrew and David to figure out a shift-work arrangement to care for their infant adopted daughter Alexia. Theirs was the newest and probably most temporary of all the shift-work arrangements. It was especially significant though because, as gay fathers of a newborn, they were breaking new ground. When I met them, Andrew was 35 and David was 30. They had been together for nearly seven years and married for nearly one. When they were younger, they had (like many other gay men) gone through a time of believing that parenthood would not be possible for them. But shifts both in public perceptions of same-sex relationships and in public policy (most Canadian provinces now allow same-sex adoptions) opened the door to the kind of parenthood they wanted. Adoption was especially appealing, Andrew said, "because we could really equally participate in the process." They underwent the exhaustive home study required of all adoptive parents, took courses, talked to other adoptive families, and read extensively. Less than a year after they started the process, through a private adoption agency, they were chosen by Alexia's birth mother.

Both were university educated and had secure professional jobs with small, family-friendly companies. Both employers had been alerted to their plans, but there could be no anticipating the timing—Alexia's arrival ten weeks earlier had, like most adoptions, taken everyone by surprise. Ongoing work commitments and unfinished projects meant that neither Andrew nor David could easily take a parental leave. So David went in to work early in the morning while Andrew cared for the baby; towards noon they changed over. This arrangement, under way for two months, was scheduled to last for another six. Then they would have to move to a longer-term arrangement.

Already, they were a going concern as a family, negotiating a new division of caring labour around work schedules that, though flexible, were starting to point each in particular directions in terms of family responsibility. For example, David's afternoon caregiver shift positioned him as the one more available for the baby's medical appointments. And it was David who was negotiating space in the mother-dominated social world outside the home (Doucet 2006b). When we spoke, his main encounters with this world had been through walk-in clinic sessions combining the opportunity to weigh the baby with some group discussion and socializing. "Moms don't know what to do with dads that stay at home," he commented. "And then you throw a gay dad into the mix...." Both agreed that he was better suited to this part of the caregiving job than was Andrew: "just sort of being outgoing and comfortable in different situations, and sort of dealing with that chaos." Both also recognized that Andrew would much prefer to be at home more but that he was better placed to be the primary earner. In the early days of their caregiving, however, their shift-work arrangement kept both in their paid employment and allowed each of them to share in the care of their daughter.

Dual-Dividers: Sharing Work, Sharing Care, Hiring Help

The staggered-shift strategy employed by couples such as Denise and Gary is not practical for most employed parents. Give or take an hour or so, most jobs are done during a nine-to-five weekday. Usually, when parents leave the house in the morning, so do the children; family schedules become more complicated as the time demands of both parental workplaces are aligned with children's pick-up and drop-off times at day-care centres, private day homes, and nursery schools. The time children spend with other caregivers obviously reduces the time during which parents themselves are providing hands-on care. But it introduces another layer of parental work related to the choice and supervision of outside care.[2] There is also the emotional work of coping, and helping children cope, with family lives that are increasingly time stressed (Daly 2001; Hochschild 1997). This extra work, to say nothing of the more routine childcare that must still be done outside of working hours, is added to the broader level of ultimate, executive responsibility for children's welfare that one or both parents must assume.

The group of dual-dividers in the study was made up of six couples who, like the shift-workers just described, were dual earners. However, at the time I interviewed them, they were using paid childcare or workplace-supported parental leave to help them balance two more or less full-time paying jobs and the care of preschool children. The six couples I introduce here possessed few if any of the characteristics of the statistically representative dual-earner couple described in the introduction to Part II. Three of them (Karen and Monica, Grant and Pierce, and Mitchell and Tony) were same-sex couples in which the standard family comparisons were not between mothers and fathers in the first place. Though, in one sense, these couples could be considered as going "against the grain" of conventional family life by virtue of their sexual orientation, all three also met the criteria I outlined in Chapter 2 by pushing the boundaries in their highly individual but even-handed sharing of earning and caring responsibilities.

The three heterosexual couples (Alison and Trevor, Marie and Stephen, and Rebecca and Aidan) deviated from the statistically representative dual-earner image in other ways. All three couples, with both partners in full-time jobs, featured three fathers who had shared parental leave and three mothers who earned an equal share (Rebecca) or substantially more (Alison and Marie) of the family income. In all three cases, any privileging was usually in support of the mother's job. Like Keith and Matt, described in Chapter 3, Trevor and Stephen were also domestic managers, doing most of the cooking and household work in their families.

These families did not *cross* gender boundaries in the way the couples in Chapter 3 did. Nor was their balance of earning and caring as symmetrical as it was for the shift-worker families described earlier. Like those families, though, their arrangements for combining full-time employment and family responsibilities *blurred* gender boundaries and contributed, in the process, to new understandings of mothering and fathering. When I considered the six couples in this category and took into account both the arrangements that were in place when I interviewed them and the circumstances these arrangements had to accommodate, there seemed to be three natural groupings. At one level, these related to the practical details of who was doing (more or less of) what. However, the groupings also allowed me to explore different relationships to paid work, as well as the needs of particular children, which played into the arrangements. With a focus on how each arrangement shaped the ongoing practices of mothers and fathers, I examine each in turn in the next three sections.

Equal Sharing (of a Heavy Load)

The two couples I include here were unique among the dual-earner couples in that each partner was contributing half of the family's income. From all the interview accounts, it also appeared that each parent was an equal partner in terms of responsibility for children. For both couples, too, caregiving arrangements had changed over time, with the equal earning and caring having replaced earlier arrangements that had positioned one or other parent as a home-based caregiver. Coincidentally, these couples happened to be the two in the study who were also caring for preschoolers with special needs.

Rebecca and Aidan were the parents of four-year-old Conrad and two-year-old Oliver. When I met them, Rebecca was 39 and Aidan 32. Aidan worked in the non-profit sector in public relations and communications. At the time of the interviews, Rebecca was combining several part-time contract positions in research, organizational administration, and teaching. But that arrangement had followed multiple job changes and an interprovincial move. The circumstance that came to direct all their choices, both in work and caregiving, was the diagnosis some two years earlier of Conrad's autism — just at the time Rebecca was about to give birth to Oliver. Rebecca and Aidan shared a year of maternity and parental leave between them to provide care for infant Oliver and to come to terms with Conrad's needs. Ultimately, and after moving closer to their families' home base, they found a form of therapy that appeared to be effective, but it was also expensive and time consuming. So they were dealing with pressures both to maintain as high an income level as possible and to spend as much time with their children as possible. The time demands were particularly acute: not only did one child require a disproportionate amount of attention and emotional energy, but there was a second child who needed nurturing too.

The second couple, Grant and Pierce, were the adoptive parents of five-year-old Gemma. Aged respectively 43 and 41 at the time I interviewed them, they had been together for ten years and married for three. They were also business partners in a marketing company. Neither came to Gemma's adoption as parenting novices. Grant had two children from a previous heterosexual relationship; the shared custody arrangement negotiated for these children, from the time they were preschoolers, gave Pierce as well as Grant a full share of hands-on caregiving. However, the life they anticipated as co-parents to their own baby was derailed almost from the beginning; like Rebecca and Aidan, they found themselves caring for a child with serious health and developmental problems. At the beginning, they divided up the earning and caring responsibilities along breadwinner-caregiver lines. Grant, familiar with babies and able to work flexibly from home, became the main caregiver while Pierce's higher and more stable income provided the financial support. Gradually, as Grant completed his return to full-time work, the care he provided Gemma at home was supplemented by a nanny and other therapists and then by outside kindergarten and day-care programs. By the time I met them, the initial breadwinner-caregiver arrangement had given way to a much more even sharing of earning and caring responsibilities.

For both couples, the child with special needs was the hub around which most other activity was organized. It involved Rebecca and Aidan in research on therapy programs, in coordinating a team of therapists, in dealing with government bureaucracy in the context of getting financial support, and in advocacy at both the community and the neighbourhood level, among many other things. The therapy alone involved a consultant, as well as a team of university student therapists who came into the house to provide Conrad with some 40 hours of sustained one-on-one interaction per week. Rebecca described the work created by this schedule:

> You're overseeing them as an employer. You're also overseeing the [program], how it's developing, the troubleshooting. You're the communication person between them, and the consultant, and you're hiring a speech therapist...you know, that kind of stuff, so we're sort of the hub of that wheel so that is a huge amount of work.

This work is what DeVault (1999), building on Hochschild (1983), considers under the general heading of advocacy, an important but often neglected form of family emotion work. In the case of a child with a disability, this requires parents to participate in specialized caregiving and generally to make sure the child's needs are being met. Grant and Pierce, in the wake of the diagnosis of their daughter Gemma's brain damage and other health problems, undertook similar work. The variety of therapies she needed, on an ongoing basis, took them into what they wryly called "baby boot camp." Though Gemma made rapid progress under this regime, Pierce commented that they had to be constantly aware of giving every interaction or activity some therapeutic value.

Carrying all this responsibility alone was out of the question. The major dilemma was how best to divide it up. All four parents had undergone transitions in their working lives as they accommodated the shifting needs of their children. Rebecca said she would have liked to be spending more time at home to cope with these heavy demands. But, as she pointed out, Conrad's therapy needs were "so expensive that you want to be out there working like a crazy person." Rebecca's situation was further complicated by the fact that, with two university degrees and more work experience (because she was more than six years older), she also had greater earning potential than Aidan. Her compromise was to organize her work so that she could do as much of it as possible from home. When I met her, she had just negotiated a high-level part-time job (working for a provincial government commission) that would give her some job and income security while also allowing her more time at home. While his mother worked, Oliver was in a non-profit day-care centre.

Aidan was caught in the same dilemma as Rebecca, needing to share the work at home and also needing to provide income to meet the household's unusually high financial needs. He was also employed in a sector that was chronically underresourced, trying to do the sort of politically motivated social justice work to which he felt a personal commitment. His paid work, though it varied in terms of interest, was something of a cause. In an ideal world, he said he could envisage sharing caregiving with Rebecca, not along the lines of James and Christine's two-day–three-day split or Diane and Geoff's morning-afternoon trade off but rather as a six-months-on–six-months-off division, so he could "work six months like crazy" and then be home with the children. In the less than ideal world in which he and Rebecca were currently working, that wasn't possible, so the home demands just had to be fitted in anyway. The point was that, for a father in Aidan's situation, there was no question of opting out. Like the fathers studied by McNeill (2004, 2007), Aidan found his child's condition a catalyst for involvement.

The work transition for Grant and Pierce had seen Pierce, formerly the main earner in a stable executive job, join Grant in his marketing business. This move was designed partly to give the family more flexibility to accommodate Gemma's needs and also to eliminate the potentially conflicting demands of two unrelated careers. For Grant, the decision was "wonderful," offering the simplicity of schedules that could intertwine. For Pierce, the decision was a conscious realigning of priorities, factoring in "more considerations than simply me and my career goals."

For both couples, the sheer volume of family work overwhelmed questions about who was "really" in charge or who had the closest bond with the children. In fact, my interviews with all four illuminated the particular importance, in these circumstances, of another bond, the one between two parents experiencing the mixture of sadness, hard work, worry, and protective love that comes from raising a child needing more than usual care and help.

Rebecca commented that she was "not a kid person before I had my kids." Conrad's was the first diaper she had ever changed, and, at the beginning, she felt that Aidan was actually more at ease with the caregiving than she was. Over time, both parents' relationships to the children evolved. On the current emotional connections in the family, she commented:

> I would say I am in the more traditional position with Oliver, and I'm sort of the person he runs to. But with Conrad ... [Aidan's] great with Conrad, really good, much more relaxed and sort of comfortable with it.

Her current push to be able to spend more time at home was not because she thought there was anything particular that positioned her as "the one." From her initial discomfort, she grew to enjoy spending time with the children and wanted to maximize her opportunity to do so. "I think it could just as easily be Aidan," she said. "I think it's because I've really said, 'I want to be the one to do it.'" In only one area did she see herself as better suited to being at home: the cultivation of neighbourhood relationships that would allow her to advocate for Conrad and build a social network for him too. "I do think this is one special skill that I bring," she said.

Aidan was involved in "emotion work" of another kind. Though he did not speak of it himself, from Rebecca's account, Aidan took his turn with public advocacy, lobbying government and media on issues related to autistic children. When he had more time, he too helped oversee Conrad's therapy program. Though less free to do that part of the work now, he continued to carry all the administrative load of managing payroll, filling out forms for bureaucrats, serving as liaison to government departments, and managing the budget — a load that, in Rebecca's judgement, was "huge." And he also shared in the more daily emotion work, of which he offered "a perfect example":

> Other families take their kids to the park, right? And then ... they just sort of let them go and it's kind of a fun thing: you relax, you sit, you watch them. For us taking [Conrad in particular] to the park can be in fact a very stressful experience because not only can you not just sort of sit back and relax, you have to ... watch him, and make sure that he is pushed into engaging with other kids and pushed into sort of not lapsing into ... isolative behaviour. But then when he does do that it's very stressful to watch him compared with other kids because there's nothing that reminds you more of your child's handicap than seeing him in an environment with typical children.... So that's just a perfect example of a simple thing like walking your kids to the park on a

summer evening is not the relaxing thing that it might be for [other parents]. It can be very stressful.

The commitment Grant and Pierce felt to their daughter Gemma was remarkable for being freely chosen. They adopted her when she was less than a year old, knowing she had been very ill as an infant. Grant remembered an official involved with their international adoption process referring to her as "a broken child." Technically, they were free to call off the adoption, but, having seen her, both felt they had a moral obligation to Gemma, whose life in her country of origin would otherwise have been, in Pierce's terms, "really grim." "When you birth a child, you don't send them back or give them back if you don't like how they turned out," he said. "It's the roll of the dice." Grant spoke in similar terms. "You have to stand up for people," he said. "Our child would have never been adopted. We were presented with it ... for whatever reason, and that was that." That said, "I had *no* idea what we signed on to!"

Their initial division of labour, which positioned Grant as the primary caregiver, felt "quite natural" to him. He considered himself "more maternal," "more house-happy." He described the family as being, in this period, rather like the "traditional, stereotypical heterosexual Ward and June Cleaver family." The stereotype, of course, did not really apply because they were both men. But it was also breached in the sense that, for Grant and Pierce as for many other couples, the division of caring work in particular was not nearly as straightforward as the stereotype suggests. Grant, although picturing himself as the primary parent, described feeling overwhelmed by Gemma's needs and depressed by her prospects. Pierce, although trying to be the primary breadwinner, was "trying to be everything that I thought I should be for her in that stage" as well. He was also trying to think positively, to help counter Grant's concerns. At the level of practical caregiving, Pierce, like many of the breadwinner mothers described in Chapter 3, usually handled the evening routines and tended to Gemma in the time when she was still waking up in the night—he remembered "lots of nights of rocking in the rocking chair." Grant also had a shoulder injury as a result of an accident, so Pierce did much more baby lifting and carrying.

Over time, as Gemma began to show what turned out to be a remarkable response to all the therapeutic interventions, much of the initial stress eased. Over time, also, the balance of responsibilities changed, especially once Grant returned to full-time work and others picked up much of Gemma's therapy and care. At the time I met them, Pierce judged that Grant was more involved with her school and in her classroom, but he was handling more of the medical appointments and her extracurricular activities. However, the consistent morning and evening routines she and Pierce shared and his greater capacity to engage in physical activities seemed to have positioned him as the parent to whom Gemma was, for the moment, more attached. For all that Grant had seen himself as the "mother figure" of the two, Pierce could see a mother model in much of his own relationship to Gemma. "At the same time," he added, "I've been probably also very male in the sense that I was the primary earner and do a lot of the kind of male things around the house." (In Grant's view, though, Pierce was carrying a heavier load of household chores in general.)

In this household, as in Rebecca's and Aidan's, there was too much to be done and very little down time. As I noted earlier, the allocation of caregiving was not straightforward. As the situation for Rebecca and Aidan also showed, when caring for children is difficult, the parental relationship is especially crucial. Grant, who had described himself as "more the nurturer," was also, after years of difficult caregiving, "very very tired." From his account, Pierce seemed acutely aware that Grant, too, needed to be cared for.

Rearranging Responsibilities

The two families I include here accommodated two careers with a wide income gap between them, and, in both cases, the lower income earner also did more domestic work and somewhat more of the hands-on childcare after working hours. All four partners gave a very clear accounting of the extent to which they considered themselves to be equal partners in their family lives. But, in both cases, equal partner status was accompanied by a division of earning and caring responsibilities that blurred gender boundaries and conventions in different and interesting ways.

Monica and Karen were the mothers of four-year-old Michelle and 17-month-old Liam. Both babies were conceived through in vitro fertilization; Karen was their biological mother, and Monica the gestational mother. Monica had taken a year's leave with each birth. When I met them, Monica was 47, and Karen was 41. Both had full-time jobs, though Karen worked at home in the mornings so that she could transfer Michelle from kindergarten at midday to the day home where Liam was also cared for. Karen earned about 60 per cent of the total family income. With both children,

Monica had been the one to take leave. As a public school teacher with good benefits, she was in a better position (Ranson 1998) to negotiate this kind of workplace arrangement than Karen, who worked as a management consultant. Karen's higher income further justified the arrangement. However, it was Karen's job, rather than Monica's, that was being bent to accommodate the family's complicated schedule; one child in morning kindergarten meant a pick-up from school and a subsequent drop-off at the day home in the middle of the day. Karen had negotiated with her employer to work at home in the mornings, so she could do it. She was also more likely to be the one to stay home when children were sick. Although Monica's job as a teacher had the good benefits, it did not offer this kind of flexibility. Medical issues were also a factor in their arrangements. Karen, too, had hoped to be a gestational mother, but she had not been able to carry a pregnancy to term. Her age and other health-related factors had now all but eliminated the possibility. Had she also given birth, she too might have taken leave time at home. It was a prospect she was still considering once the children were a little older.

The second couple, Trevor and Alison, aged respectively 43 and 42 when I met them, were the parents of four-year-old Helen. Helen was adopted when she was 13 months old and past the intensive caregiving needs of infancy. At the time she arrived, Trevor was an editor with a major trade publisher. He was a permanent, full-time employee, who, along with a regular benefits package, had the additional advantage of working from home. Alison was a health professional in private practice; she had the much higher income, but (since she was self-employed) no benefits or paid leave option. So Trevor spread a three-month parental leave over Helen's first six months at home, working half-time and sharing the caregiving with Alison, who worked just enough hours to maintain her practice. After that, when Helen was nearly two, her parents entered her full-time in a not-for-profit day-care centre. Trevor's flexible home-based work positioned him to take more responsibility for household management and to assume a variety of other parental obligations, such as visits with Helen to the doctor or dentist. Alison, meanwhile, earned about 70 per cent of the family income.

As adoptive parents, Alison and Trevor started out on a more even footing than might otherwise have been the case. There was no biologically-based maternal advantage involved; both saw themselves as equally able to care for Helen. For Monica and Karen, the playing field was levelled in a different way. Although in lesbian families the biological mother may be privileged over the "other" mother (Reimann 1997), Monica and Karen both had equally compelling, though different, biological claims on their children; Monica was the gestational mother to Karen's biological children. The different requirements and opportunities of their jobs positioned Trevor and Monica as more likely to pick up some extra childcare and domestic slack in their respective families. But, ultimately, this did not mean they became "primary parents" in counterpoint to their partners' primary earner status. All four partners spoke of sharing the responsibility for children and households in ways that disrupted conventional gender divisions.

Of all the mothers in this group (and indeed in the study as a whole), Alison was the one most convinced that she would not have children. "I remember breaking up with guys who wanted children, just for that reason," she said. In Trevor, whom she had met when both were graduate students, she found a like-minded partner. She completed a graduate degree and gradually established her own practice. But she recalled that her focus was not so much on building a career as on enjoying life and travelling. She also recalled her shock when Trevor raised the possibility of adopting a child. (In Trevor's words, she was "totally gobsmacked!") But, within a week, for reasons she could not fully articulate, she was committed. They signed on with a private agency that handled international adoptions, and some 15 months later they became the parents of Helen, then aged 13 months.

Looking back, Trevor could recall a sequence of events in his life — meeting little adoptees from Asia at a conference, reading about international adoptions in a magazine, spending time at another conference with couples who had adopted children internationally — all within the space of a few months and all seeming to reinforce international adoption as a possibility. Up till then, "we were just, kind of, doing the same things," Trevor recalled. "There was just ... I think I would describe it as just kind of like an emptiness." It was he who, as he put it, "articulated the question" of whether they should adopt — and the time from question to answer was very quick. As Trevor described it, "We both just kind of turned. And we've never had any doubts. I mean it's just been the best experience."

There were many circumstances, apart from her lifelong resistance to the very notion, that made it unlikely Alison would become a traditional mother. She had not given birth to Helen, or nursed her, or, indeed, had any contact with her during the critical months of infancy. She also came to motherhood as a partner in an egalitarian marital relationship, which meant, as she put it, "knowing that I would have a partner that's fully on board in the care of the child." Equally committed and equally inexperienced, Trevor and Alison were dealing with a going concern in Helen, a child able to express preferences and to favour one of her new parents, clearly, over the other. Initially, it was Trevor she favoured.

Over time, the balance shifted. Helen's growth and her social and intellectual development gradually brought her closer to Alison. Alison had child development expertise that Trevor lacked. Her account indicated that, like many mothers, she was the "emotion expert" in the family, better able to understand Helen's behaviour and her emotional state (Risman and Johnson-Sumerford 1998). Alison said she also took the lead in supporting Helen's imaginative and creative play — at least some of which was clearly gender based. "Because she is quite the girly girl at this stage, I am sort of doing all the girly girl stuff with her," she said. (This mother-daughter connection also extended to Helen's clothes, which Alison bought.) In a sense, Alison appeared to be most clearly a *mother*, and not a parent, in the activities in which she engaged with Helen.

Trevor was the more physically active and task-oriented parent — the *father*, in fact — who helped Helen on her bike and pushed her on the swing and was teaching her to ski; he much preferred goal-directed activities to unstructured play with his daughter. However, both Trevor and Alison pointed out that Helen was an intensely busy and active four-year-old, to whom Trevor's style was well suited. ("She loves fun and activity", Alison commented. "And... Trevor's fun and activity.") Trevor concurred with Alison's assessment that she was better at handling emotions ("I'm just a guy in that regard"), and he spoke of his reliance on her to give him feedback on some of his own responses to Helen. But in Trevor's case, too, the more conventional mother/father division only worked up to a point. If Trevor was more classically masculine in some of his fathering activities (the goal-oriented, physical ones), he was also more capable domestically. Working from home, he was already doing all the cooking and much of the cleaning.

Like James, described earlier, he claimed for himself the commonly feminine-associated ability to "multi-task" — an ability that in his view Alison did not have. He earned much less money than Alison did, and, although he spoke of getting a high level of satisfaction and intellectual stimulation from his job, it was not the privileged job in the family. Working from home, he was in a better position to take charge of medical appointments and to care for Helen when she was sick. He was another parent who had never changed a diaper until his own child's arrival, but, in that and in other childcare, "you kind of learn." He commented that he felt "completely competent" to care for Helen. He was also, in Alison's terms, "one hundred per cent in" when it came to sharing overall planning and executive responsibility for Helen's welfare. Along with taking charge of the more day-to-day planning (in which he included tasks such as registering her in swimming or gymnastics classes), he was thinking ahead, taking charge of finances to meet the cost of post-secondary education, if that turned out to be necessary. They were currently engaged in a lively debate on the merits of French immersion schooling. He was also reading extensively on issues related to cross-cultural adoption, to be prepared for questions down the road. In other words, their more gendered division of *interactional* work with Helen was not reflected in the sharing of overall parental responsibility and decision making. Both their accounts suggested that, in these domains, Alison and Trevor were equals.

Unlike Trevor and Alison, Monica and Karen had been trying to have children for many years, and both had hoped to be gestational mothers. The fact that it was Monica rather than Karen who ended up taking the parental leave after each baby's birth was as much a by-product of the relative success rates of new reproductive technologies as a comment on their individual preferences. (Karen, however, did position Monica as the parent better suited to home-based caregiving.) During Monica's parental leaves, Karen, like the employed mothers described in Chapter 3, came home from work and immediately took over the caregiving. When her leave ended, Monica's teacher hours meant that she saw more of the children in the afternoon and evening than Karen did. Though the children were not around, Karen's morning shift at home allowed her to do the occasional household chore (notably laundry). But it also led to an extra office load, so she was seldom home in the evening in time to have dinner with the family.

Their different schedules were clearly producing an imbalance in the allocation of some of the caregiving responsibilities. As Monica commented, "I think I do a little bit more just because I'm [home] at a different time of the day than she is." Like the mothers described by Walzer (1996, 1998), Monica was also the parent who worried more or, as she put it, who talked about her worries more: "I don't know if I worry more, but I verbalize my worrying." For Walzer, this "thinking about" (and worrying) distinguished the mothers from the fathers in her study. But to position Monica as the "mother" figure and Karen as the "father" figure in this family on the basis of these apparent differences between them is to make much too arbitrary a judgement. Karen was, rather, a different kind of mother; in fact, she appeared from her account to be a mother much like the bread-winner mothers described in Chapter 3. She may have been less of a worrier, but, in her interview, she described situations where she, rather than Monica, did the emotional labour of tackling some key worries at their source. (Resolving an early misunderstanding on the part of school administrators about their status as lesbian parents when Michelle started kindergarten was one example.)

Though her work hours deprived her of contact time with them, as I noted earlier, it was actually Karen's job, rather than Monica's, that was most affected by the children's schedules. Outside of working hours, how-ever, Karen observed, "We almost do everything together." Together, they also managed the household calendar of children's activities and doctors' and dentists' appointments. "I think we both notice the clothes, the appointments, what needs to be done, and, you know, if Michelle's hair is getting out of control and needs to be cut, that kind of thing," Monica commented.

The sharing of this executive responsibility was accompanied by a shar-ing of the children's attachment that was, as in some other families I have described, changing and fluid. Both Monica and Karen spoke of the firm preference their elder daughter Michelle expressed, first for Monica and more recently for Karen, and the emotional wrench that created for the less-preferred parent. The most recent snapshot assessment aligned Karen with Michelle and Monica with the baby, Liam, but, from Monica's per-spective at least, that too was starting to change. Liam, she thought, had always been more even handed in the distribution of his affections, and the pendulum of Michelle's devoted attachment was starting to come back to a balance between both parents.

Transitions against Tradition

The two remaining couples technically fit the broader dual-earner cate-gory. In both cases, though, one partner was temporarily doing more of the earning and the other more of the caring. At the time they were inter-viewed, both couples also seemed to be on the brink of transitions that would make these temporary arrangements permanent.

Marie and Stephen were the parents of four-year-old Kimberley and 11-month-old Maya. When I interviewed them, Marie, a 39-year-old university professor, had returned to work after six months of parental leave following Maya's birth. Stephen, a 33-year-old communications professional, was coming to the end of his own six-month share of the leave; he was leaning towards a decision not to return to work but to stay at home to care for the children. Stephen had previous experience with a part-time schedule, having reduced his work hours for a time when their first child, Kimberley, was an infant. For this couple, the alternating shifts of home-based care over the four years they had been parents were an interesting meshing of two employment patterns. Marie completed a PhD and then looked for and some time later found a permanent job. Her periods of primary caregiving were stops along a well-defined, upward career path. Stephen's caregiving turns had accommodated Marie's work, and they represented a different rhythm of alternating attention to work and home over time.

The second couple, Mitchell and Tony, aged respectively 36 and 42 when I interviewed them, had been together for sixteen years and married for nearly three. They had adopted their son Nathan two years earlier, when he was three. Mitchell worked in a non-profit organization. Tony worked from home as a technical writer. Their different employment circumstances shaped how, over time, they divided up the administrative— and emotional—work of becoming parents to a toddler whose start in life had not been easy. Home-based Tony was heavily involved at the beginning of the process, facilitating Nathan's transition from his foster home and also taking the lead in medical and other appointments. Mitchell, however, took parental leave and so moved quickly into more of a "primary parent" role.

For both couples, the balance of earning and caring work had to be organized around the obligations and opportunities offered by particular kinds of paid work; around individual tastes, talents, and aspirations; and around the perceived needs of individual children. In both couples, one partner earned two-thirds of the family income and had much more of a career orientation. Primary earner status seemed obvious. In both couples also, the other partner was keen to assume primary caregiver status. As in other cases I have described, however, there was some tension around the possibility of the primary caregiver becoming the primary parent, with all the emotional consequences that implied in terms of children's attachment and overall family responsibility. There was also considerable gender-blurring in the arrangements both couples had made over time.

Marie gave birth to her first child, Kimberley, when she was approaching 35 and on the linear academic career track also followed by Tanya (introduced in Chapter 3). She was working on a postdoctoral fellowship that is a common intermediary stage between the completion of a PhD and the start of that first permanent academic job. She noted that both she and Stephen "badly" wanted children. Four years later, she commented: "I underestimated how difficult it is to be a parent, I don't know how many fold. I completely underestimated it."

Marie's underestimation linked to the circumstances surrounding Kimberley's arrival. From Marie's own experience, it was "quite a desperate time." They lived in a one-bedroom apartment where noise was an issue, and Kimberley, though perfectly healthy, was neither a quiet baby nor a good sleeper. Meanwhile, Marie was fulfilling a short-term teaching contract agreed to before Kimberley was born. She was also struggling to meet the "relentless" demands on a neophyte academic looking for a permanent appointment, and she was stressed because she didn't yet have the job. Her account of this time contained many comments about how difficult it was, how she "almost sort of crumbled under the weight of it":

> I remember that period as being...sort of mired in these contradictory feelings. One of, like elation at having a beautiful baby, and the other of just sheer terror that I wouldn't get a job.... I found the adjustment with Kimberley very, very difficult.

Looking back, Marie said she wondered whether she might have been suffering from a mild form of postpartum depression. "I've talked to people," she said. "I don't think I was actually suffering from a really deep form...but I think I had a little bit of it." Marie's experiences were similar to some of those described by Taylor (1996). And while Taylor, like Marie, distinguishes in her study between social and individual dimensions of the condition, she paints a vivid picture of the expectations of motherhood that new mothers feel they must live up to and their feelings of wretchedness, guilt, and dismay when those expectations are not fulfilled. *This Isn't What I Expected*, the title of a guide to postpartum depression cited by Taylor (Taylor 1996:41), is also an apt summary of Marie's first months as a mother.

Marie was not unsupported through those difficult times. Stephen cut his work back to part time so that he could be home with the baby when she was doing her sessional teaching, and he quit his job when Marie got hers, becoming Kimberley's full-time caregiver (for nine months or so, until Kimberley was nearly two and ready for day care). Stephen, like Trevor, was an exemplary household manager and a capable caregiver. He recognized how difficult the early months of caregiving were for Marie — even when both parents were, in effect, working part time while sharing the caring work. And he recalled anticipating an escalation of stress when Marie started working full time. "I knew that it couldn't work, both of us working full time," he said. "It was just the stress of it.... I just couldn't face it, in some ways." When their second child, Maya, was born, Marie was able to take a six-month maternity leave. Because Marie now had a secure permanent job in her field and supportive colleagues and friends, mother-hood the second time around was "totally different." At the same time, though, Marie's account contained hints of an ongoing struggle to accommodate the "cultural contradictions of motherhood" referred to by Hays (1996). As she herself put it, she wanted to have her cake and eat it too. She invested much time and energy to be a "good worker" while also contending with the social expectations placed on the "good mother." From her account, these expectations appeared to weigh more heavily on Marie than on many of the other employed mothers in the study. One particular statement about herself as a mother to her children was vivid in its very incoherence:

> I kind of have this weird debate with myself. Am I like a full, I'm not really full, I'm not stereotypically a full-time mom, although I feel like, I am a full-time mom but I'm not really, so that, sort of not, maybe not giving, I feel sometimes I'm not giving my full attention to them.

Her comment suggested a struggle to make the distinction between being "always a mom," which she clearly was, and being "a full-time mom," which, in practice, she could not be. There was a note of stress in her description of coming home at the end of the day: "the kids are on me.... It's like everything's multiplied." She spoke of Maya, in particular, having missed her — "she knows that I'm her mom and I'm not there." In fact, "no one's confused about who's the mom." But meeting those end-of-day demands (when "my nerves are shot") and getting very tired ("way more tired than Stephen") seemed to be difficult. She spoke of feeling "enormous amounts of guilt, about being away from the kids," but, at the same time, she recognized that spending the kind of time on home-based caregiving that Stephen was thinking of doing on an ongoing basis would not be possible for her. "I would hate it," she said flatly.

However, when she could set her guilt aside, she could view with some detachment the social construction of all those mothering expectations:

> I think it's a really powerful discourse about, you know, they're only young once, they're in the formative years...only parents at home, only a mom at home can do it, you know. So sure, I have some of those anxieties, even though intellectually I know that there's all sorts of not very positive things going on behind [them].

With that detachment, another note emerged:

> I feel...ultimately really quite good about what we're doing because I kind of see it as not having to trade off, that by thinking, you know, as partners, thinking strategically about each other, about the kids, I think we've managed to hit a really envied place, where we're both doing what we want.

The quiet subtext in Marie's account was that her family, like some of those described in Chapter 3, might actually be much better served by a caregiver father and a breadwinner mother than by the more traditional arrangement.

This was the subtext in Stephen's account as well. When I interviewed him, his six months of parental leave with Maya were almost over, and his need to make a decision about whether to return to his job was pressing. His relationship to paid work was interesting. He was well educated, with a master's degree and communications training. He had spent most of his working life employed by the same organization. It was a flexible, progressive work environment — in Stephen's assessment "open-minded" — where work was routinely organized around contracts and where people often moved in and out. It was not like "some kind of stock-broker agency" where unconventional work arrangements and career trajectories might not have been so easily accommodated or tolerated.

Stephen's account of his ongoing connection with his employer, through his stint of part-time work and then during his time as a full-time caregiver, suggested that he was a valued employee. He noted that his shift to part-time status was his preference but not his employer's. "[I] had a lot of experience at that time...and a lot of training, and so — they didn't stop me, but...I think they would have preferred if I stayed there [full time]," he commented. Later, during his time as a full-time caregiver, "they kept on asking me to come back." When he did return, it was to a better job than the one he had left. "They missed me," he said. "It was a good thing for my career."

The effect this had on Stephen was to remove much of the anxiety other full-time caregiver fathers feel about being away from the workforce. He recognized that, for him, a period of absence from his job would not "shut the door":

> I just always felt that ... even if I couldn't get back with [his former employer], I'm sure I could get some kind of work somewhere here, work from home or ... you know, [it's one of these fields] that, there's so many ways you can [do it] ... So I think that made it so, the time I was home, that it wasn't stressful.

Stephen's circumstances were also more advantageous in two other ways. First, he did not feel isolated in the way that some other caregiver fathers did. He lived in a progressive urban neighbourhood in a major Canadian city, where there were many other caregiver fathers practising the balance of flexible, often creative or artistic work and childcare that Stephen was. This meant that he wasn't short of male company on a day-to-day basis. And, unlike some of the other caregiver fathers, he did actively maintain a network of friends with whom he would "try to do stuff" — such as a trip to the pub on a Friday. He commented, "That's kind of important because that way I can go and talk about something other than, you know ... just talking to the kids." The other implication of the more obvious male community presence was a clearly gendered one. "Half the people I see in the park are men," he commented. "In my models, when I look around, I don't feel like I'm doing something that's women's work."

Stephen's second advantage was a family background that prepared him well for domesticity. He was one of four siblings with two working parents. His mother had trained all her children to be independent. He commented, "She taught us all how to cook and how to look after ourselves, stuff like that, and I think a lot of that's ... why I enjoy being home too." Cooking for Stephen was a special pleasure, and he had "a nice vegetable garden." More than that, though, like some of the stay-at-home fathers introduced in Chapter 3, he was a household manager. He saw that as being part of the job of being home with children.

If domesticity came easily for Stephen, caring for children did too. In his view, being a parent did not involve "skills that you're born with." It was something learned on the job; some parents (whether men or women) were better at it because the learning came more easily. In Stephen's view, it came "really easily" to him. He thought there might be differences between mothers and fathers, but the differences were small ("I couldn't breastfeed"), and "they become less important as the kid gets older." He stressed the importance of Marie's having spent time at home with both children too, and he acknowledged that being a parent was more difficult for the employed parent, whose inevitable wish to maximize time with children after working hours meant there was never any time for anything else. Like many of the other caregiver fathers, he was restrained about his own caregiver expertise. He was, he said, "fairly good at it," and he noted that, "in some ways" and "sometimes," he was better at reading his children, at "knowing what the kids want." He was also clear in his assessment that his household needed him at home, at least for the time being. "Both of us going back full time, I just can't see it working and us staying sane and, you know, keeping married," he said.

Mitchell and Tony, like Monica and Karen, also struggled to become parents, though the nature of their journey was different. Part of the journey was coming to feel that, as gay men, they were entitled to be parents. Berkowitz and Marsiglio (2007) call this the process of negotiating a "procreative identity." Tony commented on this process:

> I think Mitchell always had the presumption that somehow he would [have children], so he was definitely the driving force, and, more so, I had to be dragged into it, and, you know... sort of have my eyes opened. But I think we both definitely went through that whole process of wondering, of becoming entitled. And then once you feel entitled to parent, then you want to and it seems like a natural thing to then do, and you just continue on.

"Continuing on" involved a four-year journey, with its share of tension and heartbreaking disappointment. But when three-year-old Nathan first emerged as an adoption prospect, "it was almost like a birth moment." As Tony explained it, "We knew right then and there that there was nothing they could do to stop us from making him part of our family."

Because he worked from home, Tony was actually the one who first met Nathan, during a routine doctor's appointment. The encounter moved Tony deeply and guaranteed his emotional commitment. After that, he took the lead facilitating the transition from Nathan's foster home and also with medical appointments and other therapy to address some of their new son's developmental delays. Unlike other parents discussed so far, however, Tony and Mitchell were becoming parents to a toddler. Nathan at three was even more of a going concern than was Helen, adopted by Trevor and Alison at 13 months. His tastes and preferences soon led to Mitchell becoming, in Tony's terms, "the favourite." In part, this preference developed because Mitchell took the nine months of parental leave available to adoptive parents in Canada. Although Tony, working from home, was able to participate in much of the early, intense work involved in making Nathan feel secure and happy, he did also have to attend to his business, so the primary caregiver role quickly defaulted to Mitchell. Though he confessed to feeling a little hurt when Nathan's partiality was expressed too clearly, Tony also recognized its basis: "I think we recognize that children usually gravitate towards one parent as an anchor, and, I mean, they need to, I think." Nathan, he said, turned to him in other ways:

> He'll look to me for things like learning things or to build things or to play, you know. I'm not the most [sporty] person but he will still look to me to be the horsey and to rough and tumble and that sort of thing. So we do sort of split the roles in that way.

Tony agreed that these activities were stereotypically "dad" activities, but added a proviso:

> The interesting thing is it's almost not by choice. It's almost as if Nathan imposed those roles on us to some extent, honestly. Because I pictured myself in the nurturing role as well. And, in the beginning, when you don't know what your role is going to be exactly, I mean, it wasn't as if I said to Mitchell, 'OK, you take over this, and I'll do this.'

After two years of caregiving, Tony commented, "I'm not sure it didn't work out the way it should." He was, he said, "maybe not as calm and patient as Mitchell." So "his assumption of the nurturing role just seems natural, like a natural split of our personalities." Added to this, he said, "I enjoy my work quite a bit" — and it was his income that mainly supported the family. It was Mitchell, however, who commented on Tony's heroic attempts to unlearn his own fathering model and to develop a strong relationship with Nathan. And in many ways, the division of caring work in their household was designed to make both partners interchangeable (in Nathan's eyes) in the provision of daily care.

When Mitchell and Tony were interviewed, Nathan was heading for six. He spent three mornings a week at junior kindergarten and three afternoons, plus one full non-school day, in day care. Tony was doing most of the pick-ups and drop-offs, and they shared most of the rest of the hands-on caregiving, organizing a scrupulously even-handed division of domestic work around Nathan's needs and their mutual wish to spend time with him. "Family time" was built into most evenings. Mitchell, however, because of his part-time schedule, had the bonus of one full day every week in sole charge.

Aware that he was currently the prime focus of Nathan's attachment, Mitchell, like other primary parents already discussed, shifted between relishing his special status and wanting to make the attachment less exclusive. So, on the one hand, he spoke of fretting when he was not available to take Nathan to school:

> Because it's a scary thing for him, and...I think that I have more experience getting him to settle down and calm down than Tony does. So sometimes I'll just worry that he's not going to have a good day because, you know, I wasn't there.

The laugh with which Mitchell ended this comment spoke, on the other hand, to his awareness of sounding like "number one":

> And I feel like number one, yes. But, yeah, I do really want Tony to have that opportunity as well, and I want [Nathan] to be close to Tony as well, so we try to provide that for him.

For Mitchell, part of the importance of sharing the attachment and responsibility with Tony was to build in Nathan "that confidence...that he does have *two* parents and nobody's ever going to be able to tell him differently."

Any questions about Nathan's two parents, of course, would probably be questions about his two fathers. In the same way that Rebecca and Aidan, who were raising a child with a disability, needed to undertake a considerable extra workload of education and advocacy, so Mitchell and Tony also carried on this extra "emotion work." Part of it meant allowing their family life to be more public, having people over to show, as Mitchell put it, that "there's no secrets — we live the same as you." Part of the work was an energetic participation in Nathan's school and their community. Both shared this work. Tony took on more of the "adult" volunteering activities (Coltrane and Adams 2001), for example, volunteering with a provincial adoption organization and sitting on the policymaking council at Nathan's school; Mitchell was involved in more of the child-oriented ones, such as fund-raising events at school and classroom volunteering.

An easy response to the division of labour in this two-father household would be to categorize Tony as the father and Mitchell as the (de facto) mother. Yet a closer analysis calls this categorization into question. Mitchell was, in many ways, no different from the other primary caregiver fathers already described. As far as could be determined from his account, he was no more a "mother" than they were. He relished domesticity and would have enjoyed the opportunity to give up paid work. (In fact, when I interviewed him he had just accepted a new flexible-hours job close to home, which would enable him to provide all the caregiving outside school hours when, a few months later, Nathan would be starting Grade 1.) He was a superior caregiver, engaging in considerable "mothering" work and learning "maternal thinking" — just as other caregiver fathers did. However home-based Tony, doing his scrupulously even-handed share of after-school caregiving, as well as taking on some of the conventionally mother-dominated practices, such as responsibility for child health care, was hardly a conventional breadwinner father. Though he lacked their advantage of close, embodied relationships with their children through pregnancy and infancy (a lack he shared, incidentally, with adoptive mother Alison), he had, in other ways, a lot in common with many of the breadwinner *mothers*.

Summing Up

The mothering and fathering done by the couples described in this chapter was more complicated and, in many ways, more diverse than that practised by the breadwinner mothers and caregiver fathers described in Chapter 3. Here, the introduction of a second paying job into the family introduced also a second set of workplace requirements to be accommodated and reduced the time individual parents themselves spent on caregiving. (None of these parents spent as much time on caregiving as did the fathers described in Chapter 3.)

The shift-worker parents spent more time in caregiving than the other dual-earner couples, providing full-time coverage between them for their preschool children. Sharing this care, rather than allocating the bulk of it to one parent, affected the ways mothering and fathering played out in the families concerned. If, as I showed in Chapter 3, mothers who delegated caregiving to fathers could still retain executive responsibility and CEO status, that possibility might seem even more likely in the case of the shift-worker families, in which mothers continued to do half the caregiving. Yet it was only in the case of Denise and Gary that this dynamic was in evidence, along with the hint of conflict it generated, conflict that, in Fox's (2001) terms, is not problematized in much of the work on parenthood. In the other shift-worker couples, parents seemed to see themselves as much more interchangeable, across the full range of earning and caring responsibilities. Here too the shared communication born of close and joint engagement with their children from birth led to what I earlier described as an "equal terms" sharing of family work. This did not mean that "mothering" and "fathering" as explicitly gendered activities had disappeared; Christine's extended breastfeeding, and James's complementary background support were the clearest examples. It is interesting, however, that the interview accounts produced few other examples so distinct.

Examples of "mothering" and "fathering" as distinctly gendered practices were rare among the other dual-earner couples as well. Where they showed up, as practices that clearly distinguished partners, they were more at the level of interaction with children, as was the case with Alison doing the "girly girl" activities and Trevor doing the physically active, goal-oriented ones with their daughter Helen. They did not appear to be in evidence at the level of executive responsibility for children, and they did not appear to dictate children's attachments. These preferences were often directed to the parent who had done more hands-on caregiving, but this parent was not always the mother, and, in any case, the attachment was often (inter)changeable between parents.

The most interesting challenges to conventional understandings of "mothering" and "fathering" as the practices of women and men came from the same-sex couples introduced in this chapter. These challenges were foregrounded by the way I chose to classify the couples. One option might have been to consider all the same-sex couples in a single grouping, making sexual orientation the factor that most clearly differentiated them from the other dual-earner parents. But my judgement was that, in terms of the issues they were facing, the kind of caregiving work they were doing, and the division of labour they were negotiating, sexual orientation was largely irrelevant. To the extent that it mattered at all, it was only as a source of more family work; all the same-sex couples were aware of the advocacy and educating they needed to do in their communities to reduce the possibility of homophobia directed against their children.

It must be said, however, that same-sex couples did occasionally cast *themselves* in "mother" and "father" roles. For example, during a discussion in our interview about the particular kind of caregiving he was doing with his son Nathan, Mitchell acknowledged that he *felt* more like a mother than a father. ("That's the first time I've actually admitted it," he joked. "I'm out as a mother!") But from a broader perspective, compared with others in the study, Mitchell was no more of a "mother" than the (hetero-sexual) caregiver fathers discussed in Chapter 3. Karen, the lesbian partner of Monica, was no more the "father" in her family than were other bread-winner mothers, who spent more time at their paid work than in caregiving but who were fully involved in after-work caregiving and the sharing of executive responsibility for the children. The families with two fathers or two mothers might have looked different from the more conventionally gendered caregiver-breadwinner template. But when, as the couples in this study demonstrated, particular family tasks are being done by both moth-ers and fathers, the gendered template begins to lose its currency.

One legacy of that template is the designation of women who have both children and paid employment as "working mothers." The assumption built in to the term is that "mother" is their primary status; "working" is the qualifier. Implicit in this designation is another assumption — *because* they are primarily mothers, their working lives will be structured to accommodate their family responsibilities. The gender imbalance built in to this assumption is demonstrated by the fact that there is no equivalent "working father" term in popular discourse. Yet the fathers described in this chapter demonstrate the need to activate such a term. They were all "working fathers" in the sense that they prioritized their family responsi-bilities, sometimes making significant changes in their working lives to discharge them. Stereotypical expectations about fathers were further breached in that only two of the men — shift-worker James and Mitchell's same-sex partner Tony — were the primary earners in the family. The women described in this chapter had children and paid employment as well. But they were not conventional "working mothers." In part, this was because their jobs were generally considered to be no more liable to be compromised in the family interest than their partners' were, and, as I have just suggested, many were primary earners. But they were also not conventional working mothers, bearing the main family load, because the second adult in the family was at least as family oriented as they were. In other words, there was either another working mother or a working father sharing the family work.

The work context in which these newly designated working fathers and unconventional working mothers operated is an important element in the changes I have described. Much of the paid employment financially supporting their families was conducted outside the confines of regular workplaces and regular working hours. Indeed, at the time they were interviewed, all but one of the families had a parent either providing full-time care at home (Stephen, on parental leave, and all the shift-worker parents) or working from home (as in the case of Tony, Trevor, and Rebecca). The shift-workers were the couples who most clearly avoided regular working hours, though, in every family, there was at least one partner able to be at home if needed.[3]

In only two of the ten couples described here were both partners holding down conventional, full-time jobs as permanent employees. In the case of Monica and Karen, one (Monica) had good family benefits, and one (Karen), working in a consulting firm, had considerable bargaining power as a long-term employee. In the case of Andrew and David, both were able to negotiate part-time hours on a short-term basis to help them care for ten-week-old Alexia, but David was likely to leave his job within a few months to become her primary caregiver. In all the other families, various combinations of self-employment and contract work, much of it home based and technology empowered, afforded at least one partner the flexibility required for involved caregiving.

As I noted in Chapter 1, the flexible work characteristic of the New Economy is often seen to come at a social cost, as secure, permanent jobs give way to work that is insecure and contingent. At the same time, as other scholars (e.g., Smith 2001) have pointed out, with the risks of the New Economy come opportunities, particularly for well-educated and highly skilled individuals. All the couples described in this chapter were well placed to take advantage of the opportunities opened up by new ways of working. In some cases, they creatively combined the benefits of one partner's job with the income of the other's. In others, where both income sources were judged surplus to requirements, they "scaled back" the work of one or both (Becker and Moen 1999; Sweet and Moen 2006).

In all cases, the division of paid work and family responsibilities was child centred, pragmatic, and individualized. It took considerable work, negotiation, and compromise. It meant the (sometimes painful) sharing of children's attachments; the need, on occasion, to modify or set aside work aspirations; and the need, too, to deal with conflict over what was best to be done. Significantly, it also extended ongoing challenges to conventional gender boundaries even further. These couples were interchangeable over a much wider range of activities than the crossover parents described in Chapter 3. They were "undoing gender" not only in their commitment and competence as co-caregivers but also in their gender-blurring relation-ships to paid employment as well.

Part III

The Longer View: Couples with School-Age Children

Introduction

Children's transition from preschool to school is a major transition for parents as well. It signals the end of a particular form of caregiving labour—the hands-on, physical, intensive kind that they had been responsible for delivering, either directly or indirectly. It means the opening up of time during the day that does not have to be organized around the supervision of young children (Silver 2000). Usually, that means time that can now be used for paid employment. This is also the transition to another form of family labour, as parents embark on what will be more than a decade of accommodating family activities and employment schedules to the inflexibility of the school's timetable and coordinating family work to help their children meet the school's academic and social expectations.

The need to coordinate with the school introduces a new order of complexity into household arrangements.[1] Children of elementary school age still need supervision outside of school hours, and school hours, both on a daily basis and over the course of a year, do not fit most adult work schedules. Canadian workplaces, as I noted in Chapter 1, generally offer little flexibility to parents trying to cover off the times when their children are out of school, or when they are ill and have to be kept home. Conventionally, it is mothers rather than fathers whose paid employment is accommodated to fit these other time demands.[2]

For the 13 couples in the study whose children were of school age, the caregiving work varied as widely as the children's ages (the youngest was 7, the oldest 17). Concerns about after-school care and the need to help with reading in some families were overtaken in others by the challenges of adolescence and children's increasing independence. Furthermore, these older children, though in one sense the *objects* of parenting work, were by no means passive recipients; in another very important sense, they were subjects, orchestrating many elements of the show. The kind of work required and the way it needed to be organized had everything to do with who they were, as individual children.[3] In all 13 families, though, the caring work had to be combined with paid employment, in arrangements that matched parents' resources and their perceptions of their children's needs.[4]

Once, these children had been infants, toddlers, preschoolers. Their parents had organized caring and earning work in the same unconventional ways as the parents of the preschoolers described in the two previous chapters. Some had traded places as "crossovers," with fathers as home-based caregivers and mothers as primary earners. Some had been "shift-workers," scheduling hours of paid work to allow full-time parental care. And some had been "dual-dividers," needing some outside help to supplement their own caregiving while redistributing, in non-traditional ways, the demands of childcare and two full-time paying jobs.

Those unconventional arrangements were likely to have consequences for these couples, as they did for the couples with preschool children described in the earlier chapters. There, I showed how shadows of tradition lingered in the ways some of the mothers struggled to retain executive responsibility for their children, even while serving as family breadwinners as well; how some fathers struggled with their relationship to paid work as they took on a fair share (sometimes the lion's share) of family responsibilities; how two invested parents, both practised caregivers, could sometimes disagree (raising the spectre of family conflict and the need for negotiation and compromise); and, finally, how two invested parents, negotiating and compromising, could become, for practical purposes, interchangeable as caregivers, raising questions about whether "mothering" and "fathering" were even the best terms to describe their joint caregiving practices. The couples I introduce in the chapters to follow were further along the child-rearing road. Their children's transition to school, in many cases, saw shifts in their earning and caring arrangements as well. But, as I will show, going "against the grain" in the early years of caregiving usually played forward to the gender relations that seemed to characterize this later stage.

The six couples who had been "crossovers" for some if not all of their children's preschool years followed two different trajectories once their children started school. In one, the crossover pattern seemed to become entrenched, with fathers continuing to be home based and the households continuing to rely on the mothers' earnings. The second trajectory involved the caregiver-father/breadwinner-mother arrangement being replaced by a dual-divider pattern, as fathers joined mothers in paid employment and both parents equitably shared the caring work and responsibility for children outside of working hours.

The three couples who had used variations of the "shift-worker" arrangement during their children's preschool years all became shift workers of another kind when their children started school. This involved accommodating (in most cases) full-time paid work to allow them to share after-school care. The four couples who had been "dual-dividers" during their children's preschool years followed three different paths with their children's transition to school. One couple switched from day care to after-school care for their school-age child and carried on with the dual-divider arrangement they had initiated at the preschool stage. One couple switched to a crossover arrangement. Two couples, each with two children, used the launching of both children in school to dispense with formal outside caregivers. From being "dual-dividers" when their children were preschoolers, they too became "shift-workers" of another kind, trading off school drop-off and pick-up times to ensure a parental presence outside school hours.[5]

The patterns, the problems, and the promise of major change in gender relations that emerged from my descriptions of the couples with preschoolers were evident also among the more seasoned parents I introduce in the next two chapters. As I have pointed out, they began their journeys as parents in much the same way as the couples with preschool children described in the earlier chapters. But, by the time I met them, they had accumulated longer histories as parents. The ways their lives unfolded, in tandem, with the passage of time and their children's important transition to school, provided a different perspective on those early patterns, a longer view of what earning and caring against the grain might look like.

Chapter 5 picks up, from the perspective of parents of school-age children, some of the problems and challenges of unconventional family arrangements that I identified in the earlier chapters. Among the families with preschoolers, there were breadwinner mothers struggling to retain executive responsibility for their children and stay-at-home fathers wondering when and how they would return to paid work; this chapter looks at couples for whom these issues had magnified with the passage of time. So one focus is on those for whom the "crossover" arrangement had outlived its usefulness but now seemed hard to change. A second focus is on the issue of conflict, negotiation, and compromise, which was raised in the earlier chapters and was articulated more sharply by couples with more experience in the field.

Chapter 6 takes up the transformative dimension of going "against the grain" identified among many of the parents of preschoolers. The couples with school-age children, who (like many of the couples with preschoolers) were interchangeable across the range of earning and caring responsibilities but over a longer period of time, reinforced my sense that unconventional, "against the grain" family arrangements had radical potential for "undoing gender." This chapter describes the ways couples working hard over the years to be egalitarian across the board challenged conventional understandings of "mothering" and "fathering" in the way they framed themselves and their family work.

Chapter Five

Challenges on the Path to Change

Valerie and Charles, aged 48 and 50 respectively when I met them, were among the oldest couples in the study and the parents of 13-year-old Melanie. When Melanie was 13 months old, she had been diagnosed with type 1 diabetes. This meant she would be insulin dependent and her condition would have to be carefully monitored and managed. It was also going to be an expensive process. When Valerie and Charles got this news, Valerie had returned to her receptionist job after a six-month maternity leave. Charles, meanwhile, was out of work; he had taken over the caregiving while applying for jobs, but, in Valerie's terms, "nothing was happening."

"Nothing" continued to happen over the next 12 years of their lives as parents. The crossover arrangement into which they had been catapulted early on seemed increasingly resistant to change. In my interview, I asked Charles if he saw anything new on the horizon. He replied, "I've been out of work for so long I don't really see very much, to be honest with you." Long dependence on Valerie's salary (some $14,000 for the year before her interview), a salary supplemented by some government assistance for Melanie's health care and by support from extended family, meant there were no resources for retraining, for either parent. And age was coming to be a limiting factor too. As Valerie commented, "When you're just about 50, you're not going to go and be a brain surgeon." Meanwhile, her financial support had come at a cost; she had struggled through bouts of depression and other illnesses, and kept working. "You feel trapped; you feel trapped sometimes," she said.

As a couple, Valerie and Charles represent one of two scenarios uncovered in the study, scenarios that I came to think of as "challenges to change." In their case, the challenge was one that seemed to occur for former "crossover" parents when their children's entry into school was not accompanied by a transition to more equitable dual-earner arrangements. The second challenge I take up, in the second part of the chapter, is the conflict that can be experienced by two parents, often with very similar caregiving credentials, who are equally invested in their children's well-being.

Problems of Transition

Valerie and Charles were one of three couples in the study who remained in the crossover pattern once the children in the family were well launched in school. All three couples were linked by a common thread: one or both partners expressed concerns that the arrangement had outlived its usefulness but now seemed hard to change. As cases, they make it clear that going against the grain of conventional caregiving arrangements in the early years does not always lead to transformed and egalitarian relationships down the road.

For Valerie and Charles, the major life event that came to direct their earning and caring arrangements was the diagnosis of their daughter's illness. Melanie had been born after they had been married for several years; she was a much wanted baby, and they were not willing to delegate the care and monitoring she would need to an outsider. So Charles got to be the stay-at-home caregiver because he was unemployed at the time of Melanie's diagnosis, and Valerie had a job with the health benefits they were clearly going to need.

Valerie had wanted to be the one to stay at home, and, in her interview, she confessed to worries about whether Charles would be able to manage the daily caregiving of an infant. He had grown up with one younger brother in what he described as "a quieter household." She was the oldest of four. "He didn't grow up around babies," she said. "I grew up around babies. There were always little kids in the house." Like many breadwinner mothers, she found the return to work very hard:

> I cried all the way to work when I was driving.... [When] I got to work...I went to the public washroom and I washed my face and put cold water on it.

And I would phone home and stuff, and he would get upset because he thought I was checking up on him. And I wasn't, I just wanted to hear her.... You know, I just wanted to hear her.

Over time, those early worries diminished. "To give him his credit, yeah, he caught on better than I anticipated that he would," she said. Over time, too, Valerie developed her own relationship with her daughter. Like many breadwinner mothers, she spoke of the stress of fitting in her caregiving after a day of working. She commented that, sometimes, she was so tired after work that she couldn't do as much with Melanie as she would have wanted. But "if she was up, if she was sick or something, it wasn't him that she wanted, it was me." Though she was "bothered" because she thought she should have been at home with Melanie, "when I'm home with her I try to be with her as much as I can."

In my interviews, I did not feel able to probe for the reasons for their continued dependence on Valerie's succession of low-paying office jobs, especially when her own health was not good. There had been periods of unemployment for her, too, when two companies for which she worked went out of business. Charles had a university degree and some training, now long outdated, in a technology-related field. But even though he could not work in that field, he did not pick up any other kind of work, even when Valerie was at home and money was desperately tight. With support from extended family keeping the couple afloat, Charles became a professional volunteer instead of finding paid work, and turned occasional shifts in his daughter's elementary school into a regular daily commitment. This volunteering not only put him on the spot, on the occasions when Melanie needed medical attention, but also gave him the social network not always available to stay-at-home parents. Two years before I met him, when Melanie had moved to junior high school, he had, in a real sense, lost his job, though he continued, as before, with "adult" volunteer activities (Coltrane and Adams 2001), such as serving on the school's parent council. Recently, with the threat of cutbacks to Valerie's working hours, he had started a part-time home-based job—in his words, "simply because we need the dollars."

The financial stress in this family added to caregiving burdens that were already greater than the average. Both Charles and Valerie had also participated in the emotion work of advocacy aimed at increasing government help for families coping with diabetes, and they were involved in a support network of families and medical professionals. Melanie's medical condition also meant that they were on duty to a greater extent than many other parents were. Though Melanie was increasingly able to manage the condition on her own, parental vigilance was still needed. Diabetes "dominates our lives, even now," Charles commented. The annual weeklong camp Melanie attended, for juvenile diabetics, was "the only break that we get from our daughter all year."

For most of Melanie's 13 years, Charles had been the parent most available to her, and he provided the most hands-on care. Charles, rather than Valerie, had taken on the bulk of the school-related work usually done by mothers (Griffith and Smith 2005). In my interview with him, however, there was little talk about his relationship with her or about his caregiving work — though he commented that he had received "a ton of compliments on being a stay-at-home dad and what I've done," and he spoke with pride of Melanie's many academic and other accomplishments.

Valerie talked more about their efforts to communicate, across the gulf their individual family backgrounds created, to be consistent with discipline and to ensure a constant parental presence in Melanie's life. Early on, she said, when they were coming to terms with Melanie's condition, she was stricter, and he was more relaxed. As Melanie reached adolescence, though, these positions seemed to have reversed. Valerie's account, too, suggested that their styles as parents differed sharply. Valerie was more playful and hands on; Charles more serious and "adult."

From Valerie's perspective, Melanie had been closer to her father when she was younger and thought his volunteer work at her school was "kind of cool." More recently, according to Valerie, Melanie was "just sort of distancing herself" from her father, at the same time that, in his words, she was becoming "somewhat more mysterious" to him. "She's a girl, and there's all that sort of thing to deal with," he said. To the extent that "all that sort of thing" was taking up more space on the family stage, Valerie seemed to be making more of the decisions.

Valerie, too, was adjusting to Melanie's increasing maturity and independence. "One minute, there was this kid in Grade 4," she said. "Now I'm living with another young lady person, who's as tall as me and is wearing a bra, and we're going buying panty liners and tampons." Valerie's account suggested that, having always tried to spend as much time with Melanie as possible, she was reaping the rewards in a relationship that was close and that both of them enjoyed. (She said Melanie had told her, "You're not so bad for an old lady!") Valerie was now the mother who drove Melanie and her friends to the mall and then went to the library on the premises, so she could be available when they needed her. She spoke of television shows and movies that she and Melanie liked and watched together, though they were often not to Charles's taste. Valerie said she thought she and Melanie had similar temperaments and shared many traits. "So we're sort of connected that way too because — our personalities sort of jive despite being way off base and out there, and Charles is just like, 'Oh, my god!'" Valerie thought Melanie, an honours student and school soccer player, appreciated the stable presence of both her devoted parents. But it seemed now to be her mother with whom she was closest and to whom she would turn first.

Belinda, like Valerie, was also the primary parent to nine-year-old Zack and seven-year-old Kevin, even though she was also the family breadwinner. In her case, though, she was an undisputed CEO, probably the most overtly directive family manager of all the breadwinner mothers in the study. Belinda and her partner Frank started down their unconventional family paths from a transition point frequently documented in this study: the higher-earning professional woman becoming a mother in her mid-30s, the slightly younger father in a blue-collar job, the high cost of day care, and the preference for parental care, all combining to frame the pragmatic decision that the father would be the full-time caregiver till the children entered school. All through their children's preschool years, Belinda and Frank had this arrangement. But Belinda was, if not a reluctant breadwinner, a deeply reluctant absentee from the front lines of her children's early lives. So her after-work involvement with them was intense, and Frank's acquiescence to her management and establishment of the ground rules for their care was, she acknowledged, in part a way to make her feel better when she returned to work after maternity leave with their second child, Kevin. "I think he might have allowed me to do that just to be connected, too," Belinda said. "Because I was just really having a hard time."

Over time, however, this collusion seemed to have evolved into something else. Although other caregiver fathers in this study became increasingly confident in their children's care, Frank did not. His ongoing insecurity was partly the product of a chronic health problem he was battling. But, to the extent that he remained insecure about his caregiving, particularly in settings outside the safe confines of home, Belinda had to pick up the slack. And the more she picked up the slack, the more he backed off and deferred to her. Belinda spoke of the way these patterns of responsibility had become set: "I almost set the tone so that I would be the decision maker."

During the children's preschool years, her managing had included strategies such as signing the children up for play groups and urging Frank to take them or behind-the-scenes organizing of play dates with other children or telephone consultations aimed at helping him through bad patches with bored or cranky children. In fact, a great deal of Belinda's ongoing management of the children was handled through frequent phone calls during the day. All this was in addition to the caregiving she did herself after work:

> From that moment I walked in the door, I was on with the kids … he never did the bathing or the bedtime or the reading. I did all of that. And in the middle of the night it was always me, and when they were sick and nursing and all that stuff, that was very clearly defined as my role. And still, to this day, if the kids are sick, even though he's been home for many years, it's me. That's my role.

From my reading of the interview accounts, this role seemed to be, as I have already suggested, self-appointed, a way for Belinda to compensate for the work time she had to spend away from the children. It also seemed that she was compensating *them* for things their father could not provide them. As she said,

> I'm not a critical person, and I would never criticize Frank because he was outstanding at home. But still I could do it better. Because I'm their mother, and, at the end of the day, I'm a bit of a snob when it comes to that. I am their mother, and I know best. And Frank is somewhat shy and not as outgoing and, you know, I would be the one at the swimming pool with them and I would be the one at the library groups and I would be the one at the play dates and arranging this and arranging that, where he would be kind of laid back and waiting for people to come to him and initiate some sort of contact. So I always felt that I would have been much better at being at home.

The question of who would have been better at home was resolved to a certain extent when the children started school — but that transition served in another way to reinforce the parent hierarchy established earlier. Frank was unwilling to compete with university-educated Belinda's assured supervision of homework and piano practice, a school-related load recently increased manyfold by the recognition that their older child had a learning disability. Belinda commented that she managed "everything related to school" — to the extent that she now thought the children saw their father as incapable of taking it on. "I do feel badly for that: that we've set a tone in the house that I'm more capable of taking care of those things," she said. "Now that I look back, I wish that I wouldn't have because I've shot myself in the foot quite frankly."

The picture Frank painted of his caregiving suggested a father struggling mightily to do his best against challenging odds. Given these odds and his own conviction (repeated more than once in the course of his interview) that it would have been better for the children had Belinda been at home with them, I pushed him to come up with some things he felt he had done well. He responded:

> I've always loved them. Things I've done different than my dad is ... I've always hugged them and kissed them, I've told them I've loved them every day, ... I'd always reassure them that I did love them and they were special to me. I always kept them fed and protected.... I always tried to make sure that they were happy. I didn't neglect them.... I always tried to put them before me the best I could.... I really did try to put them before me and keep them happy and protected.

If his children's needs were ranked from the most basic to the most advanced, Frank was clearly focused on the more basic end, leaving the rest for Belinda's attention. His other major contribution to the earning and caring work of the family was as an exemplary housekeeper, who also did occasional home renovation work along with all the house and car maintenance. But with the children's transition to school and with Belinda as primary breadwinner also taking on all the school-related responsibilities, the division of labour seemed increasingly unbalanced. "I'm finding it harder and harder to justify staying home," Frank said. At the same time, he was worried about the kind of work he might be able to take on, partly in terms of his own abilities and partly because, with children still in their early elementary years, he needed the flexibility to work around school schedules. In the meantime, he worked behind the scenes, on physical not emotional labour. He kept the household running, but he looked to Belinda to keep him "grounded." In her words, she was "driving the boat." For Frank and Belinda, as for Charles and Valerie, the division of earning and caring work they had organized during their children's early years had become unbalanced as more of the responsibility for children, as well as the breadwinning, devolved to the mothers. In both households, fathers seemed to have become less central.

In the case of Judith and Paul, the balance had swung in the opposite direction. This family contained a home-based father who was very much the primary parent and a breadwinner mother who appeared to be struggling for a share in the life of their only child, 11-year-old Robert. Judith and Paul had begun their lives as parents with a fairly conventional sharing of both earning and caring work. Judith took a nine-month maternity leave from her office administration job and then returned to work part time. Paul was working full time in a technical service position. From the start, however, he had been determined to have a significant involvement in Robert's caregiving. This determination was part of a convergence of circumstances that shifted the balance of their earning and caring arrangements. When Robert was still a preschooler, Paul cut his job back to part time and then moved to work from home, in the process taking on most of Robert's care; Judith increased her work hours to compensate financially. Significantly, this arrangement did not change when Robert started school. When I met them, Paul was still based at home, working part time on technical contracts. Judith was employed full time outside the home, and earning about two-thirds of the family income. This lack of balance in earning reflected a lack of balance in family responsibility also — in a highly unusual direction. In what to an outsider looked like nothing less than a successful power struggle, Paul had also retained "primary parent" status; he maintained a close relationship with his son that appeared to leave little space for Judith.

Paul acknowledged that his strong desire to be a nurturing presence for Robert was influenced by the fact that, when he was very young, he had lost contact with his own father. "So there was that feeling in me like I did not want to be like my father, and that was a very conscious thing very early on," he said. Judith commented that Paul "would have made a great mother of a newborn." But his eager and intense involvement, from the moment of Robert's birth, set the stage for some of the child-rearing challenges that followed. In Judith's words,

> If I could do something different, I think I would have found some way to ask
> Paul to back off a bit and give me a bit more space to figure out how to mother
> this newborn. And I do remember feeling… my god, you know, he just loved

this [child] and he just wanted to be there, but, in some ways, I felt smothered, and "You've got to do it right," a little bit of that.

Robert was a demanding baby, who later had some developmental problems as a toddler. In her interview, Judith recalled wanting to get professional help, but Paul, in her eyes, resolutely refused to acknowledge there was anything seriously amiss. "My sense is Paul's view [was], you know, this was his kid; this was a perfect kid, and he was in love with this kid who could do no wrong," she said. "So I had to really chip away at that bit by bit." This early disagreement seems to have set the tone for the considerable conflict over child rearing that followed. And perhaps it played in to some other family decisions as well. Judith had found it "actually harder than I anticipated being home full time with a little one." Her readiness to return to work was matched by Paul's dissatisfaction with his job, and his wish to take on some contract work and do some creative projects of his own.

From his perspective, this move was an opportunity to focus on work he loved and to be able to spend more time with Robert. "It was something I really wanted," he said. His account also suggested that the arrangement was mutually agreed upon. From Judith's perspective, though, the move was financially risky — and more contentious than Paul's account suggested. "I'm the one who worries about money, and I'm the one who's trying to save for things ahead of time," she said. And, in the event, her fears appeared to have been justified. Paul commented that his project "just didn't work out the way [we] intended." When I interviewed them, Paul was doing contract work from home and earning about a third of the family income (which totalled some $85,000 in the year before their interviews). "I really love not having to work full time," he said, adding that he didn't feel there was a financial need for him to do so, either. "This really suits me, and, as long as Judith has the position that she does and is working full time, then it works out for both of us," he said. "I guess you could say I wanted to be in this position more, and overall I think she likes what she's doing."

"This position" meant that Paul, who was home based and doing more and more of the caregiving and school volunteering with Robert, became the undisputed primary parent — a job, and a status, that he relished:

Early on I remember someone making the comment, "Oh, he's a daddy's boy" … I don't really like the term, but in that sense he's probably felt closer, in some ways, to me than Judith, and — that's just him. I don't know if it's, you know, because he's a boy, or just because that's who he is.... So there had been that closeness, and I know there's that feeling in me — just wanting to nurture, just wanting to fill that role in his life — that's really strong.

Paul's position, both on work and caregiving, seemed to leave Judith little choice but to pick up, by default, the primary earner responsibilities. She conceded that she did like her work and "wasn't being a martyr." She thought Paul's wanting to be closely involved in Robert's care was "a legitimate wish," and she was also more than happy to be relieved of some of the domestic work, notably cooking, which she didn't enjoy. But the time she spent at work affected the amount of involvement she could have with Robert. "I don't think that I missed out earlier on," she said. "I think I was there for most things.... But now, I work five days a week, and I have not been in his classroom once this year to observe during the classroom time, and so I really do feel out of touch there." Judith acknowledged that Paul was "better at that stuff" than she was, and, for the most part, she was willing to give up her share of it. But his much greater involvement with Robert, through trips to and from school and their many shared activities, certainly made Paul "the parent that he gravitates towards":

> I don't have really as much of a sense day to day of what he's doing as I think Paul does. You know, who are the kids that he's connected with and the parents of those kids ... I haven't even got the full families straight. Paul knows all their names and, you know, does all of that. So yeah, I do feel out of touch.

Judith spoke about two other factors that may have contributed to their skewed parental balance. The first was that Robert was a boy. "If he was a girl, perhaps that would be a way in which [we] would have a connection that would be special or unique," she commented. The second was that he was an only child, so the focus was much more intense. As she put it, "It would have been easier on everyone to just spread it around a little bit more." When I interviewed her, she was thinking about the ways she could "remain an important factor" in her son's life.

Conflict, Negotiation, and Compromise

For Judith and Paul, disagreements over what was best for their son seemed to have locked them in a power struggle that Judith was losing. The mutual support that appeared to be characteristic of most other couples in the study was missing. Paul seemed not to be doing the work other care-giver fathers reported, work ensuring that the breadwinner mother was involved and up to speed with daily doings; Judith seemed unsure about how hard she wanted to push to be included. Their differences still seemed close to the surface.

Perhaps not surprisingly, their lives as parents were marked by conflict. In their interviews, they referred to it many times. Paul commented, "We really come at a lot of things very differently," adding, "We're getting that feeling of always being in conflict over how to raise Robert." Judith echoed Paul's assessment of their differing views and took it further:

> And because we have quite different takes and come from quite different per-spectives on some issues of parenting, it's been a really hard road—apart from who's out working and so on.... I think we're getting better, you know; we've had eleven years of this, but it was not easy. It was very, very hard for a number of years.... We're still married, but sometimes, I think, how did we manage to stay together through this? Because it's been the parenting issue that has been, I think, the biggest challenge for us.

Few other couples in the study spoke as directly about conflict as Judith and Paul did. This, of course, does not mean those other couples necessarily experienced conflict-free child-rearing relationships. Indeed, that would be unlikely. As Fox points out, couple negotiations about the care of children may be "laden with conflict" (Fox 2001:377). It does mean, though, that, in most separate partner interviews, answers to my questions about child-rearing philosophies and perceptions of children's needs suggested overall agreement and mutual support rather than dissension and antagonism. When agreement wasn't necessarily a given, it was seen as a goal to be reached by negotiation, in the interests of equity and balance.

Why might committed parents not see eye to eye on their children? One answer is that people have views on appropriate behaviour for parents that are significantly shaped by the way they themselves were raised and by the families in which they grew up. Sometimes, as I noted earlier in the case of Valerie and Charles, different family backgrounds created a gulf that needed to be bridged as couples struggled to be consistent in their dealings with their own children.

In no case was the gulf wider than it was for Cheryl and Khenan. Though they had an educational background and intellectual interests in common, as well as many years of shared life in Canada, as a mixed-race couple they faced family challenges of a different order. Cheryl was the daughter of European immigrants; Khenan was born in the Caribbean and came to Canada with his family when he was nine. Until recently, Cheryl and Khenan had both been struggling to complete graduate degrees with the help of student loans and the limited funding available through research or teaching contracts. For most of their children's preschool years, they lived in family housing on the university campus where they had been students and where their children attended the university's day-care centre. The switch for them came when they moved to another university, with children in or almost ready for school, so that Cheryl could start a graduate degree. Khenan was also a graduate student, on yet another campus. So with backup only from Cheryl's mother, they balanced their class and work schedules to cover off caregiving outside school hours. When I met Cheryl and Khenan, their children were 15 and 12, and they needed a different kind of after-school supervision. Meanwhile, both parents had completed their graduate programs and were making the transition to permanent jobs — a transition that would greatly reduce their financial stress.

They were raising children under circumstances that would have been difficult even had their backgrounds been similar. Family work had to be organized around class schedules, as well as around the contract teaching and other work they needed to do to supplement student loans and put bread on the table. As students, they also had to fulfil the requirements of demanding graduate programs. They faced considerable financial and time stress, with almost no outside support. In their interviews, both were articulate about the ways their own priorities, cultural backgrounds, and perceptions sometimes exacerbated the stress.

When their children were young, Khenan was a committed and involved father. But he was not always a willing participant in other domestic work. To him, the more important work was in his community, joining in struggles against racism. Over time, as he put it, "we both had to learn the meaning of our existence for each other." This meant Khenan learning how gender worked (so he could better understand Cheryl's insistence on sharing domestic responsibilities) and Cheryl learning how race worked (so she could better understand "the insidiousness of racism and what it meant for Khenan to live as a man of colour").

In their interview accounts, both Cheryl and Khenan framed this conflict as one they had confronted and resolved. As Khenan said, "We both benefitted from our willingness to mutually engage each other in our own commitments." By the time I met them, they had reached a division of domestic labour that suited them both and seemed equitable. "Now it's absolutely split," Cheryl said. "What I mean by split is just sometimes he may cook more and I may clean more, but we're both burdened equally."

Other family labour, though, was not so equally shared. Cheryl was, in her words, "the nurturer," "the one who keeps the family together." If anything were to happen to her, Cheryl believed, they would fall apart, at least for a little while:

> That's partly because ... I played the role. I've embraced it, the mother who you go to in times of crisis: she will be there, she will love you, she will understand you. But it's become, actually, I don't know if "burden" is the right word, but it's become very taxing on me because I'm absolutely burnt out.... So, in the last few years, I've been saying to Khenan, I need you to be more emotionally available for the children. I can't do this. And he's trying, but it's very difficult, and I can see he's trying, but I don't think he quite knows how.

Khenan, for his part, was involved in another kind of emotional labour, the advocacy version described by DeVault (1999). He was the father of mixed-race children, likely to encounter the racism in school and other social settings he had experienced himself. Asked where his own expertise as a parent lay, he responded without hesitation: "One of the things I'm good at is fighting for my children institutionally." Cheryl's version of emotional labour — being a good listener, being willing to negotiate with the children, not leaping to judgement — was much harder for him. If his racial and cultural background helped him to understand and support his children in an institutional context, it got in the way when, at home, they behaved very much like the middle-class Canadian kids he had helped raise them to be.

It was clear from his interview account that he was all too aware of the irony of his situation. He spoke of not wanting to reproduce with his own children the relationship he had had with his own father. He talked of his aspirations, of his wanting to live up to the model of Anglo-Canadian fathering he had seen in the families of his friends while he was growing up — "someone to build a basketball hoop in the back yard, and you do it because that's what your kid wants; it keeps them happy." Khenan said he had wanted to be that kind of father: to put up the basketball hoop; to "take the kid to basketball, baseball, and all the rest; to do the Anglo-Saxon parenting." But that fathering style did not produce the kind of children or the kind of family life he had known as a child—family life in which children were seen but not heard and adult authority was never questioned. Khenan commented:

> And now these children are seen and heard, and, to my astonishment, I have [been] complicit [in] encouraging that. So when they challenge my directives, my quote/unquote "authority"…they're probably asking for an explanation, not that they're challenging my authority…They're not challenging me personally, but, for me, it seems like a slap in the face.

Racism had dealt Khenan many slaps in the face. He recognized, however, that he needed to come to terms with parts of himself—"the warrior impulse, the self-defence impulse"—that had defined him in his own struggle with racism but that were not appropriate responses to the growing assertiveness of his children. He was willing to learn from Cheryl. As he put it,

> I'm learning to see more from her perspective, and I'm willing to do it because there's less conflict in doing so, and, actually, it creates the space for both myself and the children…to actively understand where each other's coming from. I mean, she's much, much, much better at it than I am, but it's something that I'm learning to do because I think it works.

Even with Khenan's commitment to share the emotional labour Cheryl had been doing, they were not out of the woods. Their children were proving to be particularly demanding adolescents. Cheryl's burn-out occasionally came through in her interview:

> I'm at my wits' end.… I don't know how to parent any more. I can honestly say that. I don't know how to parent any more. All the things that I thought would work, how I've raised them up until now, it's almost like they've been raised by different parents because I don't recognize them.

It was also not easy for Khenan, struggling to learn new ways of relating to the children while dealing with the challenges of his first solid job. He commented:

I feel like I'm going through this tug of war now, where I am trying to make up economic ground, and my children, their emotional needs are probably now the greatest they've ever been. So whereas I would've thought that I've given them the best of me and all that I could, now is the time that they really need it. And so I'm having a lot of trouble with that, but I'm trying to cope with dealing with their needs.

Cheryl recognized his efforts, and she knew how hard it was for him to "step outside of himself and go, 'Oh, I need to stop acting like that.'" She also recognized her own complicity. Like Belinda, described earlier in the chapter, her willingness — perhaps her need — to be "it" limited the opportunity for Khenan to step in. "There's things that I need to change," she said. "I need to stop being there all the time, and 'I'm here, I'll save you all.'"

Cheryl's earlier comment, that, in terms of sharing housework, they were "burdened equally," bears revisiting. At the time I interviewed them, the family burdens seemed greater than the rewards, and both were bearing them. Cheryl's load had been heavier, but both interview accounts suggested a couple relationship in which equity mattered, as well as a commitment on Khenan's part to take on more. Across a wide gulf, they seemed able to negotiate.

The gulf was not so wide for Penny and Dennis. Both were White, university-educated parents who had similar intellectual and political interests and were working in full-time jobs. But, like Valerie and Charles, they came from vastly different family backgrounds. Penny was one of nine children in what she described as a "strong Irish-Catholic family"; Dennis was one of two children, raised by a staunchly feminist single mother. Like Paul, mentioned earlier, Dennis had lost contact with his father at an early age; he shared Paul's determination to be a different kind of father to his own children.

Penny and Dennis became parents as students, sharing all the caregiving on an equal footing. They used outside childcare after first Penny and then Dennis resumed full-time paid work, and they divided all other family responsibilities between them. Later, they shared a nine-month leave on the arrival of their second child. Dennis, like Paul, was also resolutely committed to sharing not just the day-to-day work of childcare but the decision-making responsibility too. While equally balancing both the earning and caring load, they also needed to do the emotionally charged work of negotiating, across the gulf of their different family backgrounds, decisions about raising the children. They were like many of the couples described by Schwartz (1994, 2007) in her study of "peer" relationships (a study I will describe in more detail in the next chapter). Schwartz noted that couples committed to sharing family responsibilities equally often encountered serious conflict over child rearing because "there is no territory that is automatically ceded to the other person and conflict cannot be resolved by one person claiming the greater right to have the final word" (Schwartz 2007:227).

Their negotiation was substantively different from that of Cheryl and Khenan, who, in a sense, needed to work out the kinds of parents they wanted to *be* in a highly stressful context. It was more like that of Judith and Paul, who came into conflict about what to *do* in specific situations. Dennis named the child-rearing conflict as "one of the big things" he and Penny had to deal with. Like Paul, he spoke of the "very different ideas" they had about raising the children. He gave as an example the role each would give to child-rearing advice books. "I would have read the parenting books, and then I would have tried to follow them," he said. Penny, he implied, was less willing. He cited, with a laugh, a specific situation:

> In one of the [Penelope Leach][1] books it says, so what you should do to get your kids to eat properly is that you just put all the stuff out at the same time, [including] the sweets, and you just let them eat it all at the same time. So, okay, I can go with that!... And Penny just says, "No, you don't do it that way; you do this."

Penny, for her part, acknowledged the challenges of child rearing for two deeply invested parents:

> Everything is negotiated because we're both so involved, right? And that can be quite maddening because, in some ways, you'd kind of like to just, you know, either say, this is my turf, and let me just make these decisions or, you know, sometimes you just think...let me just for the day, say, I'll make the decisions.... Tomorrow it's your day, you make the decisions!

However, from Penny's perspective, the habit of negotiation was accompanied by recognition of what really needed to be negotiated — being able to ask, as she put it, "Is this about trying to get a good solution, or is this about power? If this is about power, maybe I can back off on this one." She added, "So maybe in some ways it makes us grow up."

Penny could identify other benefits to the negotiation process. She thought it prevented parents from unthinkingly reproducing the way they themselves were raised. It prevented parents from acting in haste: "it probably keeps you from making some really rash decisions." It pushed people to think more carefully about "who this child is and what they need." And it worked as a model:

> I think that, at its best, it's also a very good example to your kids about the idea that people can have very different opinions and can work to a constructive end. And they can see having differences … as not being negative, that it can be actually, it's okay. You can still respect each other; you can still love each other and work through [the differences].

Summing Up

All the couples described in this chapter had worked together in unconventional ways to see their children through infancy and early childhood, into school, and, in the case of Valerie and Charles and Cheryl and Khenan, into early adolescence as well. For all these couples, though, the path had not been easy. As a group, they forcefully make the point that going against the grain of societal expectations about mothering and fathering has its pitfalls.

The three couples who remained in crossover arrangements for an extended period of time shed light on two important issues. The first involved conventional understandings of men and paid work. Both Charles and Frank were fully engaged as caregivers during their children's preschool years. As well as being a pragmatic solution to their families' childcare needs, this work also seemed to provide an answer to problems that had arisen in their earlier work history: Charles couldn't find a job, and Frank was not committed to (or especially happy in) the job he had. For both men, the years of caregiving served to postpone employment challenges that inevitably loomed much larger when their children's transition to school greatly reduced the caregiving load. Charles's strategy was to extend his caregiving by following his daughter to school—a move that could certainly be rationalized, if not fully justified, by her health concerns. His volunteer work there gave him a job of sorts, but, at the same time, it also extended his absence from the world of formal employment and reduced his likelihood of being able to return to paid work. At 50, as he commented, he had been out of the workforce so long that he didn't see his situation as likely to change. Frank was eight years younger than Charles, and his children were younger too; he had been without a full-time paid job for a shorter time. In his case, though, his "time out" was in a home that also felt like a safe refuge. He was finding it hard to leave, even though, as he said, he was also finding it harder and harder to justify *not* leaving. Paul's situation was different. He was self-employed and working from home, though only part time. He was very happy to be doing so, even though his only child was now well past early childhood dependency. But his part-time status could only be supported by a partner willing and able to provide most of the family's financial needs.

All three families were statistical anomalies in an era when the number of single-earner families was shrinking and a family with two *full-time* earners was the norm. They were anomalies, too, in that all three financially dependent partners were men. By the time I interviewed them, Charles and Frank could be classed as involuntarily rather than voluntarily unemployed. Paul could perhaps be described as voluntarily *underemployed*. All three represent scenarios well known to women caregivers — the protracted absence from paid work leading to long-term unemployment, the home as a retreat from unsatisfactory work, or part-time self-employment organized around family responsibilities (Marshall 2001; Spivey 2005). So it should not be surprising that men who assume the full-time caregiving responsibilities usually associated with women will find themselves similarly disconnected from paid employment. In fact, in an important sense, the experiences of Charles, Frank, and Paul degender the problem. They are a reminder that almost *any* parent removed from the paid workforce for an extended time because of caregiving responsibilities will face similar consequences.

The second issue illuminated by the experiences of the couples continuing as crossovers involved the sharing — or not sharing — of executive responsibility for children over time and the question of who had primary parent status. This issue is best taken up from the perspective of the mothers because their different situations and mothering styles had, ironically, produced similar outcomes. Belinda, as I noted earlier, was the most overtly directive mother-manager in the study; a clear CEO with an assistant partner, she was unequivocally the primary parent. She was the mother it was most tempting to label a gatekeeper. In Chapter 3, I noted the conceptualization of maternal gatekeeping by Allen and Hawkins (1999) as comprising three dimensions: the setting of rigid standards, the need for external validation of a maternal identity, and the belief in differentiated gender roles. Though her commitment to her professional work and her easy assumption of family breadwinner responsibilities indicated she was not a conformist in terms of gender role expectations, she did set very high standards for childcare, and the mother identity did seem to be critically important. However, as my earlier discussion of Belinda and Frank indicated, gatekeeping isn't a simple phenomenon. It happens interactionally and incrementally, as one partner's accumulating experience, interest, and expertise gradually overwhelm and outrank the other partner's participation. Valerie also seemed to be the primary parent in her family. But, in her case, the status seemed not to have been acquired by gatekeeping but earned, again incrementally and over time, as her daughter grew towards her in personality, as well as in gendered needs and interests. My sense in both these families was of fathers being sidelined while mothers, under quite different circumstances, became much more central in their children's lives.

The case of Paul and Judith is a reminder that gatekeeping isn't necessarily gendered. Fathers can also do it, and mothers can be sidelined in the process. Paul, protective of his base at home and cherishing his relationship with his son, seemed well positioned to win the battles over child rearing he fought with Judith, and he won in much the way that home-based mothers might be expected to win. Here too, though, gender seemed to have played into the mix in a more conventional way. Judith and Paul were parents of a son growing towards adolescence. Had Judith, like Valerie, had a daughter instead of a son, the family dynamics might have been different, and Judith might have been less likely to be sidelined. In terms of the sharing or not of executive responsibility and primary parent status, the critical point established by all three crossover families is that fathers' increased participation in caregiving does not inevitably lead to more equal sharing of the overall work and family load, or to gender being "undone" in progressive, liberating ways. Patterns of inequality and imbalance can become entrenched over time, unless they are resisted.

The other couples introduced in this chapter — Cheryl and Khenan and Penny and Dennis — were resisters. Their experiences are a useful complement to those of the three crossover couples because they make visible the work it sometimes takes to build and then to maintain egalitarian relationships. Both couples had to bridge wide gulfs of difference in cultural or family backgrounds, so the challenges were often intense. Cheryl wanted to involve Khenan more in the emotional work of caregiving, while recognizing her own tendency to block his participation by her wish to "save [them] all" and do everything herself. Khenan, meanwhile, was not always willing to leave the other emotional work he had to do, fighting the institutional racism Cheryl had never experienced. They seemed to have come together, at the time I interviewed them, tired but "burdened equally," only because they were committed to an equal partnership. They knew it would continue to be hard work. Penny and Dennis had a similar commitment, though the work in their case might not be quite so hard. Dennis, as committed as Paul was to a full share of responsibility for his children, brought his own strong views about child rearing to the table. But he was not in a position to sideline Penny—nor was there any suggestion in the interviews that he would ever want to. Penny had strong views too. So two committed parents, with similar obligations outside the family, had to work things out. This work, as I will show in the next chapter, is the work of building a "peer" relationship.

Chapter Six

Parents as Peers

In this chapter, I continue the discussion of the more seasoned parents of older children begun in the previous chapter. The focus here, though, is on the couples whose relationships as parents over the years offered the most persuasive evidence of transformation in family life along balanced and, in most cases, degendered lines.

For these couples, like all the couples in the study, earning and caring "against the grain" had a common denominator: father involvement in caregiving that approximated and occasionally exceeded the involvement of the mother and that far exceeded conventional expectations of fathers. Going against the grain required a shift in the balance of priorities given to paid work and family work that also shifted conventional patterns of dependence and power. Like Schwartz (1994, 2007), I discovered that more equally shared earning and caring arrangements seemed to be linked to more egalitarian relationships.

Schwartz, in her classic study of "peer marriage," in fact *began* with a focus on egalitarian relationships. She then discovered that it was frequently a desire to share family responsibilities as equal partners that led couples into such relationships and that helped them maintain an equal balance over the long haul. Peer couples, according to Schwartz, check in with each other to ensure they're not "drifting too far away from reciprocity" (Schwartz 2007:230). In small ways, they maintain equity. Schwartz cites the following as examples:

> If one person has been picking up the kids, the other is planning their summer activities and getting their clothes. Or if one person has been making sure

extended family members are contacted, the other takes it over for a while. If one partner really decides he or she likes to cook, then the other partner takes on some other equally functional and time-consuming job. (Schwartz 2007:230)

These observations about the "peer couples" in her study resonated with what I had encountered in mine. The couples I describe in this chapter had achieved balanced partnerships across the range of earning and caring responsibilities; their relationships were very much like those described by Schwartz. How the balance was achieved might have taken work and might well have involved conflict, negotiation, and compromise. Penny and Dennis, introduced in the last chapter, were good examples of this process. But, in their case too, the outcome was a balance. Though they came from very different family backgrounds, neither was privileged as having more expertise or more authority. And they had the same amount of experience with their own children because, from the beginning, they had shared all the work.

Penny was not persuaded that they always "read" the children the same way. Along with her occasional hankering (noted in the last chapter) to be able to make some of the decisions on her own, she also occasionally wished her perspective on their children's personalities could carry more weight. On some matters, she did think she knew best. But she could also identify the circumstances in which Dennis did better than she did. For all their differences, though, what they shared on a daily basis made them more or less interchangeable, in the sense described by Dienhart (1998) and noted about other couples described in earlier chapters. Both Penny and Dennis participated fully in all the household and caregiving routines, and each could easily substitute for the other's occasional absence. Although in more traditional families the mother's absence, in particular, might be cause for concern, this was not the case for Penny and Dennis. In Penny's words, Dennis was no "comedy sitcom kind of father" who would have to order pizza every night or struggle to keep things going for the children. "He's able to do it, quite easily, and they feel quite comfortable," she said. "I don't think the kids feel like, 'Oh, what happened? Where did Mom go?' ... They feel like the pattern is still the same."

This functional kind of interchangeability was a common model for couples who appeared to have found balance in their division of earning and caring work. But among the couples in the study whom I considered to fit this category, it was not the only model. For some, there was a sharing of earning and of the physical side of family work: cooking meals, supervising homework, doing laundry, and so on. However, as in the "fair families" described by Risman and her colleagues (Risman 1998; Risman and Johnson-Sumerford 1998), some mothers continued to be the "emotion experts," monitoring relationships and managing the emotional climate. For other couples, there was an equitable sharing of the emotion work but a skewed division of domestic work (with fathers doing more of it). In all cases, though, the sense of mutual agreement, teamwork, clearly shared executive responsibility, and strong emotional engagement by both mothers and fathers resonated through all the interview accounts. Shadows of traditional mothering and fathering were evident in two cases, but only as shadows. Much more in evidence were mothers and fathers whose contravention of tradition in the early years of caregiving had ensured that, with older children, their mothering and fathering would take on a different look. In the next section, I consider the two couples in whose parenting accounts the shadows of tradition still lingered. I then move to a closer look at the mothering and fathering described by the couples who, over their years as parents, seemed to have carved out new, distinctly non-traditional paths.

Shadows of Tradition

Lisa and Joe, in separate interviews, both told a story involving Logan, the younger of their two sons, a story that seemed to me to illustrate the vestiges of traditional thinking overlaid, but not entirely overtaken, by the progressive practice that characterized their caregiving. The story was that one day, when they were sitting outside entertaining company, Logan, not much past toddler stage, took a nasty tumble and ran to be comforted. "Here comes the little guy, crying," Lisa recalled. "And, he runs by me! He runs to the B-team! And it's like, 'What are you doing? I'm the A-team!'" Lisa's mock distress was matched by Joe's relish when he told the story: "So it was like, yes! One for the B-team, eh?" he joked. "It was like, [a] small victory."

The B-team victory was achieved out of Joe's work as a primary caregiver, which started when Logan was about 18 months old and his older brother Glenn was about three years old. Several circumstances converged to position Joe at home: Lisa wanted to put more time into her home-based craft business; she was not happy with their childcare arrangements; and, though Joe seemed to be clearly in line for an upcoming promotion at the social service agency where he worked, when the time came, he was passed over. "I had no problem being the breadwinner because I knew I was capable of supporting us all," she said. "So he quit, and we kind of, didn't have anything structured at first because I would always say that I'm the A-team and he's the B-team, right? So he could never be an A-team, but he could be B+."

Both had stories about his struggles to take on the caregiving while Lisa worked at home and continued to be the "quality control person," making sure the household continued to function, being "it" or, in her terms, "the A-team." Joe's stories involved persuading resistant children that he, too, could look after them and battling the isolation of being a lone man at home in his neighbourhood during the day. He used to time his morning coffee for 10 a.m., to coincide with the visit of the (male) letter carrier. "I still miss that guy," he laughed. "It's five years later, and I miss my ten o'clock."

Over time, though, both Lisa and Joe agreed that he settled in to the job, developing his own routines with the children and, in the process, taking on the "girls' club" of caregiver mothers who at first wouldn't associate with him. "It's like I wanted to break in, just to get in," he said. "Just to have — because it's nice to be able to chat to people." Showing up often enough at the park or the preschool and being able, in his words, to "tell them your story" finally earned him a place in the group. "And it's funny because, once you're in, it's like you're one of the girls," he said.

The A-team/B-team hierarchy, though described in semi-joking terms, seemed to be another way to represent the mother-as-CEO/father-as-executive-assistant relationship that characterized some other couples in the study and that was described in earlier chapters. But both Lisa and Joe explicitly challenged gender stereotypes as well. Joe, having joined the "girls' club," became critical of those of his men friends who took their wives' caregiving work for granted, for example, by sleeping in on the weekend when their partners had been caring for children all week. "I see some of my buddies, and I'm not knocking them, but, at times it doesn't seem like … they're as interested in everything; they just sort of go through the motions," he said.

Joe did not just go through the motions. He was a faithful school volunteer, though he was almost always the only father: his younger son told him, "You're the only dad who ever comes." (Here, too, Joe had words for the ones who were not there. "You can get time off," he said. "It's the new millennium here — you can take time off or make it up.") And he took on some of the challenges that the A-team might have been expected to handle. It was Lisa who told the story of Joe's visit with Glenn's teacher, to discuss some rules he thought were unreasonable. From Lisa's account, the visit led to mutual respect and a good outcome for Glenn, who ended up having "the best year that he's ever had at school." Joe spoke about how being present as a caregiver had brought him closer to the boys and made him "a better person." In Lisa's words, "Joe is totally into his kids, and he's an awesome father."

On the work front, once the children were well launched in school, Joe joined Lisa in an expanded version of the business that saw both working from home. The flexibility this gave them was offset by the long night hours they needed to work to keep the business going. When I interviewed him, Joe had started some trades training. He saw it as a way to work on short-term contracts for good money to make the family more secure financially without giving up the home-business flexibility. "Instead of, you know, you see dads rushing to the baseball game, I'd rather be there at the beginning," he said. "And when we're working at home, we can do that."

Lisa's description of her own relationship with her sons was in quintessentially maternal terms. She was the one who cuddled with them on the couch and who smoothed over difficulties. Joe, she said, was "the heavy," so one of her functions was to mediate between Joe and his sons when they were in trouble. "If they think that there's something that will make him mad, they'll come to me, and I'll hammer it out for them," she said. She was also the one who made sure they ate properly and were appropriately dressed. If she were away, she said, "the place would go to hell." But her mothering seemed to leave room for the intensive hands-on caregiving Joe wanted to do. She was aware of living, as she put it, "in totally guy land." As the boys grew up, there were more occasions, in sports change rooms or at football games, where Joe's seemed to be the more required presence. In this household, the gendering of some elements of the caring work was muted by Lisa's openness and her support of Joe's involved fathering—and Joe was much more involved than other fathers in their circle—and by Joe's own commitment to stay involved. Joe also had a comment about the effect of their shared caring on his relationship with Lisa. "Somewhere along the line, I think, we got on to the same page," he said. "I think we fought more before we had kids." Having them "probably made it better...stronger somehow."

I sensed similarly strong family bonds during my visit with Jane and Bill and their children and during my interviews with both parents. Jane

149

and Bill had a much more conventional shift-work arrangement when their two children were preschoolers. It began when Jane's adoption leave with their second child was about to end. Though their first baby had seemed ready for day care at a similar stage, it was clear that outside day care would not be possible for the second. He had come from a troubled background and was showing the signs of it. As Jane commented,

> When it came time to think about going back to work, we just made the decision that we *could* not have someone else parent this child for any moment of his life for a long time. And so that's what drove us to, well, OK, if he can't go to day care, what are we going to do?

Their solution lay in the availability of afternoon and evening shifts at the company where Bill worked as a mechanic. The afternoon shift was 4 p.m. to midnight. So Jane, who worked in a non-profit organization, adjusted her hours to work from 7.30 a.m. to 3 p.m. Bill worked afternoon shifts for six years, until their younger child started Grade 1. He then went back to the regular 8–4 day shift, and both parents shared after-school care and other household work.

For Jane and Bill, there was no dispute about who was the family manager. Bill commented:

> Jane is really good. She just knows how to set things up for the kids and what they've got to do, and organizing, and all that kind of stuff. She's better at that than I would have been, I think.

Jane too acknowledged the family organizing—the dentists' appointments, the tutoring plans, the scheduling of other activities—as her domain. She did, as she put it, the "directional planning." In her view, Bill would know things had to happen, but he wouldn't think ahead to set them up. In Jane's words, "I think that's just the way a lot of men are wired." As Bill commented, "A mom has something a little more than a dad, sometimes. They seem to know more. More natural things." Both agreed that Jane was also the emotional expert, monitoring relationship climates and keeping the family on an even emotional keel. "[Bill] doesn't do any of that stuff—or I have to remind him to," she said.

Over their longer history as parents, the children's attachments had, in Jane's terms, continued to "change and cycle," partly on the basis of their changing activities and interests. Bill spoke of a strong bond with 15-year-old Cassie, through his involvement in her out-of-school sporting interests. John, their 13-year-old, he thought was closer to Jane, but Bill was aware of a shift starting to happen there too, as John the teenager was becoming, like his father, more mechanically minded.

If the organizational and emotional labour was not evenly shared in this family, almost everything else seemed to be. (Jane joked that Bill did not like her to cut the grass, and she did not like him to do laundry, but these were the main exceptions.) Cassie and John were active in sports, and both parents participated fully, driving to practices and games, coaching, and cheering. Bill explained that they tried to set things up so that all family members went to all the games.

The vestiges of tradition, in their attribution of Jane's emotional and organizational expertise to "natural" differences or differences in "wiring," did not extend very far. Though a blue-collar job provided half the family income and shift work had been a means for them to avoid outside childcare when their children were young, they were not like the US working-class families described by Hochschild (1989) or Deutsch and Saxon (1998), which upheld traditional ideologies about gender while, in practice—and out of necessity—they lived non-traditional lives. For Jane and Bill, as for Lisa and Joe, sharing the earning and caring between them was past being a practical necessity. It had become a way of life.

Parents on New Paths

Six of the study couples—all heterosexual pairs with children well launched in school—seemed to me to have reached a balance of earning and caring (caring, too, across all its dimensions) that signalled a more radical change in the gender order. On the surface, most of them looked a lot like the more statistically representative dual-earner couples I defined earlier, pitching in to help each other out because there was too much for one person to handle alone.[1] All such dual earners, as mothers and fathers, have crossed into space once considered the traditional domain of the other parent; the "separate spheres" of home and work, of caring and earning done in separate spaces by different parents, have long disappeared in most Canadian families. But, unlike those more conventional dual earners, the couples I introduce here were reorganizing the space on their own much more extreme terms. The discussion to follow demonstrates some of the new configurations of all this space. It also takes the temporal dimension into account; the mothering and fathering I describe in what follows was taking place in a new time, as well as a new space, because it involved older and more independent children.

Mothers in a New Space

Of all the mothers, Laura was the one who seemed to have moved the furthest from traditional motherhood in the caring "space" of the home. For the last ten years of their 17-year-old daughter Leah's life, Laura and her partner Ian had been a crossover couple. Leah was born when Laura was 30 and Ian was 46. She had a promising career as a civil servant; he was ready to downshift at the end of a long stint with the company that had been his sole employer. So when Leah was nearly seven, Ian became her primary caregiver, and Laura's career took off, requiring the family to make three interprovincial moves.

The shift in their balance of earning and caring with the first job relocation had almost palpable effects on Laura because it required her, against her better judgement, to make the move six months ahead of her family:

> There was a crisis and they needed me up there.... Not being I guess as good a negotiator as I am now ... I didn't realize that I could have just said, well, no. I tried to say no actually, but I remember it was kind of, the conversation went, "Well, if you say no you're probably not the person for this job." And I really wanted the job; I knew that, so I went.

Leah at the time was in her first year of school. For Laura, the move marked a significant transition point in their relationship:

> I remember distinctly that that physical bond that you have with your young children, that was when it changed. And Ian was always like, a main caregiver to her, but, you know, I nursed and was very physically attached. And I remember distinctly that whatever last bit of my role in attachment to her sort of disrupted, you know? And I've always sort of felt, I lost something there.... Hindsight, eh? Like if I was to do it again, that is one thing in my life I would change.

Laura had a fairly high-powered career. Like Tanya, introduced in Chapter 3, she was a breadwinner with a "wife" at home who took care of all the family responsibilities. Though with her latest job move her hours had become more regular, for many years, she had worked the same long hours as many careerist breadwinner fathers. Asked what she might change if she could, she commented, "I don't know that I'd be so ambitious." But she had only one child, and for the six years until Leah started school she had been very much a mother. Laura, Ian, and Leah were also nested in a close extended family offering a network of mutual support—and at least one of Laura's job moves was partly to bring her closer to one of the family branches. Our interview did not dwell on her relationship with Leah over the busy work years. But she commented that she had recently asked Leah what she thought she and Laura shared. Leah had replied, "Well, Mom, I can tell you about anything."

Beth, a 42-year-old health care professional, and her partner Patrick were the parents of nine-year-old twins. Beth's account suggests she would have understood the pangs Laura experienced in her physical separation from her child because she herself was a mother for whom physical connection continued to be critically important. Out of extended breastfeeding and the kind of attachment caregiving described in earlier chapters had come a relationship to her children that surprised her.

Beth's feminism, and her politics, had at first persuaded her against the idea of having children at all. She had seen conventional motherhood as a trap that would prevent her from doing the kind of activist, change-oriented work to which she was committed. But her relationship with Patrick—and his desire to parent as an equal partner—changed her mind. For Beth, a key feature of their agreement had been Patrick's willingness to be the home-based caregiver when the children were very young.

Beth recalled easing back to her job after six months or so, working short and flexible hours at first to fit around nursing the twins. But she never did return to the full-time, breadwinner hours she had originally envisaged before they were born:

> Some of what I learned is that the sun set and rose on their little heads and that I wanted to be around them as much as I could, and no, I didn't want to go off and be the sole breadwinner and miss them as much as I did when I wasn't around them … just discovering how intense and profound that love for them was, and just, they were absolutely both of our priorities…. So OK, how do I work a little and really flexibly to work around their time and both of us having lots of time being able to parent?

Their solution was a shift-work arrangement. After Beth's maternity leave, she returned to a reduced-hours position with her employer. Patrick, meanwhile, left his full-time job and for five years was the home-based caregiver. For most of that time, he had done contract work of various kinds, though always fitting it around Beth's work schedule and never working longer than part-time hours. Echoing Dienhart (1998), Beth called it "tag-team parenting" — a way of sharing earning and caring that did not end when the children started school. When I interviewed her, Beth was working 32 hours a week, leaving at 2.15 p.m. two days a week to pick the children up after school. When she was not at work, she was mothering in a hands-on, intense, and physical way, which had not changed as the children got older. The nightly rituals were an example; even with nine-year-olds, she spent "hours and hours" rubbing their backs, cuddling in the dark, and reading with them. "I'm surprised at some of the very nurturing, mothering kinds of ways that I have about me that I probably didn't know as well before," she said.

However, the "mothering kinds of ways" that suggested a remarkably traditional view of herself as a mother had not replaced her need for other things in her life that "fed her separately." Patrick's different but equally devoted caregiving provided space on an ongoing basis for her rewarding paid work, too:

> There's been interesting growth for me at work as well. But even though I've been not always as available or not the super ambitious push, push, push, there's been interesting changes in my work where … I'm more challenged in some of the work I'm doing.… There hasn't been some big sacrifice there. There wasn't some kind of turning point in the road where I've turned down really great opportunities and, you know, something went off in a different direction that I watched kind of slip away.

Beth's thinking was that she did a better job in the time she was with the children because of the time she was able to spend away from them. Her sense of balance achieved — between mothering and paid work and between herself and Patrick — resonated through her account.

Laura and Beth were interesting contrasts. Liberated as both were from the need to take on the major share of caring, they had gone in different directions. From their interview accounts, they appeared to have become different kinds of mothers, with different connections to the earning and caring space. Laura's career orientation and breadwinner responsibilities positioned her squarely in the earning space, while her partner Ian was primarily a caregiver. Their division of labour was balanced, but they were not interchangeable. Beth and Patrick equitably shared both spaces; they each earned half the family income and shared the caregiving too — though, as Beth's account showed, her caring was very much as a mother. As she put it, "in lots of ways we are interchangeable, and then we're very different."

The other mothers, who cared for older children alongside partners committed to being involved, shared aspects of both Laura's and Beth's experiences. All were in full-time paid employment, and three of the four were primary earners, contributing about two-thirds of the family income. All had partners who were also working full time. All were dividing up domestic work and the different kind of childcare required by school-age children, though the division of domestic work was not always as equitable as was the balance of caregiving, emotional labour, and executive responsibility for the children.

The joke in Jessica's family was that, if her partner Sam were away, the catering would run to soup and popcorn. Sam was solely responsible for grocery shopping and meal preparation. He had been known to tease, when Jessica came into the kitchen, "Sit down before you hurt yourself!" Like several of the other fathers already introduced, Sam was an exemplary household manager. Jessica commented that their household division of labour was "philosophically very fifty/fifty," but, "instrumentally, I would have to put it about sixty/forty" — with the sixty (done by Sam) heading for seventy or even ninety when Jessica was very busy.

Jessica was completing a graduate degree as well as working as a teacher, so her domestic time was limited. During busy phases in the academic term, she also missed some of her turns at picking up the children after school. But their current imbalance had to be seen in the context of a longer history as parents. Jessica would compensate during the summer for her busy term, and, when she finished her degree, she would have more time during the school term as well. Meanwhile, she had a partner who offered her tremendous support, both moral and practical, as she pursued her career goals.

In part, as she recognized, this was because he was an exceptionally nurturing and competent person who enjoyed domesticity and who had wanted children before she herself did. With a personality disposed to caregiving, he seemed to like to take care of everybody; as Jessica put it, he liked to be "it," and she was happy to turn much of the household responsibility and the organizing over to him.

Though her domestic load was lighter than Sam's, she felt, as she put it, "tightly tied" to the children. And though her relationship to them was different from his, it was not necessarily more "maternal." She pointed out that Sam, too, had "been the one to get up with them in the night; he's rocked and cradled and cuddled and just…nurtured them in every way that is possible." From the beginning, their emotional investment had been the same, and they shared all the responsibility. The children were aged ten and seven when I interviewed Jessica; she was thinking ahead to the changes that might come with adolescence, and she was aware of the fact that, with girls, there might be "more gender stuff" on the horizon. For the moment, though, Jessica was in a parental partnership in which her practices as a mother looked very like Sam's practices as a father.

The pattern of caregiving in Eleanor's family was very similar to that in Jessica's. Eleanor too was very busy, working as an independent consultant on research projects that, at the time I interviewed her, were eating into evening and weekend hours as well. Her partner Owen, an actor, was (like Sam) the solid domestic presence, able to pick up the slack when Eleanor could not be available. But this snapshot view of their division of labour at the time I met them, when their children were 12 and 9, was not representative of their sharing over the long haul. Eleanor, too, was in a "peer" partnership; earning and caring were evenly divided. But the division took the form of taking turns over time and was very much a function of her relationship with Owen. Eleanor commented on this relationship:

> I don't think I would have been with another type of man, in a way. Like, not somebody who wasn't as prepared as I was to…suck it up when we have to, to be accommodating.… I mean, it's not one-sided for us. We take turns, but I would say, the last three years, he's taken more of a turn than I have, poor guy. But then again, when the kids were younger, he was away a lot, you know, for long stretches. There was one year when he was away most of the year, so it was really hard. So it's flipped back and forth, but, I think early on I saw in him somebody who was just as interested in my interests as he was in his own, you know. He's just a type of person who is very giving.

He was also, in her view, "more of a homebody" than she was. "I think he genuinely likes those routine things more than I do," she said. Like Sam,

Owen also appeared to be a "natural" caregiver, whose ability to nurture gave Eleanor space to develop professionally. That space also increased as the children got older. The much greater time commitment she made to them when they were younger was not just a consequence of Owen's periodic absences during out-of-town productions; it was a choice. The time allowed her, as she put it, to "develop what I wanted to with the kids." I asked her if being a mother had changed for her. "It has changed, but that has to do with the kids getting older too," she said.

> I feel like now...they're much more independent, and they need that time to be with their friends and that sort of thing. So I don't feel like I'm missing out. I think I would have earlier.... I can still have really meaningful, good interactions with them, but it doesn't have to be all day, you know what I mean? And they wouldn't want that! So I think we've sort of found our way, but it has more to do with the age of the kids.

The flexibility of Eleanor's home-based work meant she could still volunteer in the children's classrooms and attend school events. But all these activities she shared with Owen, who also shared the ongoing household planning and organizing. "There's nothing that I feel I still have to hold on to or control," she said. Eleanor and Owen had different styles as parents. But, as was the case with Jessica, partnered with an intensely nurturing, home-loving man, there was little in Eleanor's account to distinguish her as a mother from Owen as a father. Though they were clearly not interchangeable as people, they were interchangeable as parents when it came to the ongoing care of their children. Each, in other words, knew how to do everything that needed to be done.

In Sandi's household and in Lois's, the story was the same. Both families had begun as "crossovers" with home-based fathers as primary caregivers during their children's preschool years. Both fathers moved into full-time paid employment when their children were established in school, and both mothers then picked up a more even share of the domestic and caring work.[2] Their accounts, like those of the other mothers in "peer" relationships, painted an interesting picture of the way mothering liberated from many of the conventional mothering responsibilities could unfold.

Sandi was in the military, a distinctly non-traditional working world for a mother of three young children. The division of labour Sandi and her partner Todd negotiated had to accommodate Sandi's required absences on courses or training exercises. But his constant presence at home opened the way for absences that were optional, as well. The longest to date had been a three-month assignment at another military establishment, for which she volunteered when their youngest child was 18 months old. Speaking as a soldier and also a mother, she said, "I was excited to go because it was like a big adventure for me. But probably for the first month I cried every day."

Sandi described herself as, in one sense, "the traditional mother" because she was "more of a comforter." But, in other ways, she saw herself as far less typical. As she said, "I don't know if it's the soldier in me — because with the boys I do stuff that I don't think most mothers would do." The blurring of gender boundaries and the unconventional way caring work was shared emerged in a story she told about a forthcoming trip and her efforts to help Todd by reminding him of activities the children would be starting while she was away. The story's punch line was that he was actually more on top of the details than she was.

Sandi was not short of opportunities for hands-on caregiving and contact with the children. Her enforced absences were compensated with time off, which she could spend at home with them. And she was in charge in the evenings when Todd was at work. "When I get home, it's not like I lie on the couch and watch TV," she said. "When I get home it's like, 'Mom! Mom! Mom!' and back into the mother role I go.... I think we each get our own turns, when it comes down to it." Though she was only 35, Sandi had been with Todd for 17 years and married to him for 15. "For even a marriage to survive let alone, you know, everything else, you really have to talk things through, work them out, bend a lot," she said. Out of their history had come a strong orientation to family. "We do everything as a family," she said.

Though her background was very different from Sandi's, Lois's account contained many points of resemblance. She too had shared caregiving with a former full-time caregiver partner, had been (and continued to be) the main earner, and was now sharing earning and caring in an even-handed, boundary-blurring partnership. I used the experiences of Lois and her partner George in the introduction to Part I, to illustrate the way unconventional earning and caring arrangements could unfold over time and produce changes in both mothering and fathering. Lois was the mother who articulated most clearly the extent to which, after two children and 13 years as parents, she and George were functionally interchangeable. When I challenged her to think of ways they were *not* interchangeable, she could come up with only two: she was the parent in charge of piano lessons (because she played the piano herself), and George was much handier at fixing things. Lois said that, since George had returned to paid employment, their division of household labour was divided according to preference, with George doing more cooking and Lois doing more cleaning. But, in terms of responsibility for their children, now well launched in school and much more independent, their focus was joint, and their views were similar.

From Lois's account, they had been equal partners from the start. As I noted earlier, their first child was born when both were students. Neither had a proper job to be privileged, and both were equally inexperienced in childcare. So they learned together. Both were hands-on parents, so Lois could say, looking back, "I don't feel like I missed out on anything." When she returned to work, leaving George at home with the children, it did not occur to her to phone home a lot or try to micromanage from a distance. As she commented,

> George demonstrated so early that he was completely competent.... I had every confidence in his parenting ability and that he would know what to do. I mean, in a lot of situations, frankly he's better than me. It would have been ridiculous for me to try to take that role.

Nor did she fly to take over when she came home from work. Rather, she joined him, and they ended the day as a team. The balance of paid work with a strong family connection had endured. When she was not working, she wanted to be home. "And I don't feel resentful that I have to be here and not somewhere else," she said. "Because this is what I want.... This is the path that I chose for myself."

For the mothers in the balanced partnerships I have just described, there was one further common theme: their satisfaction and pleasure in the bond forged with their partners through their shared parenting relationships. Beth commented, "We're so in tune because of the time that we're spending." Eleanor said, " It's one of the huge things that we have together." Jessica said this:

> I can't imagine what it would be like not to have him share the kids in those quirky, petty ways, you know, where at bedtime we'll talk about some little thing and like we totally get it because we've lived with this child since, you know, and he feels it and I feel it and we just like *know*.

Fathers in a New Space

In the previous section, I wrote about six mothers who were "liberated" from the expectation that they would be primarily responsible for their children—a liberation they used to embark on or maintain or extend their participation in the alternate space of paid employment. In writing about the mothers, though, I also took account of and included some of what they had to say about the partners who, in one way or another, had enabled their liberation. In this section, I continue this discussion from the perspective of the men themselves: six fathers able to venture away from the primary-earner work orientation that continues to be the main expectation of conventional fatherhood. In families with mothers who had relinquished their traditional claim to responsibility and final authority over family matters and who, over the longer haul, took on some or most of the financial provision, fathers too had new opportunities, many of which presented themselves when caregiving needs changed over time.

Not surprisingly, a similarly unconventional orientation to paid work and careers linked all the men's accounts. Though all but one were working full time or close to full time, they were "working fathers" in the sense I noted in Chapter 4. For all the men, family had priority over work, and all had made significant accommodations in their working lives in order to discharge family obligations. (The one father not in paid employment was Laura's partner Ian, who had, in a sense, taken early retirement to become a primary caregiver at the end of his own career, in order to support hers.)

Jessica's partner Sam, a manager for a major Canadian bank, had the most conventional and stereotypically masculine job of all the men in this group; he needed to jump through the greatest number of hoops to balance work and family obligations. From the beginning, their division of labour was shaped by Sam's eagerness to have children and his determination to share caregiving. That determination was signalled in a public way when he applied to take parental leave after his daughter Andrea's birth, at a time (in the early 1990s) when it was not common for fathers to do so. For Sam, though, "the planets were kind of lined up." The large Canadian banks, as he pointed out, have tended to be more progressive about family-friendly policies, and his own employer had just instituted a major "work and lifestyle program" that included the option of extended parental leave. "That's probably where it first tweaked my interest," he said. "It was like, well, why wouldn't a person do that?" When he applied to take the leave, he received lots of support, becoming a kind of "poster boy":

It was really groundbreaking at that time. Like no one knew anyone else in this forty-thousand-person organization that had done this.... I think I was fortunate in terms of, the bank introduced the concept formally some time before Andrea was born. And, at the same time, I was in a position where it didn't feel uncomfortable leaving. I wasn't in the middle of a big project or I wasn't in the middle of having this fantastic results year where I was going to be cutting myself out of a big bonus, you know.... I was in a position where it was certainly doable.

Sam's four months at home with Andrea established a pattern of shared caregiving that continued after the birth of his second child. That time, though, he took a bigger risk to spend time at home. Jessica was offered a job in another city, right at the time her own share of parental leave was ending. Though Sam's employer had offices in their new location and a transfer was technically possible, at the time of the move there were no openings. So Sam had to resign his position and wait for something to come up in the new city after his leave period ended. Soon enough, fortunately, it did. Sam commented that, in hindsight, he could see that the move had little effect on his career trajectory. But, at the time, it felt like there was "a little bit more on the line."

At the time he was interviewed, with both daughters in school, he was once again pushing the boundaries. Doing managerial work better known for its long hours than its family friendliness, he was leaving work at 3.15 p.m. on at least two days a week to pick up his children from school. Sam had the flexibility in his job to work from home when necessary (he noted that his childless boss also did so) — and that's what he often did on the afternoons when he had to leave work early. He commented:

I think what I try to do is ... be transparent about it in the sense that, I'll pick up extra stuff on the weekend, or I'll even take the kids in to the office on the weekend — they like going there; there's white boards and everything to play on. You know, you can put in a couple of hours. And I think when people see ... that you're sending them stuff on a Sunday and then you're calling the next day from home at four o'clock ... most people can put two and two together.

Sam's schedule was also better able than Jessica's to accommodate the need to stay home occasionally with sick children. He remarked that, in the 20 years he had worked for the bank, he had never called in sick on his own account. But he estimated that, in his 10 years with children, he had taken about 15 days to be home with a sick child.

As a "working father," Sam experienced all the tensions working mothers have long known about: the uneasy feeling that he might be short-changing his job in the interests of his family; the conviction that, even if that were the case, he *couldn't* short-change his children; the hope that productivity mattered more than hours on the job. In his account, he spoke of wanting what he had been brought up to want—a career—but not, as he said, at the cost of "other things that are important to me." He wanted his working life to be less stressful; but he also knew he wanted to be working. Jessica, he thought, was actually more career oriented, but she was not at the stage of being able to replace his more substantial salary. If she could, Sam said, he would like to downshift to a less demanding job. His ideal was along the lines of the "four-thirds" solution described by Greenspan and Salmon (2001), which recommends both parents working two-thirds of the time in order to provide, between them, two-thirds of the childcare. As Sam put it, "That amount of time applied against your family is a lot."

In combining an exceptional involvement in family life with a stressful, demanding job, Sam was in uncharted waters. "We haven't made it easy on ourselves here, you know," he commented.

> If people … both want professional careers and kids, and they want to share all the responsibilities that come with that, my personal opinion is, it's really tough to get it so that it's never a problem or there's never any guilt or there's never any stress…. I would like to see how you do that. I mean, I think it'd be pretty tough.

Schwartz makes the same point, noting that some jobs "simply do not allow" the sharing required by peer relationships and equitably shared child rearing. One of the first steps in achieving this sharing, she cautions, is to choose jobs carefully and figure out what will work (Schwartz 1994:130, 173). The other fathers, most of them working in less traditional workplaces, had less of the daily stress Sam reported. But, over the longer haul, the decision to privilege family over career had consequences for all of them. For Todd and George, former stay-at-home caregivers to their children, it meant several years out of the paid work force and a late start on career development. For Owen, the actor, it meant scaling back his aspirations in order to work locally. With two children, for a while, they were in a more traditional pattern, with Eleanor as primary caregiver accommodating Owen's frequent absences from home during out-of-town productions. From Owen's perspective, the turning point that led to a shift in their balance of earning and caring work occurred during one such out-of-town production. Eleanor had brought the children for a visit and also delivered a message from a director about another potential out-of-town production. Owen recalled the conversation:

> Every time I got an offer, I'd always say, "What do you think?" and she would always say, "Sounds great. You'd better take it." And that was the first time where I said, "What do you think?" and she said, "I think you should maybe see if you can get some work [at home] first and, if not, then you can always take it." A huge light bulb went off in my head, and I kind of went, "Yeah, I've got to try to find some work [at home]."

Performing in New York would mean more profile and more money, but Owen was more interested in what he called the "real rewards." As he put it, "I think the benefits of building a home and a family far outweigh... [going on] the road, which isn't all that it's cracked up to be anyway."

For Patrick, the father of the twins, privileging family meant a switch to contract-based social research work, and, perhaps more significantly, a radical reduction in the social activism that was its natural accompaniment. Working for social change was a passion—but one he could not indulge to the extent he wanted "and be a good dad at the same time." Patrick commented that he felt his career was on hold, but, with an interesting reframing of the conventional career trajectory, he could see where he would pick it up again. Patrick's reframing involved a division of the life course into 15-year segments, with childhood and then adolescence and young (and child-free) adulthood occupying the first two segments. The years from 30 to 45 would be the stage of "maximum parenting of dependent children." Then "from 45 to 60, that's probably when I'm going to do my working." The "working" that Patrick had in mind was not necessarily in a conventional job; it might also mean taking on more challenging, more socially significant versions of the research and writing projects he was already doing. But it was work that would require the kind of focus that his current family focus didn't allow. Patrick's restructured life plan conformed nicely to Sørensen's anticipation of a possible future in which flexibility would not be penalized and traditional linkages between gender and caregiving could be broken (Sørensen 1991).

These fathers not only scaled back and reframed their working lives but also achieved a close involvement with their children, an involvement also referred to by some of the mothers, whose accounts I described earlier. All had been hands-on caregivers to children from infancy onwards, sharing the responsibility and decision making as well. They could hardly fail to recognize that all this made them unconventional fathers. In their accounts, their awareness of their difference turned on a variety of comparisons — with their own mothers, with other fathers (and men in general), and with their partners. Owen, for example, commented, "I feel like I'm doing a lot of things that my mother probably did for our house when we were growing up." He also participated in his children's activities to a much greater extent than his own father had done. "It's not like a big tragedy or anything — he was very busy," he said. "But I'm glad that I can go see their assemblies. I like the fact that my work schedule changes so that sometimes my days are free...so I'm here with them." Owen also pointed out that both his children came to see him in plays and saw him express emotions "on stage and in our real life" that he didn't remember his own father — or other fathers — expressing. "In that way, I'm much more non-typical in terms of father-like behaviour," he said. Owen spoke warmly of the rewards of building and enjoying a strong home base and a close connection to his family; he also relished the satisfaction, at the end of a day, of "knowing that needs are being met."

His perception of his difference from "other dads in the neighbourhood or friends and family that have families of their own" also resonated with the perceptions of other fathers. Todd spoke of feeling "more connected" to his children than he thought other fathers were. Patrick commented that having children had become his "main identifier." He spoke of the "sad feeling" he had for fathers whose lives had not been changed in the way his had, of feeling bad for the "weekend dads" who had to cram so much into so short a time. Ian, whose daughter Leah was born when he was 46, compared the greater patience and maturity of his later caregiving with the resources he had available for his first family, born when he was in his 20s.

Owen's explicit assumption of a non-traditional masculinity — "I'm not a big sports guy or I'm not a big fishing guy or I'm not a big going out to the bar guy" — was also echoed by several other fathers. Todd, the civil-

ian on the military base, contrasted his own creative and artistic tempera-
ment with the "macho, male-oriented" community that surrounded him.
George spoke of a lifelong commitment to mock the "jock mentality." He
commented, "On many levels I guess I'm not a very traditional guy." Their
willingness to cross or blur gender boundaries appeared, not surprisingly,
in their talk about their caregiving too. Todd, for example, described his
earlier role as that of a "stay-at-home mom." Of the time when his children
were babies, Patrick said, "I did get to play—I almost said a more maternal role." Sam spoke of the "separation anxiety" he suffered each time he
returned to work after parental leave and his children started in outside
day care. Still, though they could do all the things their children's mothers
were doing, they were *not* mothers, and sometimes that showed too
(Doucet 2006a). Todd considered he was less likely than the mothers he
saw around him to be overprotective. "Give the kid a break, let them be a
kid, let them run loose," he said. George spoke of his efforts, during his
caregiver years, to make his children independent, teaching them how to
make their own lunches, for example, and how to choose clothes than
matched. "The kids are quite self-sufficient, which is part of me staying at
home and putting a regimen on them," he said. Sam spent a great deal of
time with his daughters, but, like Trevor (who was described in Chapter 4),
Sam much preferred active and more conventionally father-like pursuits,
such as sledding or skating or picnicking. He wasn't keen on getting down
on the floor with them and "doing the little Beanie Baby thing."

If Lisa, described earlier, felt like she was living in "guy land" with a
partner and two sons, Sam was similarly outnumbered in his family. "It's
a little more boys against the girls now than it was ... a couple of years ago,"
he said. As they got older, Sam's daughters were raising his awareness of
himself as a man and a father (not just a parent). "There's things girls can
draw from a father that are fatherly, and there's things they can draw from
both parents equally that are ... more generic parenting," he said. But the
distinction between the "father" hat and the "parent" hat was, he considered, "pretty blurred." And the sort of fathering he had in mind was not
conventional. It was not "the discipline and the authority," but rather the
model of gentleness and nurture in someone with a stronger body and a
deeper voice than most mothers.

The turn against traditional fatherhood was implicit in many of the
men's accounts. It was explicit, and forceful, in Patrick's. Patrick was so
opposed to traditional fatherhood that he didn't want his children calling

him "Dad." "I was very uncomfortable with the kids calling me 'Dad' because I did not like what the definition of a dad was," he said. "So I brought them up to call me Patrick. They call Beth 'Mommy'... It's Mommy and Patrick." Nine years on, Patrick confessed to some regret about this early decision, which the children were not about to let him change. Now, he said, instead of "Dad," they often called him "Mommy Patrick" because they had a hard time remembering which parent they wanted.

If that suggested a high level of interchangeability between the two of them, Patrick wanted to challenge its terms:

> We parent differently.... Like everybody, we bring a lot of our upbringing to our parenting. Either we're like it or we want to be very different from it. But I feel like I parent like a man a lot.

As I noted in the previous section, Beth's account suggested a perception of herself as intensely maternal, and her extended participation in the one activity Patrick could not share—breastfeeding—was another way their caregiving could be differentiated. There was, as he pointed out, "some role stereotyping stuff." Patrick said he was stricter, keener, for example, on encouraging the children to sleep through the night when they were younger. But that did not also make him "the one who just goes and throws them up in the air and plays catch." As a parent of twins, Patrick's equal share of caregiving, from the beginning, would have been a requirement even if his politics hadn't mandated it anyway. From Patrick's account (and also from Beth's), theirs was a complicated and interesting combination of commitment to gender equity and shared caregiving with a clearer acknowledgement of their (gender) differences than emerged from the other couples. Beth's physical attachment and "mothering kinds of ways" had made her, in Patrick's words, "the favourite" when the children were younger. He expressed his joking hope that he would be the favourite when they were teenagers.

Patrick was not a "dad" in the conventional sense of the term. He did not want the same word to categorize fathering like his and the fathering done by the "weekend dads." But, in the absence of another word, there was some sense of loss and alienation:

> What's a real drag of the Left and the alternative and whatever we call ourselves is that we leave things and we don't replace them. So I think that is some of

where fathers are who embrace feminism or, these other beliefs, social justice beliefs, is that we are OK rejecting things but we are not that creative in creating our own alternatives. We haven't created an alternative vision of a father very clearly; no one's really done that; there's no model.

For Patrick, there may have been no model. But for fathers following behind, he and the other fathers introduced here were themselves the models, fathers whose practices went well beyond conventional understandings of "fathering."

Summing Up

This chapter has explored earning and caring against the grain by considering couples who had been doing it for longer than those introduced earlier in the book, couples that had, in the process, delivered the most significant challenge to conventional expectations about mothers and fathers. The couples described here had all seen their children through the early preschool years and into the school system. They, too, had moved on to new work and care arrangements. Parents' transitions usually saw both partners in paid employment, with similar work time commitments (even if their incomes were not the same), and an equitable sharing of domestic labour and caring responsibilities outside of work hours. Like the dual-earner couples described in Chapter 4, these mothers were all working mothers. And the fathers were "working fathers," giving family responsibilities priority over workplace ones and foregrounding family life and relationships over career ambitions on the broader canvas of personal fulfilment.

At the start of the chapter, I noted the "common denominator" of going against the grain for these couples, as for all the other heterosexual couples in the study: father involvement in caregiving at a level that approximated and occasionally exceeded that of the mother. Father involvement meant a sharing of executive responsibility, as well as care, in an egalitarian arrangement that seemed to flow from an egalitarian couple relationship — in Schwartz's (1994) terms, these couples were "peers."

Achieving a peer relationship was no easy task. In almost every case, there were trade-offs in earning and caring responsibilities, as each partner surrendered power in one sphere and acquired it in the other. Many fathers, as I noted earlier, scaled back career aspirations, which had consequences for family income, as they ventured much further into childcare and domestic space than most of the men they knew. Mothers surrendered their traditionally uncontested power over family matters, as they took on responsibilities for financial provision that were pressing and unavoidable. Even if couples' negotiated arrangements were achieved without major conflict, they were not achieved without work. The interview accounts showed that outsiders' comments on how "lucky" they were in their unconventional organization of earning and caring tended to rankle.

For all but one of these couples who managed their parental responsibilities as peers and as dual earners, the earning and caring spaces were shared.[3] The "separate spheres" of earning and caring were no longer separate and no longer jealously guarded. Indeed, perhaps they were shared spaces *because* they were no longer jealously guarded. Barriers to women's paid employment have fallen, both organizationally and at the level of the individual family, in the wake of economic and social changes since the 1960s.[4] However, gatekeeping at the portals of the private sphere of family life is a more complicated story. I have noted in earlier chapters the scholarly argument that being ultimately in charge of children is a source of power, which mothers can use as gatekeepers to mediate fathers' involvement with their children (Allen and Hawkins 1999; McBride et al. 2005; Townsend 2002b). Signs of that mediation were evident in some of the interviews. Lisa, for example, spoke of her children "coming to her first" for help in their dealings with their father; Jane acknowledged taking all the responsibility for moderating the emotional climate in her family. However, among the "peer" couples, those who consciously shared caregiving over an extended period, there seemed to be no gatekeeping. Individual parents seemed to be supportive and respectful of the other parent's relationship with the children, at the same time that they also respected each other's differences. The interview accounts contained many stories about these differences, but they tended to be the quirky, idiosyncratic differences that exist between any two people, each of whom is bound to interact differently with others. Probably the most consistently gender based of the perceived differences — one that also emerged among couples described in earlier chapters — was of the mother as being more "nurturing," more the "comforter." Often, fathers presented themselves and were presented as more task oriented and less inclined to be melted by tears. But even this difference was not observable across the board.

Differences also seemed to me to be more a matter of style than of underlying parental behaviour — and this is a point I need to elaborate. It links to my conclusions, in this and earlier chapters, about couples who share caregiving work equally being *interchangeable*. A more accurate description, and one I have moved to in this chapter, is that they were *functionally interchangeable*. In other words, each parent knew, on a daily and ongoing basis, how to meet the children's needs. In earlier chapters, I spoke of "equal terms" caregiving as a way to encapsulate both the equitable division of the caring work and the common bond of experience, emotional engagement, and language that it forged. This was the case here too. Each parent knew each child well — Jessica, speaking of herself and her partner Sam, said they shared "the essence of the child's soul." And they acted out of their own knowledge and according to their own style. Parents who were functionally interchangeable were not, as I noted earlier, interchangeable as *people*. And their relationships with their children were highly individual. There was talk through the interviews of rituals and activities that were cherished aspects of these individual relationships, and these were not open to sharing. But there was not a lot, in any of this, that was divided along gendered lines. In their accounts, mothers did not come across as appreciably different from fathers.

So, when in some families what is done by a mother closely resembles what is done by a father, and vice versa, what does this say about mothering and fathering? In their popular sense, each term suggests a particular set of activities, conventionally done by a particular, and gendered, person. When the activities are considered separately from the person conventionally associated with their execution, they become something else. They become, in fact, much more generic, and "parenting" is a more appropriate umbrella term under which to gather them. This is the basis of the theoretical argument foreshadowed in Chapter 1, to which I turn in the closing chapter.

Part IV

Review and Reflection

Introduction

This book has been built on the accounts of 32 couples (31 mothers and 33 fathers) who, in a variety of ways, broke with more conventional divisions of labour in their families and often, in the process, with traditional understandings of mothering and fathering as well. Differently placed in terms of social and economic circumstances and caring for children of different ages and with different needs, these couples shed light on a variety of family structures, contexts, and practices that are both under-researched and critically important.

In going "against the grain" of ideologically dominant models of family life, the mothers and fathers I have included in the book were constructing the kind of individualized biographies anticipated by theorists like Ulrich Beck.[1] And they were doing this in a world no longer well served by the traditional family model, a world in which family life had become "a daily 'balancing act'" or a "permanent do-it-yourself project" (Beck and Beck-Gernsheim 2002:90; Beck and Willms 2004). These do-it-yourself projects were also, in Connell's (2002) terms, gender projects. Couples, in interaction, were doing — and undoing — gender as they negotiated their unconventional earning and caring arrangements.

In the book's opening pages, I raised many questions that I hoped the study would answer. How do couples come to parent "against the grain" in the first place? What is it like for a mother, traditionally the undisputed expert on her children, when the other parent is as well placed to be the primary parent? What is it like for a father whose involvement with his children's care compromises his career aspirations and ability to provide for his family financially? How do parental expectations and arrangements play out in families with two mothers or two fathers? Above all, what happens to "mothering" and "fathering" when couples, as parents, go "against the grain"?

The chapters in Parts II and III have addressed these questions in a series of scenarios based on couples' earning and caring arrangements, the ages of their children, their past history of family decision making, and their current circumstances. In the book's final chapter, I reflect on what this research contributes to the study of gender and family life. In particular, I examine the possibility of reframing "parenting."

Chapter Seven

Parenting and the Undoing of Gender

In this chapter, I pull together the threads of an argument laid out in the scene-setting early pages of this book. The argument, grounded in social constructionist gender scholarship and taking up the work of Sullivan (2004, 2006), Risman (1998, 2004), Deutsch (2007), and others, begins with the claim that couples who in their daily practices as parents explicitly contravene dominant expectations of mothering and fathering have the potential to change, over time, the nature of those expectations. They do this as they contribute to slow and incremental change in household relations on a broad scale. My extension of this argument is that couples such as these, whose members are often functionally interchangeable across all the significant dimensions of earning and caring work, are also (in Deutsch's terms) actively engaged in the work of "undoing gender." In my terms, they are potentially undoing *mothering* and *fathering*. To reclaim the term I have refrained from using up to now, what many such couples are doing instead is *parenting*.

Given its recent history, the term "parenting" must be reframed in order to be reclaimed. Typically, it has been used as an ostensibly gender-neutral label for childcare practices that are generally assumed to be carried out mainly by mothers.[1] "Parents" who are really mothers suggests that "parenting" is something that, in practice, only mothers do. But parenting considered as the cumulative practices of both mothers and fathers, partners who share all such practices more or less interchangeably across gender lines, shifts the term to new semantic turf. In this chapter, I elaborate what I mean by "interchangeable" and link this idea to the new understanding of parenting I want to establish. These discussions, however, need to be preceded by a review of the book's central chapters, which built on the accounts of the couples in the study and on which my conclusions are based.

My analysis began with a discussion (in Part II, Chapter 3 and 4) of the 19 families with preschool children and the arrangements each family made that either positioned mothers, rather than fathers, as primary breadwinners or saw earning and caring evenly shared in a variety of workplace and caregiving circumstances. Among the "crossover" couples, in which mothers were primary breadwinners and fathers (in the case of all but the one lesbian couple) were primary caregivers, I explored questions of attachment to and executive responsibility for children, and I compared mothers' and fathers' different relationships to paid work. I noted that the mothers were different from typical breadwinner fathers in their willingness to limit the demands of their paid work in the interests of family life, as well as in the effort the mothers exerted outside work hours to maintain the attachment to their children built up during the early months of intensive maternal care. Indeed, the practices of these mothers (and those of other employed mothers in the study) conformed to an accumulation of research firmly establishing the case that paid employment for most mothers does not displace mothering but reorganizes its activities and expands its meanings beyond conventional images of maternal presence and direct care.[2]

Some mothers of preschoolers considered themselves — and were sometimes also considered by their partners — to retain executive responsibility for the children, even though these mothers were managing from a distance. But, more often, the close involvement of fathers in the direct, hands-on care of very young children had a different effect. Fathers moved much closer to mothers in terms of caregiving competence, the ability to do the "maternal thinking" described by Ruddick (1982), and their emotional engagement with their children. In terms of the tripartite division of involvement described by Lamb et al. (1985) — namely, *accessibility, engagement,* and *responsibility* — these fathers ranked high on accessibility and engagement. For the most part, with some exceptions, they also seemed to share executive responsibility. From my reading of their accounts, this sharing seemed to have two major consequences. First, both parents were, in most cases, interchangeable in terms of providing care to children on a daily, ongoing basis—an early sign, for me, that *interchangeability* might come to play an important role conceptually in my analysis. Second, their shared involvement in the hands-on and embodied care of their children gave them a set of shared experiences, and a language to describe these experiences, that I have called "equal terms" caregiving. Julia, whom I quoted in Chapter 3, commented that she could talk about her son Tim with Matt, her partner, "the way I would discuss Tim with a girlfriend who has a child of a similar age." Julia said she and Matt discussed "all of the little minute sort of things that you discuss about parenting." I believe Hochschild, reflecting on the fathers in her "second shift" study, fathers whom she classified as "involved," was pointing to something similar when she wrote, "Involved fathers had a much fuller, more elaborate notion of what a father was than uninvolved fathers did. Involved fathers talked about fathering much as mothers talked about mothering" (Hochschild 1989:228).

The parents who were sharing the earning responsibilities, as well as the caregiving of their preschool children—the "shift-workers" and the "dual-dividers"—had more complicated lives. The introduction of a second job and a second set of workplace expectations reduced the time individual parents gave to caregiving, though the "shift-worker" parents still provided round-the-clock parental care. For the ten couples in which partners were both earners and carers, however, there was a more fluid exchange of caregiving responsibilities and a frequent blurring of gender boundaries. Mothers and fathers were doing much the same things, both as heterosexual and same-sex partners, so examples of "mothering" and "fathering" as the distinctly gendered practices of women and men were rare. As I noted in Chapter 4, the families with two mothers or two fathers might have looked different from the more conventionally gendered caregiver-breadwinner template, but, when mothers and fathers in different kinds of family structures are doing pretty much the same things across the board and on a day-by-day basis, the gendered template begins to lose its currency for many families. These parents, like the crossover parents, were interchangeable in their ability to provide care to their children. But because both mothers and fathers were also earners (with mothers in many cases earning more than fathers), their interchangeability extended across the whole range of earning and caring activities.

Though the men in the dual-earner couples were breadwinners (even if they were not sole or even primary providers), they were not the kind of breadwinners encompassed by the gendered template. These were working fathers doing what working mothers have conventionally been expected to do, namely, prioritizing family responsibilities over their paid employment and sometimes making significant concessions in their working lives to do so. For the working fathers, and the working mothers, their strong commitment to their family responsibilities was enabled by work that was much more flexible and contingent than conventional work organizations usually allow. These were "New Economy" employees working at higher-end New Economy jobs and often sacrificing long-term security for the flexibility of self-employment and contract work.

Many of the issues identified as significant among the families caring for preschool children were salient also for the parents of the school-age children described in Part III, Chapter 5 and 6. There were 13 of these couples, and they had been earning and caring against the grain for longer. Having seen their children through the early years and into the school system, most had moved on themselves — to arrangements that saw both parents in paid employment and equitably sharing caregiving and domestic work outside of paid work hours. This transition seemed to be an especially important one; for couples in this study, going against the grain seemed to have disadvantaged one or the other parent *only* when the logical next step was not taken and balance in the sharing of earning and caring over the longer term was not achieved. As I noted in Chapter 5, increased participation in caregiving by fathers does not inevitably lead to more equal sharing of the overall work and family load or to gender being "undone" in progressive, liberating ways. In fact, the longer view provided by these families made it clear that achieving balance, as partners and peers, was not easy. Conflict over child rearing, when both parents were equally invested or when there were wide cultural or other background differences, also loomed large in some families.

More visible, though, were the parents of school-age children who were equal partners — peers, in Schwartz's (1994) terms. These were the couples, introduced in Chapter 6, who did achieve balance, an equitable sharing of all the earning and caring responsibilities, and who pushed me to think about *functional* interchangeability as a way to describe their day-to-day practices as parents. The parents in these families, like the "equal-terms" couples I described earlier, also spoke of the bond between them that their shared commitment to their children gave them. These too were the couples, along with many of those caring for much younger children, who persuaded me that "mothering" and "fathering" did not adequately describe their day-by-day practices and that "parenting" was the more appropriate term.

This returns me to the argument I laid out at the start of the chapter—that when mothering and fathering are degendered, *parenting* is the result. The first requirement here is to clarify what I mean by "interchangeability." When I claim, on the basis of accounts provided by many of the couples in this study, that mothers and fathers were interchangeable in terms of their ability to provide for the daily care of their children, I am talking about a kind of functional interchangeability linked to practice, not identity. This is not about whether fathers are effectively becoming mothers or vice versa. My focus is on the work people are doing—because, I contend, it is the work that counts. Whatever the circumstances that prompted the couples in this study to develop their unconventional divisions of paid and unpaid work, the clearest outcome was that fathers as well as mothers learned to care for children in a hands-on way and, in most cases, to take responsibility for their children's overall well-being. Especially in cases where both parents were earning as well, this interchangeability produced example after example of caring work shared in a way that defied neat gender categorizing. Two such situations, described in earlier chapters, illustrate this point. In Chapter 4, I introduced Alison and Trevor, parents of four-year-old Helen. There I noted some gendering at the interactional level; Alison did some of the "girly girl" activities, and Trevor taught Helen to ride a bike and ski. I also noted, though, that Alison was the family's main earner and that Trevor, working from home, did all the cooking and household management, as well as attending to Helen's medical appointments and extracurricular activities. Both parents were equally involved at the level of responsibility for Helen's well-being. Trevor, in particular, was doing a lot of long-range thinking and planning. In Chapter 6, I introduced Owen and Eleanor, parents of twelve-year-old Katie and nine-year-old Hugh. Owen and Eleanor had been turn takers over the longer haul, with each parent, at different times, being in charge on the home front. When they were interviewed, though, both were working full time, and it was Owen's turn to take on most of the family responsibility, freeing Eleanor (also the family's main earner) to involve herself much more deeply in her consultancy work. Alison and Eleanor were mothers and Trevor and Owen were fathers, but "mothering" and "fathering" didn't adequately describe what any one of them was doing on a daily basis in their families. They were different, as people, but, in their family activities, it seemed to me, they were more alike than they were different. They were *parents*. Interchangeability in the sense I am using it requires that practices usually associated with mothering or with fathering be considered separately from the person conventionally associated with their execution. As I suggested in the previous chapter, when this happens, those practices become something else. They become more generic, and "parenting" becomes a more appropriate term under which they can be subsumed.

Daly (2004) expresses some concern about the expectation of interchangeability that accompanies the idea of shared parenting. It follows, he suggests, from the belief that "equality involves the ability to seamlessly move between mothering and fathering in a way that involves caring, nurturing, genderless parenting." Daly contends that interchangeability of this kind is difficult for mothers and fathers, who are making their way in a deeply gendered culture, and suggests that a more achievable route to interchangeability might be *complementarity*, "whereby we recognize men and women as steeped in different gender traditions, having different legacies in their own families, inhabiting different bodies and recognizing different strengths and contributions that they can make to co-parenting" (Daly 2004:5).

With respect to the families in this study, though, it was their interchangeability that I noticed and that led me to think about "parenting" as the best way to describe their activities. This parenting was indeed being done by men and women, steeped, as Daly points out, in different gender traditions; it was not "genderless parenting." But, as I noted in Chapter 6, at the practical, day-to-day level, any gender-based differences seemed to me more a matter of style than substance. I was helped to this conclusion by two great advantages of the study format. First, I was interviewing partners as individuals, outside of the couple context that can often set partners up as (gendered) foils for one another. So, although I might hear a father doing careful verbal shadow work to establish the mother as the more important parent, I would also hear from that father about the detail of his time with his children, and I was able to recognize in that detail much of what a mother, in other circumstances, might have told me. This point introduces the second study advantage: I was interviewing *multiple* couples, whose circumstances varied widely. So, for example, I could often see the ways a mother, even one who positioned herself very much as a mother in her own family, was doing on a daily basis the same sorts of things a father in another family was doing. To take up Daly's term, the *complementarity* that was playing out at the level of the couple did not seem unassailably gendered when other couples were brought into the comparison.

At the same time, while I am suggesting that *parenting* comes from the degendering of *mothering* and *fathering*, I don't think — to repeat my earlier point — that parenting necessarily has to be genderless, as Daly implies. The comment made by Patrick, also introduced in Chapter 6, that he "parented like a man" offers a useful perspective. Patrick and his partner Beth, while conscientiously and devotedly sharing all the caregiving of their children, were aware of doing it differently from one another. They had, as I noted earlier, an interesting combination of commitment to gender equity and acknowledgement of gender difference. But, as was the case with Alison and Trevor and Eleanor and Owen, their division of labour could not be subdivided into "mothering" and "fathering." Those terms, used together, were inappropriate to describe what each was doing. Patrick's objection to the term "Dad" as failing to capture the range of caregiving activities he was involved in hinted at the same basic problem: the lack of a language to describe the kinds of parental work he and others like him did. As DeVault's (1991) study of the activities involved for women in "feeding the family" demonstrated, much remains invisible when there are not the words available to describe particular kinds of work. This is the case here too. There is a lack of appropriate language to describe men's and women's caregiving under the circumstances I have described in this study, circumstances in which couples are genuine partners, sharing work and responsibility across the board. "Parenting like a man" is different from "fathering," and "parenting like a woman" is different from "mothering." As an exercise in reconceptualization, I suggest this substitution is a place to start.

As I have indicated earlier, not all of the couples in this study were *parenting* in the new sense I am establishing here. Among the couples with preschool children, there were mothers working hard to retain primary parent status, even though fathers were doing an equal or greater amount of the hands-on childcare. Among the couples with older children — notably those described in Chapter 5 — there were examples of earning and caring responsibilities all devolving to one parent and of both maternal and paternal gatekeeping that limited the family involvement of the other parent. But these were exceptions. Most other couples were *parenting* along the lines I have described.

The inclusion in the study of couples at different stages of family life — those such as Andrew and David, just starting out with 10-week-old Alexia and those such as Lois and George, seasoned parents of a 13-year-old and a 10-year-old — helped me to discern a fundamental characteristic of the *parenting* couples: *both* partners had been hands-on caregivers from the start. In most cases, given the family structure of the couples in the study, this meant men becoming involved much earlier and much more deeply than is conventionally the case. Indeed, Lois specifically counted George's early and equal involvement in infant care as an important factor in the committed co-parenting arrangement that followed. In our interview, Lois and I agreed that George's experience was an argument for shared parental leave after the birth or adoption of a baby — an argument that other scholars have taken up.

This takes the discussion of *parenting*, as the interchangeable practices of both mothers and fathers, to the broader institutional level. The issue of parental leave, though only one of many possible means to promote parenting at the policy level, is another useful place to start. In Canada, as I noted in Chapter 1, fathers have been able to share extended parental leave since December 31, 2000. But, because the sharing is optional, fathers have been slow to respond; in 2001, only 10 per cent of eligible fathers had taken it up (Marshall 2003). By 2006, the proportion had increased significantly in Quebec, in response to the province's takeover of parental leave provisions in March 2005. In the rest of Canada, however, the take-up of parental leave by fathers remained at around 10 per cent (Marshall 2008). Paternal leave uptake is much higher in the Scandinavian countries, notably in Norway, where a "paternity quota" of one month of leave is reserved for fathers and is lost if the father does not take it up. Since the paternity quota replaced optional paternal leave in 1993, "parental leave for fathers has developed from being a minority practice into becoming the majority practice" (Brandth and Kvande 2001:259). By 1999, 78 per cent of eligible Norwegian fathers took parental leave. Asked why they did so, fathers responded that it accorded with what they themselves really wanted to do. Being obliged to take the leave was "almost as if they had received a gift they could not refuse" (Brandth and Kvande 2001:260).[3]

In another European study, Holter (2007) reported that men's involvement in parental leave was strongly associated with their later participation in caregiving. Holter (2007) was drawing on research that was part of a major European Union study of men's roles in work and family "reconciliation." It explored many of the themes recurring in this book — particularly the association of men with breadwinning and the difficulties men confront when they seek to accommodate paid work to family caregiving. The project enumerated many such difficulties, particularly in the form of organizational barriers preventing men from working less than full-time hours. Some of Holter's conclusions bear on the experiences of the couples described here because these conclusions describe the context in which these couples, too, are attempting to reconcile family responsibilities and paid work. He notes, for example, a slow change in gender ideals, with a shift among men from "breadwinner" to "caring" masculinities, and he theorizes a combination of "new man" and "new circumstances" models to account for the shift. The "new man" explanation attributes change to ideological factors associated with a specific configuration of masculinity and involving a small group of men committed to gender equality; the "new circumstances" model sees change as a product of the material conditions experienced by most men.

Holter's discussion of the European research findings affirms the approach to change theorized by Sullivan (2004, 2006): change in the direction of more equitable gender relations is happening slowly and on multiple levels. For Sullivan, it comes about at the level of couple interactions that are linked to shifts in gender consciousness and that both contribute to and are shaped by the broader social and institutional context in which they occur. At the interactional level, as Deutsch (2007) has explained, couples are "doing" — and "undoing" — gender as they negotiate ways to balance earning and caring responsibilities in the context of both available policy and program support and the widely held expectations about appropriate maternal and paternal behaviour. The extended case I have been making through this book and in this chapter is that the couples in this study, going against the grain of conventional expectations in all the ways I have described, have mostly been "undoing" gender. Rather than "mothering" and "fathering," they have been "parenting" — at least partly because they equitably shared the hands-on caregiving right from the start.

Change in household gender relations in the direction of greater equity and sharing is a matter of fairness. Over the long haul, inequitable sharing of family work disadvantages the person doing more of it. Equitable household arrangements realign the balance of paid work and family responsibilities by freeing mothers from the extra caregiving responsibilities that constrain their opportunities in the labour market and by freeing fathers from the workplace expectations that constrain their family involvement. These may not be easy adjustments to make. Mothers, by sharing caregiving responsibilities, may be surrendering a source of power and authority central to their identities as mothers. But the individual mothers interviewed in this study expressed gratitude and relief that family responsibilities were being so equitably shared. Julia, whose partner Matt was the home-based caregiver, spoke of all the "worry and emotional responsibility" that children bring. She commented, "I'm lucky that I have a husband who is so bonded that . . . he takes on a huge part of that." Matt's sharing of the worry and responsibility gave her the freedom to be "the kind of person I want to be." Fathers may be surrendering career aspirations and earning potential — in short, some of the "patriarchal dividend" accruing to men as a group from the maintenance of an unequal gender order (Connell 2002:142). But the individual fathers interviewed in this study spoke movingly of what they gained through close and long-term involvement with their children. Sam, the deeply engaged caregiver father introduced in Chapter 6, commented, "Just that hands-on, like literally hands-on . . . it's something that sort of shapes you, for the life of your child . . . and just sort of innerly as well."

Most of the families in this study have been changed in this way. They have been trailblazers, at the leading edge of the "slow dripping" kind of change in family relations that, over time, should start happening on a broader scale as well. Pushed by philosophical commitment or material circumstances into new ways of organizing their family lives, they demonstrated that the new ways could work, and work well, for themselves and for others. They were going against the grain. Others, following behind them, will find the going to be smoother, because the grain will have changed.

Appendix

The Study Participants

Parents of Preschool Children (Introduced in Part II)

Chapter 3: The "Crossovers"

1. Paula (30), a clinical psychologist,[1] and Alan (32), a home-based caregiver and graphic designer; parents of Mark (3) and an expected second baby. Estimated annual family income $40,000 to 45,000,[2] of which Paula contributed 80 per cent and Alan 20 per cent.[3]

2. Ruth (33), an administrative officer, and Warren (30), a home-based caregiver; parents of Connor (nearly 3). Estimated annual family income $45,000, of which Ruth contributed 91 per cent and Warren 9 per cent.

3. Tanya (42), a university professor, and Adam (36), a home-based caregiver; parents of Joel (5) and Lucy (8 months). Estimated annual family income $70,000, of which Tanya contributed 100 per cent.

4. Wendy (34), an accountant, and Peter (37), a home-based caregiver; parents of Nick (5), Simon (3), and Erin (1). Estimated annual family income greater than $100,000, of which Wendy contributed 100 per cent.

---

[1] To maintain participants' anonymity, I have modified job descriptions and other identifying details in some cases.

[2] Participants were asked to estimate both their total before-tax family income for the year preceding the interview and the proportion contributed by each partner. The understanding was that these estimates could be rough.

[3] As noted in Chapter 2, the couples lived in urban centres in three different provinces. I have chosen not to locate participants geographically on the basis that, in some cases, their city of residence might make them more readily identifiable.

5. Julia (37), a lawyer, and Matt (39), a home-based caregiver; parents of Tim (2). Estimated annual family income $78,000, of which Julia contributed 95 per cent and Matt 5 per cent.

6. Donna (35), a professional government employee, and Scott (35), a home-based caregiver and designer; parents of Isabel (5), Nadine (3), and Everett (2). Estimated annual family income $56,000, of which Donna contributed 70 per cent and Scott 30 per cent.

7. Kendra (36), a social worker, and Janice (49), a former teacher about to be a home-based caregiver; parents of Hannah (7 months). Estimated annual family income $75,000, of which Kendra contributed 70 per cent and Janice 30 per cent.

8. Sheila (35), a physician, and Keith (37), a home-based caregiver; parents of Kevin (2½) and Brent (6 months). Estimated annual family income $170,000, of which Sheila contributed 100 per cent.

9. Patricia (36), a physician, and Graham (41), a home-based caregiver; parents of Jonathan (5). Estimated annual family income $200,000, of which Patricia contributed 100 per cent.

Chapter 4: The "Shift-Workers"

1. Diane (36), an industrial chemist, and Geoff (45), an autobody mechanic; parents of Kelly (3). Estimated annual family income $88,000, of which each contributed 50 per cent.

2. Denise (34), a school guidance counsellor, and Gary (38), an airline pilot; parents of Daniel (3) and Ella (1 month). Estimated annual family income $115,000, of which each contributed 50 per cent.

3. Christine (38) and James (34), both college instructors; parents of Cameron (nearly 4) and Myles (13 months). Estimated annual family income $80,000, of which Christine contributed 35 per cent and James 65 per cent.

4. Andrew (35), an engineer, and David (30), a financial manager; parents of Alexia (2 months). Estimated annual family income $110,000, of which Andrew contributed 60 per cent and David 40 per cent.

Chapter 4: The "Dual-Dividers"

1. Rebecca (39), a consultant and social researcher, and Aidan (32), a communications specialist; parents of Conrad (4) and Oliver (2). Estimated annual income $90,000, of which each contributed 50 per cent.

2. Grant (43) and Pierce (41), joint owners of a marketing business; parents of Gemma (nearly 6). [Father and stepfather respectively to two teenage chil-

dren from Grant's prior marriage.] Estimated annual income $225,000, of which each contributed 50 per cent.

3. Alison (42), a health care professional, and Trevor (43), an editor; parents of Helen (4). Estimated annual income $180,000, of which Alison contributed 70 per cent and Trevor 30 per cent.

4. Monica (47), a teacher, and Karen (41), a management consultant; parents of Michelle (5) and Liam (17 months). Estimated annual income $180,000, of which Monica contributed 40 per cent and Karen 60 per cent.

5. Marie (39), a university professor, and Stephen (33), a communications professional; parents of Kimberley (4) and Maya (11 months). Estimated annual family income $100,000, of which Marie contributed 70 per cent and Stephen 30 per cent.

6. Mitchell (36), a non-profit agency employee, and Tony (42), a technical writer; parents of Nathan (nearly 6). Estimated annual income $80,000, of which Mitchell contributed 35 per cent and Tony 65 per cent.

Parents of School-Age Children (Introduced in Part III)

Chapter 5: Challenges on the Path to Change

1. Valerie (48), a receptionist, and Charles (50), a home-based caregiver; parents of Melanie (13). Estimated annual family income $13,000 to15,000, of which Valerie contributed 99 per cent, and Charles 1 per cent.

2. Belinda (44), a social work manager, and Frank (42), a home-based caregiver; parents of Zack (9) and Samantha (7). Estimated annual family income $88,000, of which Belinda contributed 100 per cent.

3. Judith (50), an administrative assistant, and Paul (46), a computer technician; parents of Robert (11). Estimated annual family income $85,000, of which Judith contributed 65 per cent and Paul 35 per cent.

4. Penny (47), a manager in a not-for-profit foundation, and Dennis (45), a consulting firm manager; parents of Jamie (nearly 9) and Fergus (3). Estimated annual income $116,000, of which Penny contributed 47 per cent and Dennis 44 per cent (the rest coming from other sources).

5. Cheryl (42) and Khenan (41), both post-secondary teachers; parents of Adrian (15) and Lora (12). Estimated annual income $22,000, of which each contributed 50 per cent.

Chapter 6: Parents as Peers

1. Lisa (38) and Joe (38), co-owners of a craft business; parents of Glenn (9) and Logan (7). Estimated annual income $50,000, of which each contributed 50 per cent.

2. Sandi (35), a clerk, and Todd (36), a youth worker; parents of Sean (9), Megan (7), and Tyler (6). Estimated annual income $72,000, of which Sandi contributed 65 per cent and Todd 35 per cent.

3. Lois (39), a social research manager, and George (41), a professional government employee; parents of Elizabeth (13) and David (10). Estimated annual income $170,000, of which Lois contributed 60 per cent and George 40 per cent.

4. Beth (42), a social worker, and Patrick (40), a social researcher; parents of twins Holly and Justine (9). Estimated annual family income $65,000, of which each contributed 50 per cent.

5. Jane (48), a social service agency manager, and Bill (52), a mechanic; parents of Cassie (15) and John (13). Estimated annual income $110,000, of which each contributed 50 per cent.

6. Eleanor (39), a social researcher and consultant, and Owen (41), an actor; parents of Katie (12) and Hugh (9). Estimated annual income $100,000, of which Eleanor contributed 70 per cent and Owen 30 per cent.

7. Laura (48), a senior civil servant, and Ian (64), a home-based caregiver; parents of Leah (17). Estimated annual income $87,000, of which Laura contributed 75 per cent and Ian 25 per cent.

8. Jessica (40), a teacher, and Sam (40), a manager; parents of Andrea (10) and Melissa (7). Estimated annual income $150,000, of which Jessica contributed 35 per cent and Sam 65 per cent.

Notes

Part I: Setting the Scene

Introduction

1. Successive years of the General Social Survey of Canada show that, of people aged between 25 and 54, the proportion doing some daily housework increased from 72 per cent in 1986 to 79 per cent in 2005 — an increase solely attributable to men. Their participation in household work increased from 54 per cent in 1986 to 69 per cent in 2005, while women's participation rate held steady at around 90 per cent (Marshall 2006).

2. In dual-earner families in the 25–54 years age range, these differences were more muted, with each partner doing 50 per cent of the *combined* paid work and housework each day both in 1992 and in 2005. However, in 1992, wives did 45 per cent of the total paid work and 65 per cent of the housework. In 2005, they were doing 46 per cent of the paid work and 62 per cent of the housework. There were differences also in the amount of time working parents spent on the primary care of children. Overall, among married people aged 25–54 with at least one child under five at home, fathers spent an average of 1.6 hours daily on such activities in 2005 (up from 1.0 hours in 1986), compared with the 3.4 hours on average spent by mothers — up from 2.6 hours in 1986 (Marshall 2006).

3. All names are pseudonyms.

Chapter 1: Establishing the Context

1. The focus in what follows is on urban, industrialized workplaces and workers. It is important, however, to acknowledge the important differences in rural

family life and in the family lives of other groups, for example, First Nations people, that this very general overview fails to mention.

2. Parr's (1990) study of the town of Paris, Ontario describes a rare exception to this norm. Parr notes that, even though "[t]here are enough affirmations in the record that married women's employment should not exist to convince a careful scholar that indeed it did not," the major employer in Paris recruited skilled women textile workers (including many who were married and had children) from English textile mill towns during the early decades of the twentieth century (Parr 1990:23). These women formed the heart of the town's workforce and were, in most cases, family breadwinners.

3. The Criminal Code changes also included the decriminalization of homosexuality, in a social climate that facilitated the emergence of an increasingly influential lesbian and gay rights movement.

4. Other examples of highly significant gender-related institutional change include the decision (after massive activist effort) to specify women as a group whose rights needed protection under the 1982 Canadian Charter of Rights and Freedoms and the 1983 amendment to the Canadian Human Rights Act to prohibit sexual harassment in workplaces under federal jurisdiction (Morris 2000).

5. The Quebec Parental Insurance Plan includes a five-week, non-transferable paternity leave paid at 70 per cent of previous earnings, which is similar to the provisions of some of the Scandinavian countries, notably Norway. Some 56 per cent of eligible fathers claimed benefits under the plan, but most took only the five weeks of paternity leave. Few used any of the 32 weeks available to either parent.

6. In fact, the Quebec program is more complicated than these details suggest. Although, as Albanese (2006) and Prentice (2007) point out, there have been clear economic and social benefits from the program, there have also been concerns about hidden extra costs for parents, long waiting lists and other problems of accessibility (with more privileged children more likely to participate), and uneven quality across centres (Campbell 2006; Prentice 2007).

7. Several British studies of women in male-dominated occupations (Jones and Causer 1995; Liff and Ward 2001; Rubin 1997) show that women are aware of the way such "special concessions" may mark them as different and recognize the consequences of taking them up.

8. Viewed from a global perspective, contemporary family change can be seen as one of the many consequences of major transitions in industrial society and of the condition of modernity that is its philosophical basis. Theorists like Ulrich Beck (1992) and Anthony Giddens (1991) share a general view that the

foundations of the social and economic order are beginning to shift, exposing people to the risks and hazards associated with freedom from old rules and certainties. In Beck's terms, these family changes are reflective of the more general trends towards *individualization* — the requirement for people freed from old rules and roles to construct their own biographies (and, not incidentally, their own forms of family) in ways that makes sense *to them*. Beck argues that the old model of the normal family has given way to multiple forms; at the same time, individuals within families of every kind are needing to accommodate biographies that are no longer complementary in the way that the old caregiver-breadwinner biographies were (Beck and Beck-Gernsheim 2002; Beck and Willms 2004).

9. *Parents* is listed by Rogers Magazine Service, run by the Canadian company Rogers Communications Inc., as one of the most popular magazines in its "family and parenting magazines" category, along with a Canadian counterpart, *Today's Parent*. Both magazines are also listed among the most popular women's magazines. No family-related magazines appear on the list of most popular men's magazines. (See http://www.rogersmagazineservice.com/rms/servlet/rms for details.)

10. In an earlier article, Sunderland (2000) analyzed the material she was given by her doctor and local hospital during her 1993 pregnancy in the UK, along with two books she and her partner received as gifts. In these texts, she uncovered "one over-arching discourse: 'part-time father/mother as main parent.'" Sunderland notes that this dominant discourse was supported and occasionally challenged by other, usually complementary discourses: "father as baby entertainer," "father as mother's bumbling assistant," "father as line manager," "mother as manager of the father's role in childcare," and "mother as wife/partner" (Sunderland 2000:249).

11. See for example Canadian groups like Invest in Kids (www.investinkids.com) and the Canadian Institute of Child Health (www.cich.ca), both of which have taken up the educational campaign referred to by Wall (2004).

12. Even in the world of women workers and breadwinners described in Parr's (1990) study of early twentieth century Paris, Ontario, the often more egalitarian division of household labour did not extend to basic hands-on childcare. Parr notes: "No matter how minimally attached they were to the waged economy, fathers did not … change children, bathe them, or assume extended responsibility for their supervision, regarding these tasks as too unpleasant, intimate, or confining" (Parr 1990:91).

13. Studies outside Canada—for example, Hochschild (1989, 1997) in the United States, Backett (1987) in the United Kingdom, and White (1994) in Australia —have found similar limitations to fathers' caring work.

14. Researchers outside Canada have also written about unconventional earning and caring arrangements. Their research, some of which will be described in greater detail in later chapters, covers three decades and involves couples in several different countries. For example, Russell (1982), Grbich (1992), and Smith (1998) have studied dimensions of shared caregiving in selected Australian families. Radin (1982), Haas (1980, 1982), Hertz (1986), Ehrensaft (1987), Schwartz (1994), Coltrane (1989, 1996), Deutsch and Saxon (1998), Deutsch (1999, 2002), and Risman (1998) covered similar ground, with a primary focus on equal-sharing couples in the United States. Much of this work has involved a search for antecedents or pathways to the caregiving arrangements in question and, in the qualitative projects, a search for common themes emerging from the experiences of individuals involved.

15. Deutsch's 2007 article is titled "Undoing gender"—a response to the now classic 1987 article by West and Zimmerman entitled "Doing gender." Deutsch acknowledges that she had been thinking about writing an article with this title for years and had no idea until her article was reviewed that Judith Butler, a gender scholar with a different disciplinary background, had published a book called *Undoing Gender* in 2004.

16. My version of parenting challenges the way the term is conventionally used— as an unproblematic means of describing the care of children that is ostensibly gender neutral but is often heavily gender coded. For that reason, I avoid it in most of the chapters to follow. I will return to it in closing, using the study findings to give it a new meaning.

Chapter 2: The Study

1. Of the Canadian studies focusing on changing gender patterns in the family division of labour that I noted in Chapter 1, Doucet (2000, 2004a, 2004b, 2006a, 2006b) concentrated mainly on home-based caregiver fathers and much less on the couple context, which is my major focus. Dienhart (1998) mainly attended to couples negotiating arrangements that would see greater father participation in caregiving. Her couples did not transgress gender boundaries in the way many of my study participants did, and her study included only heterosexual, biological parents. On the other hand, Nelson (1996) studied only lesbian couples. My work is informed by and extends all

these projects. In particular, it extends the pilot project by Fox and Fumia (2001), which is probably closest to my research in overall intention.

2. Of the 64 interviews included in the study, 51 were transcribed in full. Technical problems with a tape recorder resulted in partial transcriptions and full notes being taken of 3 interviews. Partial transcriptions and full notes were also made of 10 interviews conducted towards the end of the project.

3. This awareness — signalled by writing strategies such as "From Wayne's account, his approach to caregiving was ..." or "Ruth's strategy, as she reported it to me, was to ..." — will be evident through all the discussion of empirical material. There will also be, however, many unproblematic "descriptions of reality" that I felt able to take literally.

4. An example of my language use may be helpful. I use terms such as "equal" or "egalitarian" in an everyday, conversational way and not as an exact measure of anything — especially not as an exact measure of the amount of housework or childcare individuals performed. Measurement was not the object of this research exercise.

Part II: Getting Started: Caring for Children in the Preschool Years

Introduction

1. Sweet and Moen (2006), in their study of work-hour arrangements among middle-class, dual-earner couples, describe "crossovers" as couples in which the wife works 45 or more hours a week in paid employment while the husband does not. In my study, the "crossover" relates to the switching of responsibilities, not to the hours worked.

2. As the more detailed analysis to follow will show, these categories are all somewhat arbitrary because temporary shifts and changes may challenge categorical boundaries over time. Fathers who were full-time primary caregivers occasionally took on short-term evening jobs to get themselves out of the house. Mothers who shared earning as well as caregiving were not necessarily contributing as much financially as their partners did. The categories are best read as "ideal types," snapshots of arrangements at the time couples were interviewed.

3. The statistical likelihood that a dual-earner couple would be heterosexual is indicated by the fact that, in the 2006 Census of Canada, same-sex couples accounted for less than 1 per cent of the total number of couples in census families (Milan et al. 2007). According to the 2003 Survey of Labour and

Income Dynamics, in 71 per cent of dual-earner couples the man earned more than the woman (Sussman and Bonnell 2006). According to the 2005 General Social Survey, although "gender roles" were converging, women spent less time on paid work and more on unpaid work than men (Marshall 2006). Finally, in 2006, only about 10 per cent of eligible fathers claimed or planned to claim parental leave under the federal Parental Benefits Program (Marshall 2006).

Chapter 3: The "Crossovers": Breadwinner Mothers with Partners at Home

1. In 2005, 21 per cent of Canadian families were single-earner families with one parent at home. Of these, 11 per cent had a stay-at-home father (Marshall 2006).
2. This speaks to the *moral* dimension of expectations about mothering and fathering, a point taken up by Daly (2004); Doucet (2006a); McCarthy, Ribbens, Edwards, and Gillies (2000); and McMahon (1995).
3. For more information, see the website for the non-profit organization Attachment Parenting International at http://www.attachmentparenting.org. The US physician William Sears, whose writings are widely cited on the website, was named by Ruth as an attachment parenting resource.
4. Allen and Hawkins (1999:200) cite 19 sources as examples.
5. The extent to which assumptions and beliefs about children's needs are class-based is discussed by Lareau (2002).
6. For example, the 1998 Canadian General Social Survey on time use indicated that, in families with both parents working full time, fathers of preschoolers recorded over an hour more leisure per day than mothers, 3.5 hours compared to 2.4 hours (Silver 2000).
7. See Doucet (2006a) for an excellent extended response to the question "Do men mother?"

Chapter 4: "Shift-Workers" and "Dual-Dividers": Sharing Earning, Sharing Caring

1. Occasional backup help from grandparents or regular playschool attendance featured in some family arrangements. But, in all four cases, no other paid childcare was used.
2. See, for example, Uttal's (2002) study of the contemporary shift to market-based childcare and the gendered allocation of responsibility for its management.
3. Implicitly gendered expectations about "good workers" as being free of family responsibilities are built into conventional work organizations, which may explain why, as I noted in Chapter 1, Canadian work organizations offer so little support to working families. Many conventional jobs, carried out on a full-

time basis in such organizations, are clearly not amenable to the kinds of family arrangements implemented by the couples described here.

Part III: The Longer View: Couples with School-Age Children

Introduction

1. The work of coordinating family activities to meet the requirements of the school system—work that, as they point out, is usually done by mothers—has been most clearly articulated by Griffith and Smith (2005). Like the work of "feeding the family" explored by DeVault (1991), it is largely invisible and unrecognized, especially when a primary caregiver is nominated to take charge of it. Sharing this work requires a shared acknowledgement of its value to the child, a perspective evident in research by Lareau (2002) on the contribution of parental education work to children's cultural capital.

2. For example, in 1999, women aged between 25 and 54 made up 40 per cent of voluntary part-time workers in Canada. In this age group, 61 per cent of the women, compared to only 27 per cent of the men, had at least one child under 16 at home. Although most younger part-time workers cited school attendance as a reason for their part-time work status, 44 per cent of the women reported "family reasons." Among men in this age group, the reasons most commonly cited for part-time work were personal preference and school attendance (Marshall 2001).

3. Children's effect on parents and, by extension, on the caring work they do has been described in detail by Ambert (1990, 1992). In a model devised to study "child effect," Ambert specifies areas of parents' lives that are affected by children, including health, place and space, finances, marital relations, and community. She also notes the particular characteristics of children (including gender, birth order, level of intelligence, personality traits, physical appearance, and many others) that might exert an effect. Others (e.g., McMahon 1995; Marshall and Lambert 2006) have written of children's capacity to shape parents' identities and parents' sense of being important in the world.

4. One couple had a nearly nine-year-old and a three-year-old. Both parents had shared a nine-month parental leave after their second child arrived, and then they returned to their former jobs. Most of the transitions in the family involved the older child, so it seemed, on balance, more appropriate to group them with the parents of older children.

5. These groupings are somewhat arbitrary. As with the parents of preschool children, the earning and caring arrangements of the parents described in Part III occasionally underwent brief changes over time, when, for example, a caregiver father might take on a temporary evening job or circumstances positioned a mother temporarily at home. Although I do not overlook these temporary changes, I have classified couples according to the arrangement that, at the time of the interviews and in my judgement, best described a family's overall strategy for combining earning and caring.

Chapter 5: Challenges on the Path to Change

1. Penelope Leach is a British psychologist and the author of several popular books of advice for parents, books written from a child development perspective.

Chapter 6: Parents as Peers

1. See Part II, Introduction, note 3 above.
2. The division of earning and caring over time in Lois's household was described in the introduction to Part I. Sandi and Todd, the parents of three children aged between nine and six, made their original caregiving decisions out of financial need. Sandi had the job and the benefits, Todd was better placed to provide care than income, and outside childcare was too expensive. Todd worked evening hours delivering pizzas to help make ends meet, but the family was dependent on Sandi's earnings and subject also to interprovincial postings that were part of her job. Todd's employment prospects, as a civilian on a military base, were limited. But, like George, Todd managed to turn volunteer work with children in the Military Families Resource Centre into contract work and then into a full-time job when the youngest of his three children was in kindergarten. When he was interviewed, he was working a kind of split shift, doing administrative and organizational work during the day when the children were in school and supervising family activities at the centre in the evening when Sandi was home. When she was away, for training or other duties, he could take the children to work with him.
3. Laura and Ian were the exception. As noted earlier, Ian, in effect, took early retirement to support Laura's career by becoming the primary caregiver.
4. In 2006, 72.9 per cent of women with children under 16 were in paid employment, compared with only 39.1 per cent in 1976 (Statistics Canada 2007).

Part IV: Review and Reflection

Introduction
1. See Chapter 1, note 8 above.

Chapter 7: Parenting and the Undoing of Gender
1. Examples include advice literature overtly directed to "parents" that is implicitly intended for mothers (Sunderland 2006; Wall 2004) and "family-friendly" workplace programs and policies directed to "parents" but invariably taken up only by mothers (Connell 2005).
2. For example, for the mothers studied by Edwards et al. (2005), paid work was "not necessarily distinct from, or at the expense of," obligation to their communities and commitment to their families (Edwards et al. 2005:297). Garey's (1999) metaphor of the "weaving" of paid work and motherhood was developed to make the same point. (See also Elvin-Nowak and Thomsson 2001; Morehead 2001.)
3. Using public policy to promote gender equality was widely recognized as a strategy of the Scandinavian welfare states through the closing decades of the twentieth century. But it was not universally successful. As a strategy for increasing father involvement, it may have been "more significant on the symbolic level of gender relations than on the level of actual division of labour between mothers and fathers." At the same time, though, as one commentator has noted, policies like those enabling shared parental leave do offer parents choices and open up new possibilities for "choosing a different pattern" (Lammi-Taskula 2006:95–96).

References

Adams, Michele and Scott Coltrane. 2005. "Boys and men in families." Pp. 230–48 in *Handbook of Studies on Men and Masculinities*, edited by M.S. Kimmel, J. Hearn, and R.W. Connell. Thousand Oaks: Sage Publications.

Albanese, Patrizia. 2006. "Small town, big benefits: The ripple effects of $7/day child care." *Canadian Review of Sociology and Anthropology* 43:125–40.

Allen, Sarah M. and Alan J. Hawkins. 1999. "Maternal gatekeeping: Mothers' beliefs and behaviors that inhibit greater father involvement in family work." *Journal of Marriage and Family* 61:199–212.

Altucher, Kristine A. and Lindy B. Williams. 2003. "Family clocks: Timing parenthood." In *It's About Time: Couples and Careers*, edited by P. Moen. Ithaca: Cornell University Press.

Ambert, Anne-Marie. 1990. "The other perspective: children's effect on parents." Pp. 149–65 in *Families: Changing Trends in Canada*, 2nd ed., edited by M. Baker. Toronto: McGraw-Hill Ryerson.

———. 1992. *The Effect of Children on Parents*. New York: The Haworth Press.

Arendell, Terry. 2001. "The new care work of middle-class mothers: Managing childrearing, employment, and time." Pp. 163–204 in *Minding the Time in Family Experience: Emerging Perspectives and Issues*, edited by K.J. Daly. Oxford: JAI Elsevier.

Arnup, Katherine. 1994. *Education for Motherhood: Advice for Mothers in Twentieth-Century Canada*. Toronto: University of Toronto Press.

Atkinson, Paul and Amanda Coffey. 2002. "Revisiting the relationship between participant observation and interviewing." Pp. 801–14 in *Handbook of Interview Research: Context and Method*, edited by J.F. Gubrium and J.A. Holstein. Thousand Oaks: Sage.

Backett, Kathryn. 1987. "The negotiation of fatherhood." Pp. 74–90 in *Reassessing Fatherhood: New Observations on Fathers and the Modern Family*, edited by C. Lewis and M. O'Brien. London: Sage Publications.

Beaujot, Roderic. 2004. *Delayed life transitions: trends and implications*. Ottawa: Vanier Institute of the Family.

Beaujot, Roderic and Jianye Liu. 2005. "Models of time use in paid and unpaid work." *Journal of Family Issues* 26:924–26.

Beck, Ulrich. 1992. *Risk Society*. London: Sage Publications.

Beck, Ulrich and Elisabeth Beck-Gernsheim. 1995. *The Normal Chaos of Love*. Cambridge: Polity Press.

———. 2002. *Individualization: Institutionalized Individualism and its Social and Political Consequences*. London: Sage.

Beck, Ulrich and Johannes Willms. 2004. *Conversations with Ulrich Beck*. Cambridge: Polity Press.

Becker, Penny E. and Phyllis Moen. 1999. "Scaling back: Dual-earner couples' work-family strategies." *Journal of Marriage and Family* 61:995–1007.

Beck-Gernsheim, Elisabeth. 2002. *Reinventing the Family*. Cambridge: Polity Press.

Berk, Sarah Fenstermaker. 1985. *The Gender Factory: The Apportionment of Work in American Households*. New York: Plenum.

Berkowitz, Dana and William Marsiglio. 2007. "Gay men: Negotiating procreative, father, and family identities." *Journal of Marriage and Family* 69:366–81.

Bradbury, Bettina. 2005. "Social, economic, and cultural origins of contemporary families." Pp.71–98 in *Families: Changing Trends in Canada*, 5th ed., edited by M. Baker. Toronto: McGraw-Hill Ryerson.

Brandth, Berit and Elin Kvande. 1998. "Masculinity and child care: The reconstruction of fathering." *The Sociological Review* 46:293–313.

———. 2001. "Flexible work and flexible fathers." *Work, Employment, and Society* 15:251–67.

Butler, Judith. 2004. *Undoing Gender*. New York: Routledge.

Campbell, Angela. 2006. "Proceeding with 'care': Lessons to be learned from the Canadian parental leave and Quebec daycare initiatives in developing a national childcare policy." *Canadian Journal of Family Law* 22:171–222.

Carrington, Christopher. 2002. "Domesticity and the political economy of lesbigay families." Pp. 82–108 in *Families at Work: Expanding the Boundaries*, edited by N. Gerstel, D. Clawson, and R. Zussman. Nashville: Vanderbilt University Press.

Chunn, Dorothy. 2003. "Boys will be men, girls will be mothers: The legal regulation of childhood in Toronto and Vancouver." Pp. 188–206 in *Histories of*

Canadian Children and Youth, edited by N. Janovicek and J. Parr. Toronto: Oxford University Press.

Coffey, Amanda. 2002. "Ethnography and self: Reflections and representations." Pp. 313–31 in *Qualitative Research in Action*, edited by T. May. London: Sage Publications.

Coltrane, Scott. 1989. "Household labour and the routine production of gender." *Social Problems* 36:473–90.

———. 1996. *Family Man*. New York: Oxford University Press.

———. 1998. *Gender and Families*. Thousand Oaks, CA: Pine Forge Press.

Coltrane, Scott and Michele Adams. 2001. "Men's family work: Child-centered fathering and the sharing of domestic labor." Pp. 72–99 in *Working Families: The Transformation of the American Home*, edited by R. Hertz and M.L. Marshall. Berkeley: University of California Press.

Comacchio, Cynthia. 1997. "'A Postscript for Father': Defining a new fatherhood in interwar Canada." *The Canadian Historical Review* 78:385–408.

Connell, R.W. 1987. *Gender and Power: Society, the Person, and Sexual Politics*. Cambridge: Polity.

———. 1995. *Masculinities*. Cambridge: Polity.

———. 2000. *The Men and the Boys*. Cambridge: Polity.

———. 2002. *Gender*. Cambridge: Polity Press.

———. 2005. "A really good husband: Work/life balance, gender equity, and social change." *Australian Journal of Social Issues* 40:369–93.

Craig, Lyn. 2006. "Does father care mean fathers share? A comparison of how mothers and fathers in intact families spend time with children." *Gender & Society* 20:259–81.

Dalton, Susan E. and Denise D. Bielby. 2000. "'That's our kind of constellation': Lesbian mothers negotiate institutionalized understandings of gender within the family." *Gender & Society* 14:36–61.

Daly, Kerry. 2001. "Deconstructing family time: from ideology to lived experience." *Journal of Marriage and Family* 63:283–94.

———. 2002. "Time, gender, and the negotiation of family schedules." *Symbolic Interaction* 25:323–42.

———. 2004. *The Changing Culture of Parenting*. Ottawa: The Vanier Institute of the Family.

Daly, Kerry and Rob Palkovitz. 2004. "Guest editorial: Reworking work and family issues for fathers." *Fathering* 2:211–13.

Deutsch, Francine. 1999. *Halving It All: How Equally Shared Parenting Works*. Cambridge: Harvard University Press.

————. 2002. "Halving it all: The mother and Mr. Mom." Pp. 113–38 in *Families at Work: Expanding the Boundaries*, edited by N. Gerstel, D. Clawson, and R. Zussman. Nashville: Vanderbilt University Press.

————. 2007. "Undoing gender." *Gender & Society* 21:106–27.

Deutsch, Francine M. and Susan E. Saxon. 1998. "Traditional ideologies, nontraditional lives." *Sex Roles* 38:331–62.

DeVault, Marjorie. 1991. *Feeding the Family: The Social Organization of Caring as Gendered Work*. Chicago: University of Chicago Press.

————. 1999. "Comfort and struggle: Emotion work in family life." *Annals of the American Academy of Political and Social Science* 561:52–63.

Dienhart, Anna. 1998. *Reshaping Fatherhood: The Social Construction of Shared Parenting*. Thousand Oaks: Sage Publications.

Doucet, Andrea. 2000. "'There's a huge gap between me as a male carer and women': Gender, domestic responsibility, and the community as an institutional arena." *Community, Work, and Family* 3:163–84.

————. 2001. "'You see the need perhaps more clearly than I have': Exploring gendered processes of domestic responsibility." *Journal of Family Issues* 22:328–57.

————. 2004a. "'It's almost like I have a job, but I don't get paid': Fathers at home reconfiguring work, care, and masculinity." *Fathering* 2:277–303.

————. 2004b. "Fathers and the responsibility for children: A puzzle and a tension." *Atlantis* 28:103–14.

————. 2006a. *Do Men Mother?* Toronto: University of Toronto Press.

————. 2006b. "'Estrogen-filled worlds': Fathers as primary caregivers and embodiment." *The Sociological Review* 54:696–716.

Drolet, Marie. 2003. "Motherhood and paycheques." *Canadian Social Trends* 68:19–21.

Duffy, Ann, Nancy Mandell, and Norene Pupo. 1989. *Few Choices: Women, Work, and Family*. Toronto: Garamond Press.

Dunne, Gillian. 2000. "Opting into motherhood: Lesbians blurring the boundaries and transforming the meaning of parenthood and kinship." *Gender & Society* 14:11–35.

Edwards, Rosalind, Claire Callender, and Tracey Reynolds. 2005. "Social and family responsibility or self interest? A case study of mothers' work ethos in a hospital and an accountancy firm." *Community, Work, and Family* 8:281–300.

Ehrensaft, Diane. 1987. *Parenting Together*. New York: The Free Press.

Elvin-Nowak, Ylva and Heléne Thomsson. 2001. "Motherhood as idea and practice: A discursive understanding of employed mothers in Sweden." *Gender & Society* 15:407–28.

Fisher, Allen P. 2003. "Still 'not quite as good as having your own'?: Towards a sociology of adoption." *Annual Review of Sociology* 29:335–61.

Fox, Bonnie. 2001. "The formative years: How parenthood creates gender." *Canadian Review of Sociology and Anthropology* 38:373–90.

———. 2006. "Motherhood as a class act: The many ways in which 'intensive mothering' is entangled with social class." Pp. 231–62 in *Social Reproduction: Feminist Political Economy Challenges Neo-Liberalism*, edited by K. Bezanson and M. Luxton. Montreal and Kingston: McGill-Queen's University Press.

Fox, Bonnie and Doreen Fumia. 2001. "Pathbreakers: Some unconventional families of the nineties." Pp. 458–69 in *Family Patterns, Gender Relations*, edited by B. Fox. Toronto: Oxford University Press.

Friendly, Martha. 2001. "Child care and Canadian federalism in the 1990s: Canary in a coal mine." Pp. 25–61 in *Our Children's Future: Child Care Policy in Canada*, edited by G. Cleveland and M. Krashinsky. Toronto: University of Toronto Press.

———. 2004. "Early childhood education and care: An issue for all Canadians." Pp. 125–38 in *Social Determinants of Health Across the Life Span*. Toronto: Canadian Scholars' Press.

———. 2006. "Early learning and child care: How does Canada measure up?" *CRRU Child Care BRIEFing NOTES*, Childcare Resource and Research Unit, Toronto, ON. Retrieved September 3, 2009 <http://www.childcarecanada.org/pubs/bn/earlylearning06.html>.

Frønes, Ivar. 1997. "The transformation of childhood: Children and families in post-war Norway." *Acta Sociologica* 40:17–30.

Gabb, Jacqui. 2005. "Lesbian (m)otherhood: Strategies of familial-linguistic management in lesbian parent families." *Sociology* 39:585–603.

Gaffield, Chad. 1990. "The social and economic origins of contemporary families." Pp. 23–40 in *Families: Changing Trends in Canada*, 2nd ed., edited by M. Baker. Toronto: McGraw-Hill Ryerson.

Garey, Anita Ilta. 1995. "Constructing motherhood on the night shift: 'Working mothers' as 'stay-at-home moms.'" *Qualitative Sociology* 18:415–37.

———. 1999. *Weaving Work and Motherhood*. Philadelphia: Temple University Press.

Gerson, Kathleen. 1993. *No Man's Land: Men's Changing Commitments to Family and Work*. New York: Basic Books.

Giddens, Anthony. 1991. *Modernity and Self-Identity*. Stanford: Stanford University Press.

Gleason, Mona. 1997. "Psychology and the construction of the 'normal' family in postwar Canada, 1945–60." *The Canadian Historical Review* 78:442–77.

Glenn, Evelyn Nakano. 1994. "Social constructions of mothering: A thematic overview." Pp. 1–29 in *Mothering: Ideology, Experience, and Agency*, edited by E.N. Glenn, G. Chang, and L.R. Forcey. New York: Routledge.

Glenn, Evelyn Nakano, Grace Chang, and Linda Rennie Forcey. 1994. *Mothering: Ideology, Experience, and Agency*. New York: Routledge.

Grbich, Carol. 1994. "Women as primary breadwinners in families where men are primary caregivers." *Australian and New Zealand Journal of Sociology* 30:105–18.

Greenspan, Stanley I. and Jacqueline Salmon. 2001. *The Four-Thirds Solution*. Cambridge, MA: Perseus Publishing.

Griffith, Alison and Dorothy E. Smith. 2005. *Mothering for Schooling*. New York: Routledge.

Grindstaff, Carl. 1984. "Catching up: The fertility of women over 30 years of age, Canada in the 1970s and early 1980s." *Canadian Studies in Population* 11:95–109.

Griswold, R.L. 1993. *Fatherhood in America: A History*. New York: Basic Books.

Gubrium, Jaber F. and James A. Holstein. 1997. *The New Language of Qualitative Research*. New York: Oxford University Press.

Haas, Linda. 1980. "Role-sharing couples: A study of egalitarian marriages." *Family Relations* 29:289–96.

———. 1982. "Determinants of role-sharing behavior: A study of egalitarian couples." *Sex Roles* 8:747–60.

Hawkins, Alan J. and David C. Dollahite. 1997. *Generative Fathering: Beyond Deficit Perspectives*. Thousand Oaks: Sage Publications.

Hays, Sharon. 1996. *The Cultural Contradictions of Motherhood*. New Haven: Yale University Press.

Hequembourg, Amy L. and Michael P. Farrell. 1999. "Lesbian motherhood: Negotiating marginal-mainstream identities." *Gender & Society* 13:540–57.

Hertz, Rosanna. 1986. *More Equal Than Others: Women and Men in Dual-Career Marriages*. Berkeley: University of California Press.

———. 1995. "Separate but simultaneous interviewing of husbands and wives: Making sense of their stories." *Qualitative Inquiry* 1:429–52.

Higgins, Chris and Linda Duxbury. 2002. *The 2001 National Work-Life Conflict Study*. Ottawa: Health Canada.

Hochschild, Arlie Russell. 1983. *The Managed Heart: Commercialization of Human Feeling*. Berkeley: University of California Press.

———. 1989. *The Second Shift*. New York: Avon Books.

———. 1997. *The Time Bind: When Work Becomes Home and Home Becomes Work*. New York: Metropolitan Books.

Holstein, James A. and Jaber F. Gubrium. 1994. "Phenomenology, ethnomethodology, and interpretive practice." Pp. 262–72 in *Handbook of Qualitative Research*, edited by N.K. Denzin and Y.S. Lincoln. Thousand Oaks: Sage Publications.

———. 1997. "Active interviewing." Pp. 113–29 in *Qualitative Research: Theory, Method, and Practice*, edited by D. Silverman. Thousand Oaks: Sage Publications.

Holter, Oystein Gullvag. 2007. "Men's work and family reconciliation in Europe." *Men and Masculinities* 9:425–56.

Jones, C. and G. Causer. 1995. "Men don't have families: Equality and mother-hood in technical employment." *Gender, Work and Organization* 2(2):51–62.

Jorgenson, J. 2002. "Engineering selves: negotiating gender and identity in tech-nical work." *Management Communication Quarterly* 15:350–80.

Kurdek, Lawrence A. 2007. "The allocation of household labor by partners in gay and lesbian couples." *Journal of Family Issues* 28:132–48.

Lamb, Michael E., Joseph H. Pleck, E.L. Charnov, and J.A. Levine. 1985. "Paternal behavior in humans." *American Zoologist* 25:883–94.

Lammi-Taskula, Johanna. 2006. "Nordic men on parental leave: Can the welfare state change gender relations?" Pp. 79–99 in *Politicising Parenthood in Scandinavia*, edited by A.L. Ellingsaeter and A. Leira. Bristol: Policy Press.

Lareau, Annette. 2002. "Invisible inequality: Social class and childrearing in black families." *American Sociological Review* 67:747–76.

LaRossa, Ralph. 1988. "Fatherhood and social change." *Family Relations* 37:451–58.

Leira, Arnlaug. 2002. *Working Parents and the Welfare State: Family Change and Policy Reform in Scandinavia*. Cambridge: Cambridge University Press.

Levine, James A. and Todd L. Pittinsky. 1997. *Working Fathers: New Strategies for Balancing Work and Family*. Reading, MA: Addison-Wesley.

Lewis, S. 1997. "'Family-friendly' employment policies: A route to changing orga-nizational culture or playing about at the margins?" *Gender, Work, and Organization* 4:13–23.

Liff, S. and K. Ward. 2001. "Distorted views through the glass ceiling: The con-struction of women's understandings of promotion and senior management positions." *Gender, Work, and Organization* 8:19–36.

Lofland, John, David A. Snow, Leon Anderson, and Lyn H. Lofland. 2006. *Analyzing Social Settings: A Guide to Qualitative Observation and Analysis*. 4th ed. Belmont, CA: Wadsworth.

Lupton, Deborah and Lesley Barclay. 1997. *Constructing Fatherhood*. London: Sage Publications.

Luxton, Meg. 1980. *More Than a Labour of Love: Three Generations of Women's Work in the Home*. Toronto: The Women's Press.

———. 1990. "Two hands for the clock: Changing patterns in the gendered division of labour in the home." Pp. 39–56 in *Through the Kitchen Window: The Politics of Home and Family*, edited by M. Luxton, H. Rosenberg, and S. Arat-Koc. Toronto: Garamond Press.

Luxton, Meg and June Corman. 2001. *Getting By in Hard Times: Gendered Labour at Home and on the Job*. Toronto: University of Toronto Press.

Macdonald, Cameron L. 1998. "Manufacturing motherhood: The shadow work of nannies and au pairs." *Qualitative Sociology* 21:25–48.

March, Karen and Charlene Miall. 2000. "Introduction: Adoption as a family form." *Family Relations* 49:359–62.

Marshall, Katherine. 2001. "Part-time by choice." *Perspectives on Labour and Income* 1(2):20–27.

———. 2003. "Parental leave: More time off for baby." *Canadian Social Trends* 71:13–18.

———. 2006. "Converging gender roles." *Perspectives on Labour and Income* 7(7):5–17.

———. 2008. "Fathers' use of paid parental leave." *Perspectives on Labour and Income* 9(6):5–14.

Marshall, Sheila K. and J. David Lambert. 2006. "Parental mattering: A qualitative inquiry into the tendency to evaluate the self as significant to one's children." *Journal of Family Issues* 27:1561–82.

Marsiglio, William and Joseph H. Pleck. 2005. "Fatherhood and masculinities." Pp. 249–69 in *The Handbook of Studies on Men and Masculinities*, edited by M.S. Kimmel, J. Hearn, and R.W. Connell. Thousand Oaks, CA: Sage.

Mason, Jennifer. 2002a. "Qualitative interviewing: Asking, listening, and interpreting." Pp. 225–240 in *Qualitative Research in Action*, edited by T. May. London: Sage Publications.

———. 2002b. *Qualitative Researching*. 2nd ed. London: Sage Publications.

Matthews, Sarah H. 2005. "Crafting qualitative research articles on marriages and families." *Journal of Marriage and Family* 67:799–808.

May, Tim. 2001. *Social Research: Issues, Methods, and Process*. Buckingham: Open University Press.

McBride, Brent A., Geoffrey L. Brown, Kelly K. Bost, Nana Shim, Brian Vaughn, and Byran Korth. 2005. "Paternal identity, maternal gatekeeping, and father involvement." *Family Relations* 54:360–72.

McCarthy, Jane Ribbens, Rosalind Edwards, and Val Gillies. 2000. "Moral tales of the child and adult: Narratives of contemporary family lives under changing circumstances." *Sociology* 34:785–803.

McGraw, Lori A. and Alexis J. Walker. 2004. "Gendered family relations: The more things change, the more they stay the same." Pp. 174–191 in *Handbook of Contemporary Families*, edited by M. Coleman and L.H. Ganong. Thousand Oaks: Sage Publications.

McLaren, Angus and Arlene Tigar McLaren. 1997. *The Bedroom and the State: The Changing Practices and Politics of Contraception and Abortion in Canada, 1880–1997*. Toronto: Oxford University Press.

McMahon, Martha. 1995. *Engendering Motherhood: Identity and Self-Transformation in Women's Lives*. New York: The Guilford Press.

McNeill, Ted. 2004. "Fathers' experiences of parenting a child with juvenile rheumatoid arthritis." *Qualitative Health Research* 14:526–45.

————. 2007. "Fathers of children with a chronic health condition." *Men and Masculinities* 9:409–24.

Miall, Charlene E. and Karen March. 2003. "A comparison of biological and adoptive mothers and fathers: The relevance of biological kinship and gendered constructs of parenthood." *Adoption Quarterly* 6:7–39.

Milan, Anne, Mireille Vezina, and Carrie Wells. 2007. *Family Portrait: Continuity and Change in Canadian Families and Households in 2006, 2006 Census*. Ottawa: Statistics Canada. Catalogue no. 97-553-XIE.

Miller, Jody and Barry Glassner. 1997. "The 'inside' and the 'outside': Finding realities in interviews." Pp. 99–112 in *Qualitative Research: Theory, Method, and Practice*, edited by D. Silverman. London: Sage Publications.

Mintz, Steven. 2004. "The social and cultural construction of American childhood." Pp. 3–53 in *Handbook of Contemporary Families*, edited by M. Coleman and L.H. Ganong. Thousand Oaks: Sage Publications.

Morehead, Alison. 2001. "Synchronizing time for work and family: Preliminary insights from qualitative research with mothers." *Journal of Sociology* 37:355–69.

Morris, Marika. 2000. "Millennium of achievements. " *Canadian Research Institute for the Advancement of Women Newsletter* 20(1). Retrieved August 13, 2009 <http://www.criaw-icref.ca/factSheets/millennium_e.htm>.

Nelson, Fiona. 1996. *Lesbian Motherhood: An Exploration of Canadian Lesbian Families*. Toronto: University of Toronto Press.

Nelson, Margaret K. 1994. "Family day care providers: Dilemmas of daily practice." Pp. 181–209 in *Mothering: Ideology, Experience and Agency*, edited by E.N. Glenn, G. Chang, and L.R. Forcey. New York: Routledge.

Parr, Joy. 1990. *The Gender of Breadwinners*. Toronto: University of Toronto Press.

Patterson, Charlotte J. 2000. "Family relationships of lesbians and gay men." *Journal of Marriage and the Family* 62:1052–69.

Pleck, Joseph H. 1987. "American fathering in historical perspective." Pp. 83–95 in *Changing Men: New Directions in Research on Men and Masculinity*, edited by M.S. Kimmel. Newbury Park: Sage.

Pleck, Joseph H. and Brian P. Masciadrelli. 2004. "Paternal involvement by U.S. residential fathers: Levels, sources, and consequences." Pp. 222–71 in *The Role of the Father in Child Development*, 4th ed., edited by M.E. Lamb. Hoboken, NJ: John Wiley and Sons.

Pleck, Joseph H. and Jeffrey L. Stueve. 2001. "Time and paternal involvement." Pp. 205–76 in *Minding the Time in Family Experience: Emerging Perspectives and Issues*, edited by K.J. Daly. Amsterdam: JAI.

Pocock, Barbara. 2005. "Work/Care regimes: Institutions, culture, and behaviour and the Australian case." *Gender, Work and Organization* 12:32–49.

Porter, Ann. 1993. "Women and income security in the post-war period: The case of Unemployment Insurance, 1945–1962." *Labour/Le Travail* 31(Spring): 111–44.

Potuchek, Jean L. 1992. "Employed wives' orientations to breadwinning: A gender theory analysis." *Journal of Marriage and Family* 54:548–58.

———. 1997. *Who Supports the Family? Gender and Breadwinning in Dual-Earner Marriages*. Stanford: Stanford University Press.

Prentice, Susan. 2007. "Less access, worse quality: New evidence about poor children and regulated child care in Canada." *Journal of Children and Poverty* 13:57–73.

Quirke, Linda. 2006. "'Keeping young minds sharp': Children's cognitive stimulation and the rise of parenting magazines, 1959–2003." *Canadian Review of Sociology and Anthropology* 43:387–406.

Radin, Norma. 1982. "Primary caregiving and role-sharing fathers." Pp. 173–204 in *Nontraditional Families: Parenting and Child Development*, edited by M.E. Lamb. Hillsdale, NJ: Lawrence Erlbaum Associates.

Ranson, Gillian. 1998. "Education, work, and family decision-making: Finding the 'right time' to have a baby." *Canadian Review of Sociology and Anthropology* 35:517–33.

———. 2001. "Men at work: Change — or no change? — in the era of the 'new father.'" *Men and Masculinities* 4:3–26.

Reimann, Renate. 1997. "Does biology matter?: Lesbian couples' transition to parenthood and their division of labor." *Qualitative Sociology* 20:153–85.

Ridgeway, Cecilia L. and Shelley J. Correll. 2000. "Limiting inequality through interaction: The end(s) of gender." *Contemporary Sociology* 29:110–20.

———. 2004. "Unpacking the gender system: A theoretical perspective on gender beliefs and social relations." *Gender & Society* 18:510–31.

Risman, Barbara. 1998. *Gender Vertigo*. New Haven: Yale University Press.

———. 2004. "Gender as a social structure: Theory wrestling with activism." *Gender & Society* 18:429–50.

Risman, Barbara J. and Danette Johnson-Sumerford. 1998. "Doing it fairly: A study of postgender marriages." *Journal of Marriage and the Family* 60:23–40.

Rothman, Barbara Katz. 1989. *Recreating Motherhood: Ideology and Technology in a Patriarchal Society*. New York: W.W. Norton and Co.

————. 2005. *Weaving a Family: Untangling Race and Adoption*. Boston: Beacon Press.

Roy, Kevin M. 2004. "You can't eat love: Constructing provider role expectations for low-income and working-class fathers." *Fathering* 2:253–76.

Rubin, J. 1997. "Gender equality and the culture of organizational assessment." *Gender, Work and Organization* 4:24–34.

Ruddick, Sara. 1982. "Maternal thinking." Pp. 76–94 in *Rethinking the Family: Some Feminist Questions*, edited by B. Thorne and M. Yalom. New York: Longman.

Russell, Graeme. 1982. "Shared-caregiving families: An Australian study." Pp. 139–171 in *Nontraditional Families: Parenting and Child Development*, edited by M.E. Lamb. Hillsdale, NJ: Lawrence Erlbaum Associates.

Rutherdale, Robert. 1996. "Fatherhood and the social construction of memory: Breadwinning and male parenting on a job frontier, 1945–1966." Pp. 357–75 in *Gender and History in Canada*, edited by J. Parr and M. Rosenfeld. Toronto: Copp Clark.

Sager, Eric. 1996. "Memories of work, family, and gender in the Canadian Merchant Marine, 1920–1950." in *Gender and History in Canada*, edited by J. Parr and M. Rosenfeld. Toronto: Copp Clark.

Schwartz, Pepper. 1994. *Peer Marriage: How Love Between Equals Really Works*. New York: Free Press.

————. 2007. "Peer marriage." Pp. 222–31 in *Shifting the Center: Understanding Contemporary Families*, 3rd ed., edited by S.J. Ferguson. New York: McGraw-Hill.

Silver, Cynthia. 2000. "Being there: The time dual-earner couples spend with their children." *Canadian Social Trends* Summer:26–28.

Smith, Calvin D. 1998. "'Men don't do this sort of thing': A case study of the social isolation of househusbands." *Men and Masculinities* 1:138–72.

Smith, Dorothy. 1993. "The Standard North American Family: SNAF as an ideological code." *Journal of Family Issues* 14:50–65.

Smith, Vicki. 2001. *Crossing the Great Divide: Worker Risk and Opportunity in the New Economy*. Ithaca: Cornell University Press.

Sørensen, Annemette. 1991. "The restructuring of gender relations in an aging society." *Acta Sociologica* 34:45–55.

Spivey, Christy. 2005. "Time off at what price? The effects of career interruptions on earnings." *Industrial and Labor Relations Review* 59:119–40.

Stacey, Judith. 1998. *Brave New Families: Stories of Domestic Upheaval in Late-Twentieth-Century America*. Berkeley: University of California Press.

————. 2006. "Gay parenthood and the decline of paternity as we knew it." *Sexualities* 9:27–55.

Stacey, Judith and T.J. Biblarz. 2001. "(How) does the sexual orientation of parents matter?" *American Sociological Review* 66:159–83.

Statistics Canada. 1985–2009. *General Social Survey*. Ottawa: Statistics Canada.

Statistics Canada. 2007. *Women in Canada: Work Chapter Updates 2006*. Ottawa: Minister of Industry. Catalogue no. 89F0133XIE.

Strong-Boag, Veronica. 1988. *The New Day Recalled: Lives of Girls and Women in English Canada, 1919–1939*. Markham, ON: Penguin Books

Sullivan, Maureen. 1996. "Rozzie and Harriet? Gender and family patterns of lesbian coparents." *Gender & Society* 10:747–67.

Sullivan, Oriel. 2004. "Changing gender practices within the household: A theoretical perspective." *Gender & Society* 18:207–22.

————. 2006. *Changing Gender Relations, Changing Families*. Lanham: Rowman and Littlefield.

Sunderland, Jane. 2000. "Baby entertainer, bumbling assistant, and line manager: Discourses of fatherhood in parentcraft texts." *Discourse and Society* 11:249–74.

————. 2006. "'Parenting' or 'mothering'? The case of modern childcare magazines." *Discourse and Society* 17:503–27.

Sussman, Deborah and Stephanie Bonnell. 2006. "Wives as primary breadwinners." *Perspectives on Labour and Income* 7(8):10–17.

Sweet, Stephen and Phyllis Moen. 2006. "Advancing a career focus on work and family: Insights from the life course perspective." Pp. 186–208 in *The Work and Family Handbook*, edited by M. Pitt-Catsouphes, E.E. Kossek, and S. Sweet. Mahwah, NJ: Lawrence Erlbaum Associates.

Taylor, Verta. 1996. *Rock-a-by Baby: Feminism, Self-Help, and Postpartum Depression*. New York: Routledge.

Tillotson, Shirley. 1996. "'We may all soon be first-class men': Gender and skill in Canada's early twentieth-century urban telegraph industry." Pp. 357–75 in *Gender and History in Canada*, edited by J. Parr and M. Rosenfeld. Toronto: Copp Clark.

Tougas, Jocelyne. 2001. "What we can learn from the Quebec experience." Pp. 92–105 in *Our Children's Future: Child Care Policy in Canada*, edited by G. Cleveland and M. Krashinsky. Toronto: University of Toronto Press.

Townsend, Nicholas W. 2002. *The Package Deal: Marriage, Work and Fatherhood in Men's Lives*. Philadelphia: Temple University Press.

Ursel, Jane. 1992. *Private Lives, Public Policy: 100 Years of State Intervention in the Family*. Toronto: Women's Press.

Uttal, Lynet. 1996. "Custodial care, surrogate care, and coordinated care: Employed mothers and the meaning of child care." *Gender & Society* 10:291–311.

———. 2002. *Making Care Work: Employed Mothers in the New Childcare Market*. New Brunswick: Rutgers University Press.

Wall, Glenda. 2004. "Is your child's brain potential maximized? Mothering in an age of new brain research." *Atlantis* 8:41–50.

Wall, Glenda and Stephanie Arnold. 2007. "How involved is involved fathering? An exploration of the contemporary culture of fatherhood." *Gender & Society* 21:508–27.

Walzer, Susan. 1996. "Thinking about the baby: Gender and divisions of infant care." *Social Problems* 43:219–34.

———. 1998. *Thinking About the Baby: Gender and Transitions into Parenthood*. Philadelphia: Temple University Press.

Wearing, Betsy. 1984. *The Ideology of Motherhood*. Sydney: George Allen and Unwin.

Weeks, Jeffrey, Brian Heaphy, and Catherine Donovan. 2001. *Same Sex Intimacies: Families of Choice and Other Life Experiments*. London: Routledge.

West, Candace and Don Zimmerman. 1987. "Doing gender." *Gender & Society* 1:125–51.

Wharton, Amy S. 2006. "Understanding diversity of work in the 21st century and its impact on the work-family area of study." Pp. 17–29 in *The Work and Family Handbook*, edited by M. Pitt-Catsouphes, E.E. Kossek, and S. Sweet. Mahwah, NJ: Lawrence Erlbaum Associates.

White, Naomi. 1994. "About fathers: Masculinity and the social construction of fatherhood." *Journal of Sociology* 30:119–31.

Williams, Joan. 2000. *Unbending Gender*. New York: Oxford University Press.

Zelizer, Viviana A. 1985. *Pricing the Priceless Child: The Changing Social Value of Children*. New York: Basic Books.

Zussman, Robert. 2004. "People in places." *Qualitative Sociology* 27:351–63.

Index